JOURNAL HISTORY

OF THE

# TWENTY-NINTH OHIO

## VETERAN VOLUNTEERS,

## 1861--1865.

## ITS VICTORIES AND ITS REVERSES.

And the campaigns and battles of Winchester, Port Republic, Cedar Mountain, Chancellorsville, Gettysburg,
Lookout Mountain, Atlanta, The March to the
Sea, and the campaign of the Carolinas, in
which it bore an honorable part

BY

J. HAMP SeCHEVERELL,
(LATE COMPANY B.)

CLEVELAND.
1883

COMRADES AND FRIENDS:

On the twentieth anniversary of the organization of the Twenty-ninth regiment Ohio Veteran volunteer infantry, Comrade J. H. SeCheverell was instructed to prepare a history of the same, and the undersigned were appointed a committee to supervise its publication. Comrade SeCheverell, after months of perplexing labor, completed the manuscript which was examined by us in Cleveland, July 19, 1882. It was then decided to issue fifty proof copies of the work to be put into the hands of members of the regiment for such additions or corrections as should be found necessary. This was done, and after the return of the proofs and the incorporation of whatever corrections they contained, Comrade SeCheverell visited Akron, and spent several days with Colonel Schoonover, to whom was intrusted the corrections for that vicinity, and it is with no small degree of satisfaction that we now present the work to the comrades and friends of the regiment with our hearty endorsement, believing it *as complete and perfect as it is possible to make it.*

DAVID W. THOMAS,
THOMAS W. NASH,
THADDEUS E. HOYT,  } Committee.
ERWIN F. MASON,
CHAUNCEY H. COON,

CLEVELAND, OHIO, February 1, 1883.

## AUTHOR'S PREFACE.

In the following pages no attempt at literary gush is made, the design being simply to preserve from oblivion the record of the valiant deeds of this, the bravest of the brave regiments from the Buckeye State, that in the dim, distant future, when each comrade shall have answered to his last earthly roll-call and gone to the " grand review " with the many whose bones now repose in that far away country of the orange and the magnolia, those left behind may not forget the sacrifices made, and the untold dangers endured for that flag, the beautiful, starry emblem of a now united people, whose supremacy pre-served for them the blessings of this great country, the best beneath the ethereal vault of heaven.

The data from which the journal portion of the volume is composed was obtained from members of the regi-ment, who certify to its correctness. Colonel Jonas Schoonover furnished, from Atlanta to Washington.

The reader will mark the entire absence of personal laudation so common in works of this class, and the crowding of a few favored ones to the front to the exclu-sion of the hundreds of equally brave and meritorious men in perhaps lowly positions. That the fortunes of war brought many forward with flattering prominence is most true, and that thousands who wore the simple blouse of blue and carried the musket were possessed of merit as great is also true. To have been a member of the Twenty-ninth Regiment Ohio Veteran Volunteers is glory enough for a lifetime. If you did your duty, it is well ; if you failed, printers' ink will not make a hero of you. Then let each be content with the happy assurance that he did what he could for the flag.

The writer would acknowledge in an especial manner his obligations to L. D. Drum, adjutant-general of the United States army, for the very complete casualty list at the close of the volume ; also, to Samuel B. Smith, adjutant-general of Ohio, Hon. E. B. Taylor, Colonel Edward Hayes, Jonas Schoonover, Captain R. H. Baldwin, George W. Holloway; the members of the very efficient revisory committee, Captains D. W. Thomas, T. W. Nash, Lieutenant T. E. Hoyt, Sergeant E. F. Mason, and C. H. Coon , the Ashtabula Sentinel, Jefferson Gazette, and the Akron Daily News, for numerous courtesies extended to him, during the preparation of this work; and to each comrade and friend who has aided him in his labors, to name all of whom would require many pages He has conscientiously endeavored to make the volume free from errors. If he has succeeded it will be the first of its kind. However, such as it is, it is presented to the regiment and its friends with the belief that it contains much of value.

JEFFERSON, OHIO, February 1, 1883.

# INTRODUCTION.

The author of this volume has honored me with an invitation to write an "Introduction." A book without a preface would be an anomaly: in other words, out of harmony with established usage; not strictly important, but answering much the same purpose as the "whereas" preceding the resolutions of the convention.

I have not been permitted to read the author's manuscript, yet I do not hesitate to assure the reader that as he peruses the pages of the book he will find much to entertain and profit. To the veteran who enlisted and fought in the historic "Twenty-ninth Ohio Veteran volunteer infantry" it will be read with especial interest. The eye will moisten, and the heart swell with mingled emotions as he is reminded again of the varying scenes of the camp, the march, and the battle. Others, too young to remember anything of the war, but who have heard the stories of the conflict from their fathers, will read this historic sketch of the old regiment with the greatest avidity.

We well remember the author as "Hamp," the drummer boy of Company B, his boyish look, with his neatly-fitting suit of blue, and the tenor drum suspended from his neck, while with nimble fingers he plied the ebony sticks in beating the tattoo, reveille, or the "long roll."

He has done a real and invaluable service to his comrades in gathering up and condensing in neat and durable form so many interesting facts relating to the work of a noble regiment. So much, at least, is saved from oblivion.

In writing the history of any war only a mere outline can be thought of. Anything like a full and detailed account of what happened is out of the question. Neither time nor space would permit.

The multiplied thousands who carried their muskets and knapsacks on foot all over " Dixie," and who really did the hard work of the conflict, must be massed in history even as in war they were massed against the foe. Their individual deeds of daring and suffering were not a whit behind those of the great Wellingtons, Washingtons, and Grants. The latter were in positions to glide easily into history, and have their heroic deeds emblazoned and read in the books of every nation. The former may have loved their country as well and fought as bravely for her honor, and yet die in obscurity, "to fortune and to fame unknown."

Dr. SeCheverell has doubtless done his best under the circumstances to do justice to the name of every member of the old Twenty-ninth. It was known as the Giddings' regiment, in honor of the Hon. Joshua R. Giddings, for twenty consecutive years a member of the lower house of Congress

Perhaps no man during his time did more than Mr. Giddings to create public opinion in favor of the freedom of the slave. The regiment was raised almost entirely within the bounds of his old district, and it was fitting that it should bear his name. But I remember that when recruiting it a frequent objection to enlistment was that should any member of the regiment be so unfortunate as to be taken prisoner by the "Rebs," he would be forthwith shot, hung, or burnt at the stake, particularly on Giddings' account, and that the name would be so odious in the South, and would so advertise the regiment that every member would be especially hunted down and exterminated.

I think "Hamp" has failed utterly to ascertain that any prisoner from the Twenty-ninth was thus punished, although many of the boys were often in rebel hands.

I have ever considered myself fortunate and honored in having been associated with such a regiment.

I was duly appointed and commissioned as the first chaplain, holding the position one year, resigning at the expiration of that time, and receiving an honorable discharge from the service.

Of the officers of the regiment much might be said. Nobody who ever knew Colonel Buckley will ever forget him.   A brave man, a great admirer of order and discipline, faultlessly neat and tidy, a confirmed dyspeptic; yet the most ticklish and fun provoking humor often cropped out in his conversation and intercourse with men.   One morning, away down between Bull Run and Fredericksburg, when the tired and jaded men were in line for the day's march, the Colonel was in his saddle with his toes daintily touching the stirrups, his pale, clean shaven face shaded by the visor of his blue cap, from beneath which his practiced eye swept the whole regiment at a glance, while his well-polished sword, firmly gripped, stood perpendicular, resting against the shoulder; with a stentorian voice he published the following order: "Men of the Twenty-ninth, let there be no straggling on the march to-day   But if any of you do straggle take Twenty-ninth off from your caps and put on One Hundred and Tenth Pennsylvania."

The joke on the One Hundred and Tenth Pennsylvania was fully appreciated and immensely enjoyed (a regiment noted for straggling). With roars of laughter the boys shouldered their muskets and knapsacks for another hard day's march through the pine barrens.

Lieutenant-colonel Clark is remembered as a staunch advocate of temperance, whose interests were ever for the men.

Major Clemmer, as a genial, bluff soldier, whose songs often enlivened the dreariness of the camp or bivouac; and Quartermaster Gibbs, as a man of prompt execution, who expected equal promptness from others. Many anecdotes and incidents of them could be narrated by the page, but I remember that the introduction to the volume is not the place for sketches of this kind; and I fear that I have already introduced much that does not strictly belong to this part of the book. I beg pardon for any seeming trespass in this direction.

This introduction, written in the midst of other pressing duties, with frequent interruptions, now most affectionately inscribes this volume to every member of the Twenty-ninth regiment of Ohio Veteran volunteer infantry; to their wives and their children.

I am happy to enjoy this privilege of saying a few words in Dr. SeCheverell's book to my old comrades. My prayer is that God will bless every surviving member of the regiment, with their families, also the widows and orphans of deceased members, and that when the battle of life is over, we may wear the victor's crown in heaven.

R. H. HURLBURT, M.D, D.D,

Late Chaplain Twenty-ninth regiment, O. V. V. I.

MARION, IOWA, July 18, 1882.

# CONTENTS.

---

# TWENTY-NINTH O. V. V. I.

---

## CHAPTER I.

The South Preparing for War—The Fall of Sumter—The Grand Rally to the Support of the Flag—Formation of the Regiment.

President Lincoln, in his inaugural address of March 4, 1861, said: "I have no purpose, directly or indirectly, to interfere with the institution of slavery in the States where it exists. I believe that I have no lawful right, and I have no inclination to do so." The South had apparently decided otherwise, and continued the preparations for secession, begun under the administration of, and so ably seconded by that old imbecile, James Buchanan.

The outlook became so fraught with danger to the Union, that on April 7th a naval expedition sailed from New York to the relief of Fort Sumter. Its arrival off Charleston harbor was followed by a furious bombardment of the fort by the rebel batteries of General Beauregard. The capitulation on April 13th, of the little handful of gallant men who so bravely defended their country's flag, was followed by an outburst of patriotic indignation perhaps never before witnessed in the history of the world. In an incredibly short space of time the President's call for seventy-five thousand men was filled by citizens eagerly marching to the defense of the National capital.

The rebels meanwhile were busily engaged in appropriating or destroying the available arms and munitions of war belonging to the Government. At Bull Run, a few miles from Washington, General Beauregard massed his rebel horde, and here, on July 21st, General McDowell gratified the insane "On to Richmond" cry, by giving them battle. The result was the complete overthrow of the Union army, which retreated in the wildest disorder to Washington. This event cast a deep gloom over the entire North (barring the copperhead element). More than twice the time allowed by the knowing(?) ones to crush the Rebellion (sixty days) had elapsed, and yet it was growing stronger every day. The North was not yet awake to the magnitude of the work it had undertaken. The first patriotic outburst was on the wane; the sympathy of England and the encouragement given to the rebels by the "copperheads" in the North, gave a prestige to the Southern cause which, to many, bespoke the final success of treason. In this dark hour of our country's peril, that brave old hero, Joshua R. Giddings, with B. F. Wade, E. B. Woodbury, and other well known associates, feeling that they had been disappointed in the acts of another regiment, made up in part of soldiers recruited in this district, obtained permission to organize regiment number Twenty-nine, which should be made up as far as possible, of those in political sympathy with the projectors. The report of the soldiers already returned from the three months' service, and who were generally ready to go again, seemed to indicate who they wished for commanders. Major Lewis P. Buckley, of Akron, educated at West Point, was generally desired as colonel, and Thomas Clark, of Cleveland, formerly a cadet at Norwich university, Vermont, was for the same reason selected to commence the work. He was accordingly appointed major, on the 13th of August. Two days later he was mustered into service, and ordered to report at once to Jefferson, select a suitable location, and organize a camp. On the 17th he arrived at Jefferson, and a couple of days were spent in examining fields offered; at last the grounds of the County Agricultural Society were selected. A part of company A reported on the 19th, and company B in the afternoon of the same day. The camp equipage arrived on the 20th. On the 27th company C reported, and on September 10th, company D, and with this company came Colonel Buckley, who had just completed his service in the Nineteenth regiment.

Following are the companies, in the order they entered the service, with the commanders and the localities from which they were recruited: Company A, Captain William F. Fitch, was recruited in Jefferson and vicinity, and Hartsgrove. Company B, Captain Wilbur F. Stevens, was recruited in Pierpont and vicinity, and Harpersfield. Company C, Captain Edward Hayes, was recruited in Andover and vicinity, Gustavus, Ohio, and Espyville, Pennsylvania. Company D, Captain Pulaski C Hard, was recruited in Akron, Summit county. Company E, Captain Horatio Luce, was recruited in Conneaut and surrounding townships Company F, Captain John F Morse, was recruited in Painesville and Mentor, Lake county, and Montville, Geauga county. Company G, Captain John S. Clemmer, was recruited in Akron and vicinity. (Second Lieutenant W. P. Williamson, of this company, who was shot dead at the battle of Winchester, Virginia, March 23, 1862, was the first man in the regiment to die by rebel hands.) Company H, Captain Jonas Schoonover, was recruited in Akron and vicinity.   Company I, Captain Russell B. Smith, was recruited in Medina county, and by transfers · and company K, Captain Alden P. Steele, was recruited from the various townships in Ashtabula county.

The adverse causes before referred to, materially retarded the enlistment of the regiment, and it was not until about December 1st that the different company organizations were completed and the following staff officers elected :

Colonel Lewis P. Buckley, Akron, Summit county.

Lieutenant-colonel Thomas Clark, Cleveland, Cuyahoga county.

Major John S. Clemmer, Mogadore, Summit county.

Adjutant C. T. Chaffee, Jefferson, Ashtabula county.

Quartermaster O. F. Gibbs, Harpersfield, Ashtabula county.

Chaplain R. H. Hurlburt, Hartsgrove, Ashtabula county.

Surgeon A. K. Fifield, M. D., Conneaut, Ashtabula county.

Assistant Surgeon S. S. Burrows, M. D., Geneva, Ashtabula county.

Commissary Henry Wright, Trumbull, Ashtabula county.

Sergeant-major W. P. Williamson, Akron, Summit county.

Quartermaster-sergeant M. D. Norris, Mesopotamia, Trumbull county.

Hospital Steward E. P. Haynes, Atwater, Portage county.

Fife - major Richard Noonan, Hudson, Summit county.

Drum-major Gurley G. Crane, Cuyahoga Falls, Summit county.

Leader regimental band Chauncey Brainard, Gustavus, Trumbull county.

During the interim came the easy days of soldier life. Ah! those happy, golden days of camp life, when, with guard mount, battalion drill, and dress parade, the time passed swiftly away, and each heart beat high with patriotic desire for early marching orders, days looked back to from the dreary bivouac in the snow, tentless, and with clothing in tatters, scarce covering the form from the bitter, cutting winds of winter, or in the drizzling rain on the lonely outpost when sharp-eyed rebels only waited for the opportunity to send the leaden messenger of death whizzing in your direction. Sometimes the "boys" thought the rations were not sufficiently "gilt-edged," quite too plain in fact, for the savers of the country's honor, yet how often, while trying, almost in vain, with the half-pint of raw meal to keep the soul and the poor emaciated body together in those hell devised starvation traps—Libby, Belle Isle, Andersonville, and Salisbury—did the brave fellows turn with longing hearts to the bounteous commissary at old Camp Giddings. Fears were oft expressed lest the war would close before the Twenty-ninth should be permitted to add its mite to the support of the flag. How needless they were the rolls show; more than one-third (five hundred and forty) of the one thousand five hundred and thirty-two members of the regiment, were either killed, wounded, or missing in action, and one hundred and fifty-seven died of disease. The colors, too, which waved so grandly in the sharp winter air, that long agone Christmas morning in 1861, are now in shreds, rent and torn by the leaden hail through which they were carried to glorious victories.

This beautiful stand of colors was presented to the regiment on Wednesday, November 27th, by Hon. J. R Giddings, on behalf of the donors, the ladies of Ashtabula and Summit counties. Mr. Giddings spoke as follows: "Gentlemen, officers and soldiers. Before entering upon the particular duty assigned me on the present occasion, I may be permitted to congratulate you and the country, upon the completion of your regimental organization and the perfection of your preparation for the field. I desire you at all times to bear in mind the causes which led to its formation. The present rebellion has its origin far back in history. Its first overt acts were put forth in Congress by subjecting the people of the free States to gag rules, by striking down the right of petition, by arraigning and publicly censuring Representatives for the faithful discharge of duty, by annexing, unconstitutionally, slave territory, and extending and strengthening the encroachments of slavery To these violent encroachments upon the constitutional rights of the free States, this Western Reserve has from the first, presented a very general resistance. . . . .

"The ladies have prepared a splendid National and regimental stand of colors, and have imposed on me the pleasing duty of presenting them to the regiment. In all past ages civilized nations have gone forth to war under their own banner, on which was inscribed some device, figure, or emblem, peculiar to such nation. Thus each tribe among the Israelites had its particular banner. The early Christians fought under the cross, the Romans under the golden eagle, the Mohammedans under the crescent. The founders of our government selected for their colors a groundwork of blue, repre-

senting immutable justice and unlimited power, on which
the stars, representing light, are twinkling in the vaulted
heavens, while in mid ether the bird of Jove is floating,
a fitting representation of the ease and power with which
liberty and civilization are gliding over the earth; while
the stars and stripes of red and white represent the vital
principles and purity of our institutions.

[Addressing Colonel Buckley]: "To you, sir, as
commander, I present these beautiful standards, for the
use and benefit of the regiment. On behalf of the fair
donors I confide these National and regimental standards to the care of yourself, your gallant officers and
men. Wherever you go let them be borne aloft and respected as the emblem of universal freedom to all who
seek your protection. Preserve them unstained, except
by the blood of your enemies. Bear in mind that you
go forth to fight the battles of the human race for all
coming time; and should the roar of cannon, the rattling of muskets, the clashing of sabres, the din and
smoke of battle surround you, remember the cause in
which you are engaged, and be assured that if you fall,
we who are left will care for your widows and children.
Your own heroic deeds shall be enshrined in our mem-
ories, recorded in our history, admired by coming gener-
ations, and approved by a holy and just God."

Colonel Buckley replied: "Respected Sir—I receive this stand of colors in behalf of the Twenty-ninth
regiment. I return through you to the noble and
patriotic ladies of Ashtabula and Summit counties their
grateful thanks; and whenever and wherever it is unfurled to the breeze, and we look upon its stars and
stripes, may we then remember the generous donors and
the vow we this day make. This flag, the flag of our
country, which has been our pride and our boast, and

which is respected by all civilized nations; this flag, thank God, shall yet wave triumphantly wherever it has been struck down by the ruthless arm of the traitors; and, companions, whenever we look upon this beautiful flag may it inspire us to redouble our energies to do our duty to our beloved country, and if God in his providence permits us to return to home and kindred, may this flag come back with us to bear witness that the Twenty-ninth regiment Ohio volunteers was in the thickest of the fight.

"Sir, you have spoken in high commendation of my command. I can assure you I feel myself honored in having command of such a regiment, It will be my pride and ambition, with my fellow-officers to make it in all things pertaining to a well drilled and well disciplined regiment, one of the best in Ohio. And now, fellow-soldiers, in the presence of this assembly, and before high heaven, we swear upon the altar of our country to defend this flag so long as there shall be one true heart and strong arm to hold it to the breeze."

At last the "boys'" impatience to go anywhere but here, was gratified by an order to move to Camp Chase, near Columbus, Ohio, the date December 25th; and right here it may not be amiss to give an extract from an editorial in the Ashtabula Sentinel, as showing what the people of Jefferson thought of the regiment

"They leave Jefferson with the respect and esteem of our citizens as an orderly and well behaved body of men. They have been over three months within our quiet village, during which time no disturbance has occurred and no depredations have been committed. They have proved themselves honorable men, the best evidence that they will be brave soldiers. When they are heard from in the fight we have no fears of a bad account."

## ORIGINAL REGIMENTAL ROSTER.

Following is the roster of the regiment as given in the issue of the Ashtabula Sentinel, dated December 25, 1861, inserted by request of the committee on revision :

### FIELD OFFICERS

Colonel Lewis P. Buckley, Akron
Lieutenant-colonel Thomas Clark, Cleveland
Major J. S. Clemmer, Mogadore
Adjutant C. T. Chaffee, Jefferson
Sergeant-major W. P. Williamson, Akron
Quartermaster O. F. Gibbs, Harpersfield
Quartermaster-sergeant M. D. Norris, Mesopotamia
Commissary H. Wright, Trumbull
Chaplain R. H. Hurlburt, Hartsgrove
Surgeon A. K. Fifield, Conneaut
Assistant Surgeon S. S. Burrows, Geneva.
Hospital Steward E. P. Haynes, Atwater
Fife-major Richard Noonan, Hudson
Drum-major G. G. Crane, Chagrin Falls

### REGIMENTAL BAND

Leader Chauncy Brainard

Fifers—Moses C. Rist, George B. Mason, Henry Beach, Henry H. Ray, Rufus Daniels, Walter St. John, Edward B. Fitts, Charles N. Bancroft, F. P. Hall, William R. Meeker.

Drummers—Albert E. Brainard, Erastus Brainard, John Price, Calvin Crane, Albert Walker, William H. Rawdon, Lucius K. Woodbury, Corwin Spencer, Johnson W. Matterson, Luthur Canfield, Silas H. Kent, Louis Price, bass, Edward B. Woodbury, bass

Cymbal Buel W. Brainard

Bugler Edwin N. Devan.

### COMPANY A.

Captain William T. Fitch
First Lieutenant L. Grover.
Second Lieutenant W. S. Crowell.
First Sergeant E. J. Hurlburt
Third Sergeant C. H. Coon
Fourth Sergeant W. H. Grant
Fifth Sergeant S. G. Elliott
First Corporal N. B. Adams
Second Corporal A. L. Rickard
Third Corporal R. M. Gates

Fourth Corporal T  E  Hoyt
Fifth Corporal M  F  Roberts
Sixth Corporal J  B  Dalrymple.
Seventh Corporal H  C  Rood
Eighth Corporal J  M  Loomis
Drummer R  Lewis
Wagoner William Daniels

### PRIVATES.

J  M  Bronson, M  A  Brown  P  B  Broughton, H  G  Clafflin, Charles Covert, M  M  Canfield, F  M  Canfield, L  M  Coon, E  G  Clark, Julius Coleburn, Henry Decker, P  A  Decker, A  L  Dalrymple, G  W  Dudley, Henry Turner, D  Thatcher, H  E  Woodin, W  B  Shearer, Abram Exceen, J  A  Exceen, John Ellis, A  A  Fenton, J  M  Sober, W  A  Thompson, E  P  Young, C  H  Broughton, George Birch, E  O  Brown, W  A  Frisbie, Leonard Grover, R  W  Graham, J  W  Henry, S  Hyde, Cyrus Hendrick, E  W  Herrick, W  B  Hoyt, E  M  Holcomb, John Hague, A  Harley, W  C  Ives, E  C  Joles, G  W  Jones, L  M  Johnson, A  M  Knowlton, W  R  Williams, Elizer Wilder, W  L  Wood, M  St  John, R  E  Woodbury, A  Thompson, J  W  Bartlett, S  C  Buck, A  B  Benjamin, C  C  Bugbee, E  J  Maltby, A  H  Frayer, O  B  Laskey, S  O  Latimer, J  E  March, A  W  McNaughton, G  B  Mowry, F  B  Mowry, F  Potter, E  Richerson, C  Roath, B  L  Roberts, N  W  Simmons, T  W  Simmons, John Sylvester, Wilber Sloat, Theodore Smith, John Shears, Alonzo D  Squires, Pickering Smith, S  R  Thompson, V  Wilson, S  N  Hubbard, A  B  Durfee, N  Wilder

### COMPANY B

Captain W  F  Stevens.
First Lieutenant A  Bishop
Second Lieutenant A  Wilson
First Sergeant B  N  Smith
Second Sergeant J  E  Tanner.
Third Sergeant F  M  Hewitt
Fourth Sergeant P  O  Warren
Fifth Sergeant A  B  Isham
First Corporal A  J  Langworthy
Second Corporal O  Fairbrother.
Third Corporal R  Griswold
Fourth Corporal L  K  Bean
Fifth Corporal D  B  Peck.
Sixth Corporal F  A  Chapman
Seventh Corporal E  Potter

Eighth Corporal A Bishop
Fifer G Miles
Drummer J H SeCheverell
Wagoner E P. McArthur

### PRIVATES

E. T. Allen, L. P. Allen, S. Atkin, F R Ackley, S S Andrews, D. Ames, H Beckwith, T Beckwith, H Brainard, C Brainard, J Brazee, I Brainard, O J. Burbank, D Brown, D J. Baur, C F Baur, J W. Baur, M Burgett, A. H. Benham, W. R. Carr, F Case, H Clark, S. Chapman, J. Doe, H. Durfee, B. T Durfee, M DeWolf, J. C DeWolf, E. Furman, J H. Fails, N A German, N Hicks, H. Hicks, N. Hendricks, M. B Hoskins, F Hallett, H O. Holmes, E. C Holmes, R. Hartwell, B L Haskin, C. Hall, W P Johnson, V Jordan, A. A. Kumig, N Knapp, D. Knapp, J Kohlar, F Leonard, J Mervin, R. McKee, B A McArthur, C W Matthews, R. McFall, L Montgomery, R. Wilson, S B Wilder, G McNutt, D. Newcomb, J. Newman, D Potter, W Potter, J. Phinney, S C Pierce, M. Rowe, G Rowe, G Wright, J Rounds, A Rogers, J. Rockwell, E. Phillips, R. Sills, H. Smith, S. Stanley, R. Stewart, W H. Vanscoik, L Wright

### COMPANY C.

Captain Edward Hayes
First Lieutenant B F. Perry
Second Lieutenant F T Stewart
First Sergeant C. W. Kellogg
Second Sergeant R L Jones.
Third Sergeant D W. Rolph.
Fourth Sergeant G W. Beckwith.
Fifth Sergeant G W Britton.
Second Corporal C. J. Galpin.
Third Corporal H. M Ryder.
Fourth Corporal N H Bailey
Fifth Corporal W A Baker
Sixth Corporal G. R. Leonard.
Seventh Corporal C C. Fitts.
Eighth Corporal W. A. Burwell.
Drummer B Phelps.
Wagoner T. Kellogg

### PRIVATES

W. Alger, L B Brainard, S. W Bronson, G D. Brockett, T R. Brown, E Britton, A H Beardslee, R W. Cross, D V. Chaffee, W. J. Chambers, O P. Crosby, S. O Crosby, H. C. Carey, J. Chapell, R A Cunningham, R Churchill, L. Clark, C W. DeWitt, W. P.

Dady. C E Dudley, G Eastlick, G. Enos, J. Williams, A. W. Mann,
J. Noble, M E Forbes, J. A Frazier, J. Fleming, J. Grey, E Gibbs,
W. G. Gillett, J Hall, D. S Halstead, A Kingsley, H. Laughlin,
F D Lane, J W Lee, H Lyons, H C Lord, L O Lindsley,
L W Leavit, D C Lindsley, J Leslie, E F Mason, M Maloney, J.
W. Matteson, A L Monty, J Winby, A Mason W Yokes J
Yokes, S. Warren, J Warren, J Wenham, D. Thomas, J. Thomas,
W H. Shores, J C Shaw, S G Strickland, B F Sperry, W
Sisley, J F Rowley, H C Rice, N. J Merrells, T J. Merrells, B
Miller, E O. Miller, D B Parker, O K Phelps, W Palmer, J D
Rea, D Ryckman, W H Runyon

## COMPANY D

Captain Pulaski C. Hard.
First Lieutenant M T Wright.
Second Lieutenant J H Grinnell.
First Sergeant G W. Dice.
Second Sergeant J H Knox
Third Sergeant W E. Dockrey
Fourth Sergeant J C Ewart
Fifth Sergeant L A McAdams
First Corporal J Hile.
Second Corporal L Robinson.
Third Corporal S Woolridge
Fourth Corporal P Nicholas
Fifth Corporal G Welch
Sixth Corporal L B Starks.
Seventh Corporal W H Hart
Eighth Corporal F C Remley.
Fifer B H Wadsworth
Drummer W B Crane.
Wagoner A Hunsicker.

### PRIVATES.

W. H. Alexander, M. M. Hutchinson, R. Partridge, J. S Alexan-
der, W H Bloomfield, O Brewster, C Beck, J W. Chalfant, N
Cochran, R. T Chapman, C Dudley, G Ellis, N C Finney, G
Foust, L E Gaylord, A W Golden, J. Gardner, J C Glass, M
Houghland, W D Haynes, E Hastings, H H Heath, H Haring,
J Hugh, C G Tolcott, V V. Viers, H. F. Waters, E Hamilton, J.
H. Hill, D Hartigan, S J Iles, W H Jones, P B Jones, J A
Jones, S Kissinger, J Lamberson, N Leohner, L Lindsay, W
Medesker, G Montenyohle, W. Mendleson, H W Morill, L Meriam,
H Niman, A W Niman, I Powlis, S Parks, J Parks, A A Wol-
cott, J. Winters, G J Young, B Pontius, H Ream, A J Ream, A

Replogle, E. Randall, J. Rodenbaugh, L. C. Richardson, W. C. Stoughton, W. Shanfelt, N. Smith, P. W. Smith, J. G. Stinehour, J. H. Snyder, C. Sherbonder, D. Schaaf, S. Strecker, L. Squires, E. E. Skinner, J. Steese, L. Standish, H. A. Thompson, J. B. Yohey, J. G. Wait

## COMPANY E.

Captain H. Luce.
First Lieutenant T. S. Winship.
Second Lieutenant E. Howard.
First Sergeant L. G. Bevins.
Second Sergeant T. L. Gould.
Third Sergeant G. Hayward.
Fourth Sergeant H. Andrews.
Fifth Sergeant W. G. Buds.
First Corporal A. Durkee.
Second Corporal N. L. Parmeter.
Third Corporal H. Dewey.
Fourth Corporal C. P. Rhoades.
Fifth Corporal S. J. Rockwell.
Sixth Corporal D. Platt.
Seventh Corporal C. Howard.
Eighth Corporal L. Dean.
Fifer C. Luce.
Drummer J. S. Bellows.
Wagoner H. J. Reaves.

### PRIVATES

J. P. Bagley, A. Bardsley, D. Baringer, A. Blanchard, F. Brown, E. J. Brewer, O. Brewer, H. Bronson, B. Brick, W. L. Carey, C. W. Carey, W. L. Coulburn, I. Conklin, A. Crouch, E. Curtis, L. Culver, F. Culver, W. H. Crawford, I. M. Dalrymple, H. Dalrymple, E. Davis, R. Dewey, P. Vanskoik, N. Warren, W. Ellsworth, N. Gillett, D. Goodwell, J. C. Greenlee, O. Gunn, L. Harper, J. S. Haddock, D. W. Hall, E. Hopkins, H. Hill, W. Holden, W. N. Hill, L. Hill, W. Johnson, O. Jones, J. Jones, G. A. Lilley, F. Lovejoy, T. Marsh, M. Mayhew, D. M. Morley, T. S. McCartney, L. Weber, W. Woodward, I. N. Meeker, D. Platt, Jr., J. O. Phillips, C. Pier, G. J. Putney, P. Proctor, J. Pike, H. Rhodes, G. Ryon, E. Ryon, W. Roberts, I. Roberts, W. A. Robinson, J. Sammon, H. Sly, W. Sterling, A. H. Sturrett, J. A. Sinclair, A. E. Tracy, H. Thornton, S. Tuttle, R. Vanskoik, L. J. Woodard, E. Wilson, Thomas Shultz.

## COMPANY F.

Captain John F. Morse.
First Lieutenant H. Gregory.

Second Lieutenant E. Burridge.
First Sergeant L. H. Martindale
Second Sergeant J. Jerome
Third Sergeant R. H. Baldwin
Fourth Sergeant S. Hall
Fifth Sergeant M. E. Gregory
First Corporal C. Woodford
Second Corporal G. Gray
Third Corporal N. B. Noyes
Fourth Corporal C. Van Valkenburg
Fifth Corporal B. Pickett
Sixth Corporal H. Macumber
Seventh Corporal N. Harvey.
Eighth Corporal C. N. Hayes
Fifer O. F. Stickney,
Drummer J. Schofield
Wagoner J. H. Whitney.

### PRIVATES

D. Auringer, A. Austin, J. Briggs, H. E. Balch, S. E. Balch, J. J. Belknap, J. Broughton, C. Broughton, H. C. Canfield, J. Carson, W. Call, R. Cannon, P. H. Chapin, C. V. Clark, A. Cole, C. Cain, A. Case, F. Dimock, N. P. Durkee, M. Dowling, P. Dowling, T. Dowling, J. Dustin, J. Dodge, E. Ewer, M. Flinn, J. Flood, F. Flood, I. Foss, E. L. Gray, Y. E. Gregory, I. J. Houghkirk, D. D. Hill, A. D. Harroun, A. J. Harroun, F. R. Johnson, J. D. Johnson, P. Joyce, J. King, W. Lindley, M. Malone, J. C. McLean, S. McLean, J. Manly, A. Neil, E. S. Ontis, A. B. Paine, J. B. Pickett, T. Ryne, L. Ryne. J. Shelby, P. Shelby, S. M. Smith, C. Smith, Pomeroy Smith, S. B. Smith, O. F. Stetson, A. E. Sanford, A. Sperry, E. Williams. G. Williams, C. F. Waldron, L. Walker, G. T. Wicks.

### COMPANY G

Captain John S. Clemmer
Since the above was in type Captain Clemmer has been elected major. Vacancy not filled
First Lieutenant James Treen
Second Lieutenant J. J. Wright.
First Sergeant C. H. Russell.
Second Sergeant W. Chamberlain.
Third Sergeant George Treen
Fourth Sergeant Adam Hart
Fifth Sergeant E. F. Smith.
First Corporal William Wirt.

Second Corporal Franklin Mest.
Third Corporal M. M. Martin
Fourth Corporal E. B. Hubbard.
Fifth Corporal A. C. French.
Sixth Corporal T. Caldwell.
Seventh Corporal G. F. Hewett.
Eighth Corporal John W. Wise

### PRIVATES.

Oscar C Andrews, Edward Alley, C H. Anderson, A, P. Atchison, Augustus Belden, G. F. Brayington, Lester P. Burke, John Burns, L. D Clements, William Cline, David Y Cook, T. Cummins, John Cephus, John Campbell, C A. Downey, George W. Deam, Noah Downey, Henry H. Ewell, John W. Ewell, William A Faze, Jacob D Foster, H. W. Geer, Thomas E Green, M. Greenwall, John Gross, Albert W. Hall, Robert W. Hall, Eli Harrington, Hiram Hill, Roswell Hoffman, John Huggett, N P. Humiston, Jehiel Lane, Jehiel Lane, Jr., William C. Lantz, Joseph Limerick, Joseph F. Loomis, John H. Lower, Oliver Lee, T. E McCain, G J McCormick, J. M McCormick, J. H. McDonald, Isaac Madlem, B. F. Manderbach, C. W. Martin, F, Meztler, William Harrington, William H Moore, John B Nowling, C. F. Remley, Uriah Reifsnyder, C. L Robinson, Jacob Rosenbaum, John Rowland, James W Smith, E S Smith, G Sherbondy, George Strohl, Ferris Townsend, James B Treen, John D. Treen, Charles Upham, John Watson, John F Weidle, S. C. Winkleman, Daniel Wise, Carroll W. Wright, Charles Young, Conrod Zilite, David McIntyre, John Kummer, Mortimer Vanhining.

### COMPANY H.

Captain J. Schoonover.
First Lieutenant A J Fulkerson.
Second Lieutenant H. Mack
First Sergeant T. W. Nash
Second Sergeant O H Remington
Third Sergeant J B. Storer
Fourth Sergeant J. L. Ferguson.
Fifth Sergeant H. L. Curtis.
First Corporal L. Wagoner.
Second Corporal W. H. Connell.
Third Corporal D. W. Thomas
Fourth Corporal T. Davis.
Fifth Corporal C. H. Edgerly.
Sixth Corporal William Leggett
Seventh Corporal G B Myres
Eighth Corporal M. Humphrey.

Fifer J Hart
Drummer M Smith.
Wagoner J Miller.

### PRIVATES.

J Ardis, J. Baird, J Buck, T G Boak, F H Boyer, L Bruno, J. Best, John Davis, W Davis, W. Dennison, W Demings, J. Ernspranger, J Fritz, T Folger, O C Field, R Farnham, C. Fairchild, D Harbaugh, J Heffelfinger, L Harris, J Harris, J. D Hall, H. Hazzen, S W Hart, A. Hazzen, P Jones, G C Kellogg, C. H. King, A A. Kellogg, D Kittinger, F. Morris, G Nichols, E Oberholtz, C H. Paine, L L Porter, S Paine, J Pierson, A A Palmer, W. Peet, C Rottert, H. Ridder, L Rodgers, G Youells, A Robinson, E Randerbush, H Root, W. Robinson, J Snowbarger, G. Slusser, J Smith, F Smith, N Salsberry, H H. Scott, J C. Stall, W. Spears, C. C. Tooker, W H Tooker, E Turner, J Wilson, H Wolf, O O Wright, R. M. Wilkins, A. Wallace, J. Wells

### COMPANY I.
[Not fully organized.]

Captain R B Smith
First Lieutenant A A Philbrick
Second Lieutenant William J Hall
First Sergeant C. C Lord.
Drummer William Elliott
Wagoner B. Alderman

### PRIVATES.

N B. Adams, W H Abbott, A Archer, A Alderman, J J. Bair, C. Beach, U Cook, J C Cally, W H Cooper, J Craig, W Dickinson, J Everhard, Martin Elliott, W Eldred, Z Farnsworth, C F Gove, W Gilbert, J. Grine, T N Harrington, A Holden, P Hawk, D. N Hubbard, W Wildy, C. H Kinsdig, R S Krahl, J Miller, N Miller, J G Marsh, M H Murdock, M L Maley, M McNerny, T. J. Nicholls, H Newcomb, M G Owen, J. R. Polley, J Perkins, L Pegg, T R. Phinney, J Rupp, H Rex, G W Reed, G Rorke, E Rushon, Jackson Roe, Joseph Roe, S F Sawyer, A Squires, J Sage, J Sowers, E M Suplee, D C Stevens, S Sturdevant, J H. Freman, A. Thompson, J. A. Walsh, J. Winters, C. L. Welton, E C Whitaker, O O Wakeman, W Waterman, S. E Wilson, A A. Woodruff, W. N DeWitt, T F. Henderson, M. Hendrick, R Hill.

### COMPANY K.

Captain Alden P Steele.
First Lieutenant D. E Hurlburt.

Second Lieutenant William Neil
First Sergeant C. C. Johnson
Second Sergeant A. O Benjamin
Third Sergeant G. C Judd
Fourth Sergeant H. H Fenton.
Fifth Sergeant J. B. Partch
First Corporal D. Phillips
Second Corporal E W Gray
Third Corporal G. M. Cowgill
Fourth Corporal A. D. Eddy
Fifth Corporal Luther Kinney
Sixth Corporal Joel Ritter
Seventh Corporal J. Alexander.
Eighth Corporal Lewis Wrisley
Drummer H Wilder.
Wagoner Cooley Griffin.

### PRIVATES

R. W. Alderman, J Blodgett, H. Davenport, D. W Fisher, A. N. Alderman, Orlando Clark, G. W. Dean, William Fisher, C. A. Baker, T. Cook, E. E. Durfee, T. J. Fails, F. Burt, F. N. Cutler, F. W. Eggleston, L. Fowler, George Bullis, C. Conrad, William Fletcher, W. Fitzgerald, P. M. Griggs, Hiram Griggs, J. Goldsmith, H. Hammond, J. Hammond, W. S. Hoxter, H. Holcomb, F. Hilliard, Judson Hunt, J. L. Hayward, C. O. Hinkle, F. Johnson, E. A. Johnson, John Jinks, William Knox, F. Love, George Light, William Law (transferred to company G, December 14, 1861), D. Marsh, J. McCloud, J. Mathews, A. F. Mills, O. O. Oliver, S. Pierce, G. Perry, William Pond, G. A. Patchen, M. Ramsey, F. Rounds, William Reed, E. Reed, J. Randell, Solon Squires, J. Spain, J. Swinton, J. St. Clair, J. Sanfield, George Strong, D. Turner, J. Taylor, Jr., James Williams, C. W. Wilson, O. E. Wilson, A. J. Wightman

3

## CHAPTER II.

The Departure from Camp Giddings—At the Front—Death of Lander
—Advance up the Valley—Winchester.

Christmas morning, 1861, dawned clear, with the
earth bountifully covered with snow, and soon the busy
preparations for this the first march were apparent everywhere. Knapsacks were packed, tents were struck, and
the camp equipage snugly put into shape for transporta
tion to Ashtabula, and at 10 o'clock the drums beat off
Then the regiment filed out of the enclosure, bidding a
fond good-bye, many for the last time, to the old camp,
up through the town, where everybody was waiting to
wish the "boys" God speed. "Head of column left,"
and the Twenty-ninth regiment was en-route for Ashtabula and the front, followed by the prayers of fathers,
mothers, brothers, sisters, and sweethearts, that its every
effort might be crowned with success, and that, if heaven
so willed, all might return safely to the arms of loved
ones, "when the cruel war was over" How beautiful
they looked in their new uniform, and how gaily the
bayonets glistened in the bright sunlight as each man
kept step to the music.

Arriving at Ashtabula, the regiment took cars, and
was soon whirling rapidly towards Columbus, where it
arrived the following day

On disembarking from the cars, a march of four miles
on the National pike to the west brought the regiment to
Camp Chase, where it was assigned to barracks, and the
sweets (?) of soldier life began to be more perceptible.

While lying here, the regiment attended the inauguration of David Tod as Governor of Ohio, and perfected itself in the school of the soldier. On the 26th day of January, 1862, the long roll again sounded; the Twenty-ninth regiment fell in, and marched to the depot, a distance of four miles. It took cars, and steamed away for Dixie, passing through Newark and Zanesville, and across the Ohio river at Bellair, thence via the Baltimore & Ohio railroad through the mountains of West Virginia to a point some six miles below Cumberland, Maryland, where it made its first camp in Dixie. There it was assigned to the left flank of the Third brigade (the Seventh Ohio volunteer infantry occupying the right), Colonel E B. Tyler commanding, and here it may be well to state that from this time until the Seventh regiment was discharged the service (July 8, 1864,) the two regiments occupied the same position, engaged in the same battles, and endured an equal amount of the hard service incident to the several campaigns. The Twenty-ninth remained in active service for nearly a year after the discharge of its well-bred friends of the Seventh and until the collapse of the Rebellion. This for the benefit of those who imagine that only one regiment was recruited in Northern Ohio.

On February 5, 1862, a general movement was ordered to entrap the forces of Stonewall Jackson, then occupying Romney. The Twenty-ninth and its brigade took cars to French's store, and marched some twenty miles to a point between Romney and Winchester to intercept the retreat of the rebels. The attempt was futile, however, as those whom the federals sought had flown ere the designated point was reached This march was a terrible one, and told heavily on the men, many of whom succumbed to disease incident to exposure to the intense cold, the fording of streams whose icy waters were often waist deep, and the general hardships, were sent to hospital at Cumberland, and never returned to duty. Returning the following day, the regiment bivouacked at a point some eight miles from the Baltimore & Ohio railroad, known as Pine Levels or the Heights of Hampshire. Here it remained some ten days exposed to the intense cold, without tents, few blankets, on short rations, and no cooking utensils. Rude brush enclosures were constructed, which served the same purpose as Artemus Ward's window sash, sort of "tangle the cold" or "keep out the coarsest." It was by the greatest effort that the men were kept from freezing. This sort of thing seemed a pretty tough introduction to the "Sunny South," but hardships of this kind became the normal experience of the Twenty-ninth regiment, and the sunny spots which occasionally intervened were duly appreciated

The next move was to the eastward to Paw Paw station on the Baltimore & Ohio railroad, near which the Twenty-ninth and its brigade went into camp. February 22d, Washington's birthday, was duly observed. A general review was indulged in. The streets were prettily trimmed with evergreens; and arches, and other pretty devices were numerous. The Twenty-ninth were domiciled in small and nearly worn out wall tents

On Saturday, March 1st, as the shades of evening were falling, the Twenty-ninth and its command marched with two days' rations, in the direction of Winchester, Virginia, the object being the capture of that important point. After an all night's march the command halted, and, in a blinding snow storm, waited for further orders. At 5 o'clock P. M a counter-march was ordered, and at about midnight the old camp at Paw Paw was reached. The object of this move was to attend the remains of brave General Lander to the cars, which was accomplished on the following day. All the troops in the vicinity were present. At 9 o'clock on the morning of Saturday, March 8th, the command struck tents and marched to the railroad ; at night took cars and moved in the direction of Martinsburg, en route for Winchester. Some two or three days were occupied in reaching the former place, as extreme caution was necessary. A burned bridge at Back creek stopped further steam locomotion, and on the 11th the command moved forward through Martinsburg, encamping some two miles out on the Winchester road. Here General James Shields, of some celebrity in the Mexican war, assumed command of the division, and the One Hundred and Tenth Pennsylvania infantry volunteers was added to the brigade. The following morning the column continued the forward movement, under orders to join General Banks, in his attack on Winchester. The rebels retreated, and Shields' division went into camp to the north of Winchester, some four miles out on the Martinsburg pike.

When the rebels first occupied Virginia General Johnston (commanding the extreme left of Beauregard's army) took possession of Winchester. Troops from here destroyed the Baltimore & Ohio railroad and constantly harrassed our forces in the direction of Harper's Ferry and Cumberland. It was of great importance that the Union arms gain and hold possession of this point, hence the concentration of Federal troops in this vicinity

Skirmishing with the enemy was a daily occurrence, and, on the morning of March 20th, a reconnoissance in force was made up the valley to Strasburg. General Shields, with the Twenty-ninth and its brigade, numbering some six thousand men, moved direct to that point,

while Colonel Mason's brigade advanced on the Front
Royal road. At Cedar creek a lively artillery duel
transpired, during which the rebels succeeded in burning
the bridge. The following morning the entire command
fell back to its camp below Winchester. This was a march
which tested the men's power of endurance to its ut-
most. The rain fell lightly but continuously during the
day. For rations the men had barely one cracker each,
and yet they made the entire distance—twenty-two
miles—in seven hours, halting only a few minutes about
noon.

## CHAPTER III.

The Battle of Winchester or Kernstown—Stonewall Jackson Whipped.

At Kernstown, some four miles south of Winchester, Jackson's command, numbering fully fifteen thousand men, was massed, and on March 22d attacked the Union outposts. The citizens of Winchester, who, by the way, were about as thoroughly imbued with treason as at any point within the writer's knowledge in the whole of the chivalrous (?) South, were in high glee at the prospect of being rid of those odious Lincoln hirelings, and some were so sanguine of success to the Southern arms that they prepared elegant repasts for the victors. However that may be, the rebel horde did not enter Winchester at this time, except, perhaps, a few dead ones carried there for burial.

Soon after the firing began the First and Second brigades of General Shields' division were moved to the front, and a lively skirmish ensued resulting in the repulse of the enemy. General Shields was wounded quite severely during this brief engagement, and at night, when active hostilities ceased, he retired to Winchester. The dawn of Sunday, March 23d, was heralded by the rapid boom of artillery and the lively rattle of musketry, as the advance of the two armies resumed the skirmishing of the previous afternoon. This was continued during nearly the entire forenoon. About noon the long roll beat throughout our camp ; quickly the men fell into line, and in columns of fours, under command of brave Colonel Buckley, marched rapidly, a portion of the distance at a double quick, toward the point of attack. On reaching Winchester the regiment halted, came to a front, loaded their pieces, and remained until the artillery and trains had passed. We then moved on the road leading to Kernstown, some two or three miles, and again halted. After some vexatious delay the regiment again resumed the march and soon reached the scene of the action, which was about seven miles from Winchester. The enemy were under General Thomas J. Jackson (Stonewall). His right extending across the Pike leading to Strasburg, and his forces on his left masked behind a stone fence, while at the rear for a considerable distance the ground was a gradual ascent covered with stumps and wood which were well used as cover. The Twenty-ninth regiment and its brigade was moved to the extreme right of the line, and, formed in close column, by division, moved forward through the timber to the attack. At close range the rebels opened a heavy fire, but we continued to advance, halting at a small ravine where we deployed in line of battle, and in this position a sharp and determined engagement ensued. The distance between the opposing forces did not exceed sixteen rods. Late in the afternoon an order was given the Third brigade to charge the rebel line. Quick as thought the whole line sprang forward, and with cheers sounding above the roar of the conflict, in the teeth of a murderous fire, swept down over the stone wall and at the bayonet's point drove the enemy from their chosen position. To the rear they fled until reaching their artillery, where another stand was made and a rally attempted. The Union lead poured into their ranks with such deadly effect that they soon became panic-stricken, and in the greatest disorder retreated in whatever direction best offered an avenue of escape, and Stonewall Jackson, the pride of the South and by many considered the bravest general in the rebel army, was whipped, and that, too, by a force much inferior in numbers, many of whom had never faced death before.

To make the victory still more sure our forces followed the disordered mass of fleeing rebels and captured many prisoners, until darkness closed over all, when our brave boys returned to rest upon their laurels upon the bloody field of carnage, bury the dead and care for the wound-ed. The result of this battle was a loss to the rebels of the Shenandoah valley, at that time of great importance to them, with casualties amounting to some five hundred men killed, wounded, and left on the field, and three hundred prisoners. The loss of the Twenty-ninth regiment in this action was · Five killed, seven wounded, two missing, aggregate fourteen. See casualties at the close of the volume for names.

# CHAPTER IV.

Pursuit of Jackson—The "Long" March—Fredericksburg to Front Royal—March to Waynesboro.

At early dawn on the morning of March 24th the Union army pushed forward in pursuit of the retreating rebels. The Twenty-ninth deployed as skirmishes in the advance. Many wounded Confederates were found in private houses along the line of march. About noon the dashing rebel cavalry officer Ashby came from cover and suddenly swooped down upon the regiment with a heavy cavalry force. Rallying by companies and forming squares, a well directed volley soon sent the rebels in haste to the rear. The pursuit of the fleeing rebels was continued until nightfall, when the regiment went into bivouac near Cedar creek. The next morning (25th) our columns again pushed forward until reaching a point a little in advance of Strasburg, where a halt was ordered and a camp (Kimball,) established. Here we remained for some time, making frequent raids into the surrounding country and skirmishing almost daily with the enemy.

April 1st the regiment again moved after the retreating army, and about daylight on the following morning indulged in some artillery firing with the rebel rear guards. During the month of April the regiment marched up the valley as far as Newmarket, passing the towns of Woodstock and Mount Jackson. At the latter place a hospital was established, and companies G and E were detailed for provost, and other duties, in and around Mount Jackson, while the remainder of the regiment moved up the valley to Camp Thurburn and continued the usual picket, camp, and guard duties.

May 3d left camp and marched up the valley in the direction of Harrisburg; halted about three miles from town and camped for the night. May 5th, returned from near the town of Harrisburg and went into camp four miles above Newmarket, where the regiment remained until the 12th day of May, when it left the Shenandoah valley at Newmarket on the long march to Fredericksburg, marched to Luray, and encamped for the night (marched eighteen miles). Thirteenth, moved at 7 A M. The Twenty-ninth, was detailed as rear guard. Fourteenth, marched at 6, reached Front Royal at 3:30 P. M. and camped for the night Fifteenth, marched at 9 A. M., traveled thirteen miles, and went into camp. Sixteenth, marched at 6:30 A. M., reached Gains' Cross Road, and camped for the night, (marched ten miles) May 17th, marched at 6 A. M., and reached Warrenton (distance of eighteen miles), and went into camp for the night. Sunday, May 18th, remained in camp. Monday, 19th, marched at 5 o'clock A. M., and at 3 P. M. reached the Orange & Alexandria railroad at Catlet's Station, and went into camp Remained until May 21st, when the regiment again marched at 6 A. M., halting at 10:30 P. M. for the night. Twenty-second, marched at 7 A. M., reached Falmouth in the evening, and went into camp. Friday, May 23d, the army under Major-general McDowell was reviewed by Abraham Lincoln, the President of the United States, with satisfactory results. Sunday, 25th, marched at 6 A. M., and at 4:30 went into camp. Twenty-sixth, marched at 5 A. M., and camped for the night at Catlet's Station. Twenty-seventh, marched some four miles on the Manassas Gap

railroad, and went into camp. Twenty-eighth, marched
at 5 A. M past White Plains; after tramping fifteen miles
went into camp. Twenty-ninth, marched at 7 o'clock
A. M. in the direction of Front Royal, reached Rector-
town at 4 o'clock P. M., and two hours later fell in, in
light marching order, and moved forward, leaving the
baggage until May 31st, when at 4 o'clock A M. it
moved forward towards Front Royal, reaching Pied-
mont at 9 A. M , and Markham at 4 P. M.; moved to
within six miles of Front Royal, and camped for the
night. June 1st, marched to Front Royal, and at 4 P.
M. moved forward some three miles on the Luray road,
and went into camp June 2d, marched at 6 A M.,
marched thirteen miles, and went into camp. Third,
marched at 7 A. M, reached Luray at 12 M, passed
through the town on the Newmarket road, some two
miles and camped Fourth, remained in camp all day.
Fifth, marched at 5 A M, marched four miles, halted,
put up our tents, and prepared to be comfortable, when
at 3 o'clock P M. we were ordered to move. This was
occasioned by the close proximity of the rebel batteries
on the opposite side of the river. The regiment marched
about one mile and again halted for the night. Sixth,
ordered to march at 4 A. M., fell into line at 5, moved
two miles, halted, stacked arms, soon fell in and
marched about two miles farther, pitched our tents, and
at 6 P. M. fell in and marched back to the place the regiment left in the morning, where we arrived at 12 at
night, and went into camp. Saturday, 7th, the regiment
was up at 4 A. M. and marched at 9 A. M. (the baggage
was ordered to Luray and Front Royal, Sergeant C. H
Edgerly and Private Willard Denison, of Company H,
were furloughed home for thirty days), marched up the
east bank of the Shenandoah river, a distance of four-

teen miles, halted at 6 P. M., and went into camp.
Eighth, marched at 4 A. M., halted at 6:30 for breakfast,
and at 8:15 again moved forward; soon heard the artillery
firing at Cross Keys on the west side of the Shenandoah
river and mountain. The regiment moved on up the
river and about 5 o'clock P. M. were in sight of the
rebels, whose ambulances and train were moving rapidly
in retreat in the direction of Port Republic from the
battle of Cross Keys. The Union forces were under
the command of Major-general John C. Fremont, and
the Confederate army commanded by Major-general
Thomas J. Jackson. The Union army took shelter in a
strip of woods at the base of the Blue Ridge Mountain,
near Port Republic, Virginia, and bivouacked for the
night.

## CHAPTER V.

Battle of Port Republic—The Twenty-ninth Suffer Great Loss.

On June 9th, in the dim light of early morning the enemy began to move, and soon our artillery opened a brisk fire on them. The Twenty-ninth regiment, under command of Colonel Buckley, was ordered to fall in, and at 6:45 o'clock marched out of the timber into the open field, and moved forward a short distance, when the men unslung knapsacks and other equipage and, reduced to light marching order, advanced by the right flank, and when near the rebel position came into line on the double quick. While doing so we were obliged to pass a board fence , and at this critical time the rebels opened a heavy fire of musketry, but the regiment moved steadily forward and took position in the open field. The rebels in front of our right wing were behind a strong post and rail fence.

From the base of the mountain to the Shenandoah river was about one-half mile. The extreme left of our line extended into the timber and near the base of the mountain with the right flank extending to the river. The Fifth, Sixty-sixth and Seventh Ohio regiments were on our left, and the Seventh Virginia, Seventh, Thirteenth and Fourteenth Indiana on our right. The Twenty-ninth being about the right center regiment during the battle, and at this time in support of Huntington's battery, which was belching forth its shot and shell, doing deadly execution in the ranks of the advancing rebels. When in close range the rebels charged. Reserving our 'fire until they were almost upon us, the order was given, and with a yell the entire line poured its leaden hail into the gray clad columns of the chivalry, producing fearful slaughter, and following with a charge so impetuous that they were forced to retire from their secure position behind the fence, and here, for more than three hours and a half, our brave fellows, though outnumbered ten to one by the enemy and fighting against fate, kept them at bay and held the position. During this charge it is said that Allen Mason, of company C, Twenty-ninth regiment, captured the colors of the Seventh Louisiana Tigers, and Lieutenant Gregory and a part of company F made prisoners of twenty-five of the same regiment At last the little handfull, who had so gallantly contended against such fearful odds, were forced to retire. The Twenty-ninth regiment moved to the rear, perhaps an eighth of a mile, and came to a halt, holding the rebel forces in check until the entire Union forces had passed to the rear In the meantime the rebels had opened fire upon us with a battery at close range, which did fearful execution in our rapidly decimating ranks. When all our troops had passed, our regiment faced to the right and moved obliquely into the timber; the rebels in the meantime passed down the road and we were nearly surrounded, and now, for a distance of nearly two miles occurred a desperate struggle for freedom, The men fought with the desperation born of despair. Brave old Colonel Buckley (who before beginning the day's business addressed the regiment, saying "Aim low, men, and at every shot let a traitor fall !") on foot, his own and one other horse having been disabled by a shot, rallied the men, and with sword in hand with them succeeded in cutting their way through the cordon of gray devils almost surrounding them, and escaped to

the mountains near, where some one hundred men of the
different regiments of the Third brigade, with Colonel
Buckley at their head, bivouacked for the night.  The
small remainder of the regiment, except those killed,
wounded or captured, succeeded in reaching the main
army.  Captain Baldwin says that those who reached the
main army of the Twenty-ninth regiment numbered only
thirteen officers and men.

The night succeeding this eventful day of blood and
carnage was spent amid the gloom and darkness of the
forest.  The men gathered about their brave commander
as if to shield him from the damps of night, their
thoughts turning meanwhile to the absent comrades,
many of whom, how many they knew not, were lying,
still and ghastly, upon the bloody field, a sacrifice to the
incompetency of the general commanding.  The day
following, the little band began its weary march to the
rear, seeking shelter at night in some unused furnace
buildings.  The next day they came in sight of the rear
guard of the retreating army, where they found the small
remnant of the Twenty-ninth, who had escaped death or
capture, and who, when they saw their beloved colonel
alive and well, fairly rent the very heavens above with
their glad shouts of welcome.

The number of the Union army engaged in this battle
was some twenty-five hundred, and could form but one
line of battle, while Stonewall Jackson's official report
shows his army to have numbered some *thirty-four thous-
and*.  The Twenty-ninth regiment lost heavily in this
battle.  The aggregate was :  Killed, 12 ; wounded, 33 ;
captured, 105 ; total, 150

After the battle the Twenty-ninth regiment moved
down the valley to Luray, where the command encamped
for a few days' rest, then forward to Front Royal, and on

to Alexandria, reaching that point on June 27th, encamping on a rise of ground immediately adjacent to the line of fortifications. The Third brigade was now composed of the Seventh, Fifth, Sixty-sixth, and Twenty-ninth Ohio regiments, in the order named. General Shields having resigned by reason of McDowell's misrepresentations in relation to the ill-advised battle of Port Republic, General Sturgis, who has recently received so much adverse criticism through the press of the country, for his brutal and inhuman treatment of his men, was placed temporarily in command. After lying at this point for nearly one month orders were received to move to the aid of General McClellan on the Peninsula, and we embarked on transports, but the order was countermanded and the Third brigade marched back to its old camp.

July 25th we were ordered to join the force of General Pope, then marching via Warrenton to the Rapidan river. Proceeding by rail to the former point the brigade was reorganized and attached to Banks' Second corps, afterwards changed to the Twelfth army corps, as the First brigade of General Augur's Second division. After a few days of "masterly inactivity" we marched in the direction of Luray. Debouching to the left on the road leading southward toward the Rapidan, we soon reached Little Washington and went into camp. While here the troops were reviewed by Generals Pope and Banks, who complimented our brigade very highly upon its perfection in drill and discipline. General Tyler was here ordered to Washington, and Brigadier-general John W. Geary, late colonel of the Twenty-eighth Pennsylvania infantry volunteers, was placed in command of our brigade. His regiment and Knapp's battery were also

4

assigned to the brigade. A forward movement in the direction of Culpeper Court House, Virginia (on the Rapidan), was begun on August 8th. Here the Confederates were preparing defences, and at Cedar Mountain, some seven miles to the southwest of our position, they were strongly fortified.

# CHAPTER VI.

## 1862

Cedar Mountain—Battle— Severe Loss of Life—Forward to Alexandria.

August 8th, the regiment moved at 2 o'clock, advanced to Culpeper Court House, and went into camp ; and at 10:40, on the morning of August 9th, moved forward in the direction of Cedar mountain. Halted a short time, and the Twenty-eighth Pennsylvania regiment was sent to the right on an eminence as signal guard. The remainder of the brigade soon advanced, halting at intervals, as the day was insufferably hot (several men died this day of sunstroke) At last, passing through a piece of timber, we approached the open field with a rolling country in our front, and at 1:30, while making preparations for dinner (near a fine spring of water), skirmishing and artillery firing was heard on our right, which continued at intervals until 3 45, when the rebels appeared in heavy force, ready for battle, and the Union lines were formed without delay. The Twenty-ninth regiment (commanded by Captain W F. Stevens, of Company B,) was ordered to advance and take position in rear of a battery which had been placed on a ridge. Here the regiment took position, the right resting on the road, and the left extending into the field, covered from the enemy by the hill on which the battery was placed. The Twenty-ninth, with other regiments of the brigade, was about on the right of the left wing of the line in open field, while the right wing extended across the road, and into the timber. The regiment remained in this position, supporting the battery, and receiving a heavy fire from the rebel artillery in our front. Here several men were wounded.

At 5 o'clock P. M., we moved over the crest of the hill, to a cornfield some distance in advance of our previous position.   During the advance to this new position a terrific cannonade opened on us, dealing great destruction to our ranks   Apparently every cannon of the enemy was let loose against us, but¦we never faltered in this march of death, despite the terrible missiles that were tearing through our bleeding ranks.   Comrades were falling, and brothers dying.   The mangled and bleeding victims of the fury and violence of war were left thick around us, making the ground sacred on which they fell, but we wavered not.   Reaching a low piece of ground, we halted, and were ordered to lie down and continue firing.   We remained for one hour in the open field, exposed to this furious storm of grape and canister, shot and shell.   Comrades gave up their lives so gently that it was scarce possible to tell the living from the dead.   The fatal missile struck the victim, leaving the lifeless clay in the same attitude which the living body occupied   During the fatal period death assumed a real character while life seemed but a dream. The engagement had now become general.   The brigade of General Prince came up, and formed on the left of our regiment.   The Sixty-sixth, Fifth, and Seventh Ohio regiments were formed on our right, in the order named. (The Twenty-eighth Pennsylvania regiment was not with us in this engagement.)

At a given signal the brigade arose and, with defiant yells, rushed forward to the charge, Prince's brigade on the left moved forward with us   A sheet of flame and smoke burst forth from rebel batteries, musketry replied to musketry, bayonet clashed with bayonet, and cheers rang out against cheers, as one side or the other gained the advantage in this deadly conflict. Daring warmed into rashness, and bravery into recklessness. Hurrah ! we force them back, their line is broken, a battery is almost within our grasp; when in this moment of seeming certain victory, fresh columns of rebel infantry rush upon us on the double-quick, masked batteries open on us at the same moment a most furious enfilading fire, causing our brave boys to reel and stagger. An order comes for us to retire, when three-fourths of our regiment have been placed out of the fight—dead or wounded Slowly and sadly the remaining few obey the order, keeping our faces to the foe until fresh troops arrive to take our places, when we resume our position in the reserve near Telegraph hill. Each regiment of the brigade had done nobly, but all alike had suffered a loss so great that the four regiments together could not show a respectable facing front for one regiment. As night settled over the field of carnage and of death our entire army corps withdrew to the position it held early in the day, but our artillery kept up a desultory firing, with but short intervals during the night.

The casualties of this battle were: Killed, 11; wounded, 26; missing, 12. Total, 49.

Private George Williams, company F, came off the field with his third gun—two having been shot from his hands.

During August 10th and 11th skirmishing continued. In the afternoon of the last-named day the 29th regiment was inspected. Adjutant Storer reported eighty-three men only present for duty.

The Union army remained on the field three days, retiring, on August 12th, to Culpeper Court House, where it encamped. Our pickets, going over the battle field on the 13th, reported that dead horses were piled in promiscuous positions; dismounted cannons, wrecked caissons, and broken fire-arms were everywhere, while the graves of the fallen, singly and in trenches, were scattered over the entire field, only the freshly heaped up earth marking the spots. In one spot were the unburied bodies of a boy in blue and one in gray, their arms interlocked as their brave souls went out to the God who gave them, the one for the right, the other, it is hoped, forgiven for his misguided championship of the wrong.

Twelfth, marched to Culpeper Court House, and went into camp. 13th, put up tents and prepared to live. 14th, and all is quiet. 15th, another inspection and review. There is one consolation if we do have inspection every other day, there are so few men left that but little time is consumed in doing so. 16th, 17th, and 18th, still in camp; was inspected again, and at 6 o'clock on the evening of the latter day, struck tents under orders to march; slept on our arms that night. 19th, marched at 10 A. M., north to the Rappahannock, a distance of eleven miles, and went into camp. Had only a small quantity of green corn to eat. 20th, all quiet in camp. 21st, at 6 A. M. firing began, and was kept up along the line all day; at 7 in the evening the regiment, under command of Captain Schoonover, marched two miles and halted; company H was sent forward to the picket line, and the regiment moved at 6:30 A. M. along the Rappahannock; halted at 9:30; after a brief rest the regiment again fell in, and marched till 12 at noon without breakfast; sharp firing along the line, halted until 6 o'clock P. M.; moved up the Rappahannock river two miles, halted, stacked arms, and remained up nearly

all night; (rainy) no tents or blankets, made our bed
of rails  Saturday, August 23d, at 6 o'clock A. M. the
artillery opened fire, and continued until 11 o'clock P.
M.; remained on our arms all day ; at 10 o'clock P. M.
moved a short distance up the river, and the Twenty-
ninth went on picket.  24th, and all is quiet; at 9:30
A. M. the artillery commenced firing, which was kept up
continually during the day.  25th, artillery and musketry
firing all along the line; at 8 o'clock P. M. the Twenty-
ninth with its brigade moved up the river four miles and
camped for the night.  26th, no rations for breakfast,
but after a short time some green corn was procured,
which filled the bill. At 8 A. M. the artillery dueling again
commenced and was kept up the remainder of the day.
The Twenty-ninth regiment moved one-half mile for
shelter, remained here until 9 P. M., when it marched
forward until 3 o'clock A. M , of the 27th, halted, moved
forward a distance of three miles, and again halted  At
1 o'clock P. M., moved in the direction of Warrenton
Junction, and camped for the night (no rations for supper or breakfast)  On the morning of the 28th day of
August, the regiment moved at 5 A. M., marched three
miles and halted, drew rations and moved on in the
direction of Bristow station, and camped for the night.
Heavy firing in our advance all day.  29th, remained in
camp, about two miles above Bristow station.  30th,
marched at 6 o'clock A. M. and halted at Bristow station,
and remained till 5 o'clock P M , when the enemy was
reported in our rear. The sick and disabled were moved
to Alexandria and other points.  August 31st, teams and
trains containing camp and garrison equipage and other
army supplies, were moved in the direction of Fairfax
Court House

During the campaign under Major-general Pope from

August 20th until the regiment reached Alexandria on
the 2d day of September, 1862, it was one continuous
march and counter-march, by day and night, moving up
the Rappahannock as far as White Sulphur Springs. On
the 29th and 30th of August near the Bull Run battle
ground. A very hard battle was fought, in which the
Nationals were forced from the field, and again late in
the afternoon on the 1st day of September at Chantilly,
a short distance from Fairfax Court·House, a sanguinary
battle was fought, which continued late in the evening.
In this last engagement the Nationals held the field at
night, and on the 2d the Union army fell back within
the fortifications around Washington city. During the
last two or three days of the above campaign the Twenty-ninth regiment was completely cut off from the main
army, as it had been ordered to guard the quartermaster
stores with other government property on the railroad
at and near Bristow station, and when ordered to join its
brigade it found the enemy in the rear, so that it was
only by a circuitous route in the direction of Brintsville,
and a forced march that it reached the Chantilly battlefield during the engagement, on September 1st.
Here it bivouacked for the night, and on the following
day marched to Arlington heights, via Alexandria, where
it went into camp.

During the last twelve days of the campaign the
Twenty-ninth suffered severely for rations and rest, it
being on the march, under fire, and on the skirmish line
the entire time. When we reached Fairfax station, on
the platform of the depot we found an immense table
upon which our wounded boys were being subjected to
the ofttimes bungling butchery of ignorant alleged
surgeons, a number of whom were busily engaged in
depriving the poor fellows under their charge of wounded

legs and arms, and in many cases hastening their death thereby. This worse than murder by men, the majority of whom, when at home, had never even witnessed a capital operation, cannot be too highly condemned. (The writer is personally acquainted with professional men of this sort, who came out of the service first-class carvers, but the number of brave fellows sacrificed to bring about this state of proficiency is unknown.) It was now ascertained that the Confederate army of General Lee was making rapid marches towards Maryland. To checkmate this movement our columns were at once ordered on a retrograde movement in the direction of Washington. Reaching Alexandria, we passed up the Potomac, crossing at the long bridge, and moving forward to Georgetown where a halt of one day was made, the command departing the following morning for Frederick City, Maryland, which was said to be occupied by the rebels. A day's march brought us beyond Rockville, Maryland, where we encamped for the night. At 2 o'clock, on the afternoon of September 5th, the regiment marched to Monocacy Junction, where the rebels had a short time previous destroyed the railroad bridge.

## CHAPTER VII.

### Frederick City—Recruits—Dumfries.

The regiment remained at Monocacy junction, guarding the immense supply trains which had accumulated here by reason of the burned bridge. Sergeant Baldwin relates that a lot of rebel prisoners passed Monocacy bridge, one of whom claimed to have fired seven shots at Colonel Buckley at the battle of Port Republic, but without effect. About September 13th, the bridge having been replaced, we moved on to Frederick city, Maryland. Here we engaged in camp, picket, and provost duty, and a large number of the men were detailed to care for the wounded from the battlefields of South Mountain and Antietam, September 14th and 17th.

In the meantime we were joined by a large number of recruits, amongst which was a brigade cornet band, composed of the following members : George Shaw, leader; Everett Shaw, assistant leader ; J. G. Caskey, Jacob Koplin, Sylvanus Hile, Columbus Ferguson, N. G. Hartman, Christian Hardag, William Kurtz, George Metcalf, James Lyon, "Bige" Nickerson, Benjamin Snyder, George Turney, Micajah Rice, Bennett Wadsworth, Edward White, Frank Waltz, Eli Waltz; Gurley G. Crane, drum major.

November 25th, Colonel Clark says : " Patiently waiting in camp. ' Dress parade ' to-day, the first many of us have seen since May last. Only about two hundred men in line. Remembering how far our line reached at Camp Giddings, our force looks small indeed."

November 27th "Cold and raw. A fierce gale makes our canvas houses rock like cradles. We are now having an easy time; that is all but the men and the mules. Our men go on duty every other day. As to rations, don't think any of us will get the gout."

November 27th. "Thanksgiving.—'Distance lends enchantment,' etc , to turkeys, chickens, pies, and fix-in's that make good cheer at home Well, some of us are thankful—that we are here instead of being locked up in those dirty rebel prisons. Nine of our officers and a large number of our men have just been released. This inactivity is irksome to the volunteer who has business at home needing his attention We hardly think Burnside will reach Richmond via Fredericksburg unless he goes as some of us did—as prisoners."

On the 10th day of December, 1862, the regiment struck tents at Frederick City, Maryland, and moved by cars in the direction of Harper's Ferry At Sandy Hook a halt was made for the night; slept in freight cars; suffered severely from cold. The following day marched at 6 A M. About noon crossed the Potomac and Shenandoah rivers into Virginia , marched about nine miles and camped for the night. Twelfth, marched at 3 P. M some nine miles and went into camp. Thirteenth, moved at 6 A. M., marched twelve miles, halted for din-ner, passed through Leesburg, and camped for the night. Fourteenth, marched at sunrise, passed through Fairfax Court House to the station, where we encamped. Fifteenth, marched till about 4 P. M., crossed Broad run and encamped for the night. Sixteenth, marched four miles in rain, snow, and mud; at 12 M. halted for din-ner; had a fight with a Pennsylvania regiment over some rails that had been collected from the fence. These we used for wood occasionally in preparing our meals. I

is perhaps unnecessary to mention that the Twenty-
ninth boys enjoyed good fires to-day.    In the afternoon
the Twenty-ninth went on picket one mile to the rear.
Seventeenth, brigade counter-marched to Fairfax station,
where it remained until the 19th, when it moved southeast about one and one-half miles to an orchard, where
it encamped, and where it remained until the 27th,
when it marched at 9 A  M; reached  Broad  run
late in the evening.   On the hill on the south side of
the creek was a fort occupied by rebels; the Twenty-
ninth crossed the creek, halted, loaded their guns, and
advanced, and a red-hot little skirmish ensued at the
close of which the rebels fell back.   We went into the
fort, sending two companies out in the road leading
towards Dumfries as skirmishers.   The regiment remained on arms all night; cold and frosty.   Guns are
not very waim bed-fellows.   Twenty-eighth, marched at
7:30 A. M , Twenty-ninth in advance of division.   About
10 o'clock met some rebel cavalry; the Twenty-ninth
regiment deployed into line of battle, a few shots were
fired, and the rebels fell back.   One man wounded in
company A.   While in this position Generals Slocum,
Geary, and Green came up; a battery was soon in position which sent a few shots after the retreating rebel
cavalry.   In the afternoon marched through the woods
on right of road, in line of battle, while the division
moved in the road ; skirmishing the balance of the day.
At dark we halted three miles from Dumfries and
camped for the night.   Twenty-ninth, reached Dumfries'
about 10 o'clock A. M , and went into camp on the side
hill in the woods north of town.

January 1, 1863, the regiment and its brigade remained at Dumfries, doing camp and picket duty, until
January 16th, when it was ordered to march on two

hours' notice, did not march. On the 17th and 18th nothing transpired worthy of note. On the 19th the regiment passed in grand review by Colonel Charles Canby, of the Sixty-sixth Ohio infantry. January 27th, General Geary visited the regiment while on parade, and complimented us on our discipline, neat appearance, and soldierly deportment. February 2nd, Colonel L. P. Buckley, Adjutant T. S. Winship, Captain E. Burridge and Lieutenant Gregory, of company F, resigned and went home. Lieutenant J. B. Storer was made adjutant, and Sergeant H. R. Baldwin, of company F, promoted to captain. February 3d, Companies D and I were detached at Dumfries landing, on the Potomac, about four miles from camp, doing guard duty, unloadng army supplies from boats, and loading the Second Division trains.

On the 14th some musketry firing was heard in the direction of Brentsville.

March 9th, Eli Waltz, of Company D, and a member of the brigade band, died.

April 16th, Companies D and I moved from the landing, and joined the regiment.

From the 29th day of December, 1862, the time when the Twenty-ninth regiment entered Dumfries, its duties were severe ; the line of pickets was over three miles long, and over one mile from camp; and as the rebel cavalry were hovering around, the main roads entering Dumfries, were patroled at night. Our men suffered severely from cold and the protracted storms. In the meantime five companies were added to the brigade. The Twenty-eighth Pennsylvania originally had fifteen companies; five companies were added to the new recruits, and designated the One Hundred and Forty-seventh Pennsylvania, with Ario Pardee as colonel. Our first brigade now consists of the Twenty-ninth, Seventh, Fifth, and Sixty-sixth Ohio regiments, and Twenty-eighth and One Hundred and Forty-seventh Pennsylvania.

The suffering our men endured during our stay at Dumfries from inclemency of the weather, the arduous service, and the scarcity of almost every necessity, cannot be easily over-estimated, and it might with propriety go into history as a counterpart of that much written about, and extensively illustrated affair " Washington at Valley Forge."

About the 20th day of April, 1863, with Colonel Clark in command, the Twenty-ninth regiment, with its brigade, left Dumfries, Virginia, and marched to Aqua creek, which place it reached two days later, and encamped about one mile from the Potomac river. Aqua creek is sixty miles below Washington on the river; it was used as a base for supplies, and a field hospital was soon established. The regiment with its brigade remained at this place performing the usual camp and garrison duty, building forts and, at the same time, doing its full share of picket duty. We are encamped on the hill overlooking the Potomac. To the north and west is a fine rolling country partly covered with pine timber and tangled undergrowth. All was quiet until orders were received to march; then what a bustle; haversacks were filled, each soldier furnished with sixty rounds of ammunition, and preparations made for " business." At 7 o'clock A. M., on the 27th day of April, the regiment fell into line and moved forward on the road leading to Kelleys ford via Stafford Court House and Hartwood church, reaching the Rappahannock river at Kelley's ford late in the afternoon. The enemy was found in small force on the south bank of the river. Late in the evening the Sixty-sixth Ohio regiment crossed the river in a small boat capable of carrying but one company at a time. The regiment deployed as skirmishers, holding the enemy back until the division had all crossed when we bivouacked for the night. The next morning we marched at 5:30 A. M., the Twenty-ninth regiment in advance; passed through a low, level country, with heavy timber; halted at 12 M. for dinner at a fine residence on a large plantation; fell in at 1 30 P. M. and moved in an easterly direction, reaching the Rapidan river late in the afternoon. The bridge had been destroyed, so that a crossing was not effected until in the evening, after which the Twenty-ninth camped for the night. 29th instant,—marched at 7:30 A. M. on the direct road to Chancellorsville. About 10 o'clock A. M. General Slocum came up and orders were received for the Twenty-ninth regiment to send out a line of skirmishers on the right of the road, which was done, the regiment passing through an open field and entering the timber, forcing the enemy back; marched on the flank through the woods and thick undergrowth for several miles, were then ordered to join the brigade. We reached Chancellorsville late in the afternoon of April 30th, where we found a small force of Confederate soldiers who were engaged in throwing up earthworks near the Chancellor house, at a point where the roads crossed, one leading to the United States ford, and the other to Fredericksburg. The Twenty-ninth regiment, with its brigade and division, were the first Union soldiers to enter the place. A number of prisoners were taken, and late in the evening the Twenty-ninth moved a short distance southwest from the main road and the Chancellor house into a piece of timber and bivouacked for the night.

## CHAPTER VIII.

### 1862.

Battle of Chancellorsville—March to Leesburg, Littletown, and
Gettysburg.

The morning of May 1st dawned upon a scene of bustle
and active preparation for the bloody work which was
to follow. Troops had been arriving during the entire
night from the direction of the United States ford, and
the light of early morning revealed an almost solid mass
of blue-coated soldiers filling the open fields and woods
in the vicinity of the Chancellor house. They were
mainly from the Fifth, Eleventh, and Twelfth corps. At
about 8 o'clock A. M. the Twenty-ninth, with its brigade
and division, made a reconnoissance in force, and after
marching about one-half mile the division formed in
line of battle, and in this position was moved about the
field until afternoon, when the lines were generally
moved to the east through the timber, the right resting
on the road. Moving perhaps half a mile we found
the enemy in strong force, his artillery masked in
the road. During this time some skirmishing and
artillery firing was indulged in, and several of the
Twenty-ninth were wounded. Late in the afternoon we
moved to the rear under a heavy fire from the rebel
artillery. Reaching the place we had left in the morning we set to work throwing up breastworks. The rebels
advanced and our skirmishers kept up a rattling fire
all night, while the regiment worked like beavers preparing the works for the coming conflict. The Second

division, commanded by John W. Geary, occupied about the left center in the order of battle.

During the evening of May 1st the Confederate army were charging the right of our lines, and for four hours the artillery firing on both sides was terrific. It continued at intervals the entire night. The air was ablaze and full of deadly missiles dealing destruction all around us; the earth trembled under our feet; the rattle and roar of artillery was like continued bursts of thunder. The heavens seemed on fire, revealing the deadly strife of two grand armies locked in close embrace, fighting with desperate valor. The dense smoke was lightened by rapid flashes of artillery, the bursting of shell, and the unceasing discharges of musketry, making a scene grand and terrible in the extreme. At midnight this deadly combat ceased, the death-like stillness which succeeded being broken only by the cries of the wounded and the dying comrades so recently beside us in deadly combat. About 1 o'clock at night pickets were posted forty yards from the main line. We were so near the rebel pickets we could hear every movement. Here we lay flat on the ground watching for demonstrations of the enemy until the dawning of another day of blood and death. In the first flush of early morning the rebels advanced with columns *en masse* and at once opened fire on us. This we returned and then quickly retired under a storm of leaden hail. Leaping over the rifle-pits we soon rejoined the command.

The Twenty-ninth regiment now moved in a south-westerly direction along the line of works a short distance, in support of a New York regiment. While supporting this regiment the Twenty-ninth was under artillery fire from the right flank. Colonel Clark was struck by a shell, and rendered unconscious nearly two hours. The

5

regiment again moved into its old position on the road south of the Chancellorsville house, where it remained under heavy fire of artillery and musketry, and in the afternoon our right flank was turned, and the Union army was soon forced back in the direction of the river, at Bank's ford. When the Twenty-ninth fell back the rebels were in possession of the Chancellor house, and there were not one hundred Union soldiers in sight. The army fell back about one mile and a half, filling the woods and the road leading to Banks' ford. Here it took a strong position and threw up a line of works and remained until May 6th, when, after being on arms all night, it marched at 6 A. M., crossed the river at Banks' ford, and camped for the night.

During the three days' fight the Twenty-ninth regiment lost quite heavily; the killed were four, wounded forty-two, and prisoners twenty-five.

In this action the rebel loss was officially reported in killed, wounded, and missing, as upward of 10,000 men, while the Union loss was about the same The rebel loss in killed and wounded was greater than ours, in addition to which they lost one of their ablest generals.

May 7th, marched at 6:30 A. M. It rained hard all day We passed Hartwood church, Staffordshire, and went into camp near Aqua creek, and here it remained until June 3d, when the regiment moved to the south about one mile, and engaged in the construction of two small forts

Early on the morning of June 13th, we received orders to march. Tents were struck, but it was not until late in the afternoon that we moved, and then marched during the whole night, reaching Dumfries after daylight on the morning of the 14th.

15th, march at 4 A. M. Halted on the north bank of

the Occoquan creek for dinner. Resuming the march in the afternoon we passed Fairfax station and Court House on the road leading to Leesburg (marched twenty-five miles). This was a march of much suffering to the men, several of whom died during the day from sunstrokes.

16th. Remained in camp all day.

17th. March in the direction of Leesburg Halted at 12 M., and camped for the night.

June 18th. Marched to near Leesburg and went into camp. *Oh ! How it rains !*

19th. Remained in camp cleaning up guns and equipage, and all is quiet. In the afternoon the Twelfth army corps were ordered out to witness the shooting of three deserters from.the First division of the Twelfth army corps. Following are the names : William Mc-Kee, company A, Forty-sixth Pennsylvania ; Christopher Krumbart, company A, Forty-sixth Pennsylvania ; and William Grover, company B, Thirteenth New Jersey Lieutenant-colonel Clark left us here badly broken down in health.

Sunday, June 20th. In camp cleaning up for inspection. 21st and 22d in camp. 23d, 24th and 25th, Captain Schoonover, in charge of one hundred and twenty men from the brigade, felling timber, uncovering Ball's Bluff in front of Fort Beauregard.

26th. The regiment left Leesburg, crossing the Potomac at Edward's Ferry, passed Poolsville, and encamped for the night at Monocacy aqueduct.

27th Moved at 4:30 A. M by way of Point of Rocks, Petersville and Parkersburg, and camped for the night five miles from Harper's Ferry.

28th. Moved in the forenoon, passing through Harper's Ferry, then up the tow path of the Baltimore &

Ohio canal to Clear Springs, where the Twenty-ninth passed under the canal through a culvert, and moving in the direction of Frederick City, Maryland, went into camp.

29th. Moved through Frederick City in the direction of Pennsylvania, and went into camp. General Hooker was relieved from command of the Army of the Potomac, and General George G. Mead placed in command.

30th. Moved north into Pennsylvania, and late in the afternoon reached Littlestown, where we had a skirmish with the advance guard of the rebel Lee, which falling back toward Gettysburg, we moved north of town; mustered for pay and went into camp for the night.

## CHAPTER IX.

### Gettysburg.

### 1863.

July 1, 1863, the Twenty-ninth regiment, under command of Captain Edward Hayes, marched at 6:30 A. M., passed through Littletown and on towards Gettysburg. After moving some five miles, we halted, and while preparing for dinner, first heard the distant artillery firing which seemed to be many miles away.

While resting, troops were passing to the front. Meanwhile some of Company H had advanced to an eminence, from which they soon returned, reporting that the cannonading was not far off, as they could plainly see the shells as they burst above the timber. We were soon on the march, halting occasionally to breathe, as it was excessively hot and dusty. When about two miles from Gettysburg, we met ambulances returning with the wounded of the First and Eleventh corps, which had been engaged Advancing a short distance, we found still further evidence of the fight in the bodies of those who had been killed in battle, and left beside the road. Late in the afternoon the Twenty-ninth reached the Union lines near Seminary Hill, and here batteries were in position. The troops were moving, and the rapid forming of lines gave evidence that a *battle* was *nigh*.

The Twenty-ninth regiment filed to the left of the pike, and advancing about forty rods, took a position in a wheat field, in line of battle, and here remained on arms during the night.

During the day (July 1st) the First corps, commanded by General J. F. Reynolds, had a sharp fight, in which Reynolds was killed The Eleventh corps (Howard's) was also engaged Late in the afternoon the Nationals were pressed back, and took a strong position a short distance from Gettysburg, on Seminary Ridge, which ended the battle for that day.

During the night we could hear the moving of confederate troops and artillery in our front, while at the same time the Nationals were coming onto the field, so that in the morning of July 2d, the open field and woods presented a solid mass of troops, artillery and supply trains.

About 8 o'clock A. M., July 2d, the Twenty-ninth regiment moved back to the pike, and moved with the division to a position in the timber on a hill, near the right of the line. Here breastworks were thrown up, and skirmishing was almost continuous along the line during the forenoon, and until about 3 o'clock P. M., when the struggle was renewed on the left, and gradually extended to the center. About 6 o'clock P. M., there was a lull on the left, and the fight raged with renewed vigor on the extreme, right and center, with Howard's Eleventh and Slocum's Twelfth ·corps. Late in the evening the Twenty-ninth, with the brigade, withdrew from the works, and moved back about three-fourths of a mile, where it remained during the forepart of the night, moving back and forth, and constantly skirmishing. The entire army appeared to be in motion the greater part of the night.

July 3, 1863, at the dawn of day, the Twenty-ninth, with the brigade, moved back to, and took position in the works left the night before, and about 4 o'clock A. M. the conflict was renewed.

The rebels who had possession of our works were

quickly driven back, and, fifteen minutes after the first
gun was fired, the engagement become general along the
entire line, and for six hours the musketry was one continued roll, interspersed at intervals by the crash of the
artillery. The Twenty-ninth remained in the works except when allowed to retire to secure ammunition, clean
pieces, etc. While thus securing ammunition the rebels
charged the line on our right, gained possession of the
works, and were advancing in force, when that gallant
officer, Colonel Hayes, ordered the Twenty-ninth to fall
in, fix bayonets, and advance to the charge of the rebels
in the rifle pits and advancing on our right. The regiment made a half wheel to the right and advanced
double-quick, when the rebels gave way. An eastern
shore regiment took position next on our right, holding
the rebels in check. A battery was immediately placed in
position, a few rounds from which sent the Confederates
to the rear, leaving their dead and wounded thick about
our line of works.

The Confederates in our front were Ewell's corps, including our old acquaintance, Stonewall Jackson's brigade, which fought with desperation. The rattle of the
musketry, which extended from the extreme right to the
left center of our line, had now become continuous, and
about 1 o'clock P. M. General Lee opened a furious fire
upon our lines from over one hundred and fifty pieces
of artillery, to which more than one hundred National
guns quickly responded; some sixty thousand small arms
were heard amidst the roar of artillery. This unearthly
din continued until late in the afternoon, when the firing
ceased except at intervals, and this continued during
the entire night.

Brevet Captain George Hayward, of company E, promoted for gallant conduct at Chancellorsville, was killed

in this fight. He was daring almost to rashness, always at the front, unmindful of danger, while his tender solicitude for his men endeared him to all who knew him, and his death was sincerely regretted. The rebel who killed him was concealed in the crevice of the rock not more than twenty paces from our line. Upon again exposing his person not less than one hundred rifles were discharged at him ; he sprang backward, a shrill cry rang out upon the air, and brave Hayward's death was avenged.

A little further down the hill lay the dead body of Major Light, assistant adjutant-general on Ewell's staff, who had perished in the morning assault.

Early on the morning of July 4th the Twenty-ninth regiment advanced in reconnoissance over the battlefield, and for the first time gained a full knowledge of the fearful loss of life the rebels had sustained, full five thousand of whom had answered to their last roll-call. Still the mystery exists how any rebels escaped, as each soldier of the Union army had, in the seven hours' fight, fired two hundred and fifty rounds of ammunition, sufficient to have annihilated the entire Southern army.

We moved forward to the base of Culp's hill, and thence left, to the creek near Cemetery hill, on the opposite bank of which were posted the gray-coated pickets of the enemy. Rebel troops were moving through the town, while a force was fortified on Seminary ridge. Pickets were thrown out to observe their movements and we retired to the main line.

During the day nearly five thousand stand of rebel arms were collected from the field, in front of Geary's division alone. Our fallen comrades were tenderly, though rudely, transferred to the kindly embrace of mother earth, while the wounded were collected at convenient points to receive the necessary treatment.

Whoever has followed the phases of the battle of Gettysburg must have been expressed with the stubborn valor displayed on both sides by the common soldiers. The dauntless resolution exhibited in the attacks made it a terribly bloody and destructive conflict, and the unyielding and resolute front of the defence brought victory. But there was no possibility of achieving on either side such sweeping and complete triumphs as are recorded of wars in other countries and in other days, in a contest between two armies where the common soldiers were of such a temper and in such earnest as were these. It is a sad spectacle to see the manhood of two claiming to be Christian peoples thus march out to a field, like trained pugilists, and beat, and gouge, and pummel each other until one or the other from exhaustion must yield. It is revolting and sickening, and it is hoped that the day will come when disputes arising among nations may be settled by compromise, as two reasonable and upright men would decide a difference, governed by the golden rule, instead of resorting to blows where right and justice must be subordinate to brute force. But in a great battle like that which we have been considering it is not the soldiers themselves who are responsible, but the parties who make the quarrel. Hence, while the mind revolts at the scenes of destruction which the field discloses, the immediate actors are not to be held accountable. They go in obedience to the dictates of duty and of patriotism, and while they may indulge no personal hatred toward those who for the time they call enemies, they must in battle inflict the greatest possible injury upon them. In all ages the highest honors have been reserved for those who have fought the battles of their country—and this is right. For if there is any deed in the power of a mortal which can sway the feelings or soften the heart it is that of one man laying down his life for another. The breast heaves and the eye is suffused with tears at the spectacle of Pythias putting his life in jeopardy only for his friend. There is a halo of glory hovering about the profession of arms. It has its seat in the sacrifice of self, which is its ruling spirit.

The man who stands upon the field of battle and faces the storm of death that sweeps along, whether he merely puts his life thus in jeopardy or is actually carried down in death, torn and mangled in the dread fight, is worthy of endless honors, and though we class the deed with the lowest of human acts, prompted by a hardihood which we share with the brutes, and in which the most ignorant and besotted may compete with the loftiest, yet it is an act before which humanity will ever bow and uncover. Who that walked that field of carnage and beheld the maimed and mangled, and him cold in death, could withhold the tribute of honor and respect? For, could he make that dying soldier's lot his own, or that of his nearest and dearest friend, he would only then justly realize the sacrifice. Our casualties in the fight were: Killed, nine; wounded, thirty-five; missing, one. Total, forty-five.

## CHAPTER X.

Return to Washington—Embark for New York—Return—Transferred
to the Western Army.

The pursuit of the retreating enemy was commenced
by the Twelfth army corps at 1 o'clock P. M., on July 5th.
At night we encamped at Littletown, Pennsylvania, and
on the following morning moved by the way of Frederick
to Antietam creek. On the 7th instant we marched
through Frederick, filed to the right, and passed by a
rebel spy that was hanging to a limb of a tree. We
moved a short distance, and halted, where we remained
all night. On the 8th we marched over the mountains
in the direction of Sharpsburg. On the 9th we passed
over the battlefield, and camped near Fairplay, Maryland. On the 10th we moved through the town, and
camped for the night near Falling waters. On the following day we advanced to Fairplay, a small town to the
south of St. James' college, and the Twenty-ninth regiment, with its customary good (?) fortune, was thrown out
as skirmishers, and during the day exchanged frequent
shots with the enemy's cavalry, and at night resting in
position on the extreme front.

During the night rebel cavalry approached very near
our line, but our orders were positive not to fire unless
attacked. On the following morning we were relieved
and retired to the main line, where we assumed position
as support to Knapp's battery, which was hotly engaged
at intervals during the day.

On the morning of the 13th instant we rejoined our

brigade, anticipating an attack. Riflepits were thrown up and due preparation made. The enemy are strongly fortified between St. James' college and Williamsport, some two miles distant, and on the 14th he was reported as falling back across the Potomac. Heavy cannonading is heard towards the river, and the First division of General Williams advances in reconnoissance, the Second acting as support. A dispatch states that Lee's army, in full retreat, began crossing the river yesterday, continued through the night and to-day. Our troops are hotly engaged with his rear guard, and we remain in position until the morning of the 18th, when we move briskly forward in pursuit of the fleeing chivalry, who were now across the Potomac in Virginia. We marched via Sharpsburg and Antietam.

While passing through the woods three men were shot by Mosby's cavalry. A march of sixteen miles and we halt within three miles of Harper's Ferry. At Sandy Hook we remain until the morning of the 19th instant, when we move forward via Harper's Ferry, to Hillsboro, Virginia.

On the following morning we are early on the move, advancing as far as Snickersville, near the gap of that name, where pickets are thrown out and we bivouac for the night. We remain here for two days, during which time we muster and pass in review. Colonel W. T. Fitch recently promoted, and who has been absent on leave since March 28th, joined us here, and assumed command.

On the morning of the 23d we again moved forward, passing through Upperville and on to Ashby's gap, where, at a late hour, we go into camp. Having marched thirty miles since morning sleep was sweet that night, with mother earth for a bed, and only heaven's blue canopy for a cover. At 3 o'clock on the morning of the 24th we march rapidly forward through the villages of Markham and Linden, halting for dinner at Manassas gap, then forward, changing direction by column to the south-southeast, in the direction of White Plains. Marching sixteen miles we halted for the night.

The next day we marched to White Plains, and the next by the way of Thoroughfare gap, Haymarket, and Greenwich, the latter a pretty little village, settled by English people, for whose protection guards were stationed, as they were in fact in many instances for the protection of rebel property. After a brief halt we marched forward via Catlett's station and Warrenton, where we joined the First and Eleventh corps of our army and encamped for the night, then forward again to Kelley's Ford, on the Rappahannock, when, after a short visit, the brigade took cars for Alexandria, Virginia, under orders for New York city, to quell the memorable draft riots induced by the Southern sympathizers and copperheads.

On August 23d we embarked on the steamer Baltic and moved down the Potomac. When near its outlet we went fast aground. This action occurred about noon on the 24th, and three days elapsed before we were again on the move. On the 28th, at 9:45 A. M., we round Cape Henry and strike the swells of the Atlantic. A rough sea soon sends many of the command to the rail to— well, if the reader was ever seasick he will appreciate the situation. It is not pleasant to linger long upon this scene ; the recollection of it, even now, almost destroys one's interest in sublunary affairs.

On the 29th we pass the narrows and enter New York harbor, coming to anchor near Governor's Island at 12 o'clock M.

From our anchorage the view was grandly beautiful with the immense shipping, Brooklyn on the right, New York to the front, and Jersey City on the left. On the left of Governor's Island Castle William (now used as a magazine) stands out in bold relief. To its right is the fort which protects the harbor. On September 1st we disembarked and went into camp on the island. The men are in fine spirits and delighted with the change.

The troubles in the city having subsided we re-embarked aboard the Baltic, which, on the 8th day of September, heads towards the sea. When passing the narrows the guns of the fort thunder a salute; soon Sandy Hook is passed and we are again in the open sea, all happy at the prospect of going to the front, the inactivity of camp life with nothing to do having become tiresome in the extreme.

On September 10th we came to anchor in Chesapeake Bay, where we remained one day, then passed on again to Alexandria, disembarked, and went into camp to the south of the town. Two days later and we again move forward to Elk creek, where we encamp for the night.

September 16th, marched at 6 A. M., reached the Rappahannock at noon, and here rejoined our old brigade. moved forward to Raccoon ford on the north side of the Rapidan. General Lee's forces are massed on the opposite shore of the river, and as we came up our ears were greeted with the pleasing sound of rapid musketry firing proceeding from the pickets of the two armies. During the afternoon we witnessed the execution of two deserters from the Seventy-eighth New York.

During the last of September we learned of the defeat of the Western army at Chickamauga, and the Twelfth corps was at once transferred to the Department of the West, and without delay proceeded by rail to Washington, and thence via Wheeling, Columbus, Indianapolis, Nashville, to Murfreesboro, Tennessee, where we arrived October 5th.

After a few days' rest the regiment again resume the march, passing Duck river, Bell Buckle, and Wartrace, when the Seventh Ohio halted, while the Twenty-ninth moved on to Normandy, on the Nashville & Chattanooga railroad Here it remained in camp, with the usual routine of camp and picket duty until late in October, when the regiment and brigade broke camp, took the cars for Bridgeport, Alabama, where it arrived on the 27th, disembarked, and camped for the night. On the morning of October 28th the Twenty-ninth regiment crossed the Tennessee river with the wagon train. Halting at Shellmound for dinner, marched until late in the evening, and halted near White Sides, where all camped for the night. About 11 o'clock P. M artillery firing, with heavy volleys of musketry, was heard in the direction of Chattanooga, continuing two or three hours.

## CHAPTER XI.

Murfreesboro—General Greene—The Mule Brigade—Congratulatory.

While at Murfreesboro scouts reported that Wheeler's cavalry was in the vicinity, and the Second division (Geary's) was pushed forward to meet it, the First division remaining to guard the post and railway communication. Geary moved forward in the direction of Bridgeport, encountering Wheeler's force near the line of the railway. A brief but sharp skirmish ensued, which resulted in the repulse and hasty retreat of the rebels. We then advanced without delay to Bridgeport. October 27th the Second division, Geary commanding, with Creighton and Greene in command of the First and Second brigades, crossed the Tennessee, the object to open communication on the south side of the river by way of Wauhatchie valley and Lookout mountain for the relief of General Thomas at Chattanooga.

Brigadier-general Greene, with three regiments of infantry and four pieces of Knapp's battery, numbering about fifteen hundred men, with a wagon train of provisions, was sent to the relief of the famishing army at Chattanooga, the balance of our command following as fast as practicable with the immense supply train in charge. After we had encamped for the night the signal corps of General Greene informed us that his command had encamped at Wauhatchie, within six miles of Chattanooga. The knoll occupied by them derived its name from an Indian battle fought there years before. It is situated in the valley not far from the base of Lookout mountain. Knapp's guns were placed in position facing

Lookout, and pickets stationed perhaps fifty yards to the front.

About midnight General Hood's division came down from the heights of Lookout and quietly surrounded General Greene's small force, and at once commenced an attack. Greene's men, aroused from their slumber, hastily formed line under a most deadly fire from all sides, and one of the most desperate struggles on record ensued. We were awakened by the sound of the distant combat, and forming into line hastily advanced to their rescue. When we arrived Hood's rebels had been routed and were flying in all directions, intent only on reaching their mountain stronghold. There was a regular stampede of the mules, which had broken loose and were braying furiously. This, with loud shouts from our men, must have induced a belief in the valorous rebel horde that a large force of cavalry was charging down upon them, and their fears and flight was indeed a grand burlesque finale to a terrible tragedy.

General Greene had lost one-third of his force, killed and wounded, his ammunition was exhausted, and ordering the mules cut loose, he made a desperate bayonet charge to cut his way to freedom. The mules providentially moved in the same direction, mingling the thunder of their tread and their awful voices with the shouts of Greene's men, and our own, to let them know that assistance was coming. The effect was to throw Hood's rebel army into a wild panic and put them to rout. Three hundred prisoners and about one thonsand stand of arms were captured. Every man of Knapp's battery, save one only, was either killed or wounded. Among the former was Lieutenant Geary, son of General John W. Geary. The ground was covered with the dead and injured of both the blue and the gray.

6

While assisting the wounded and burying the dead, Generals Grant, Hooker, and Thomas, with their respective staffs, arrived from Chattanooga. The former coolly remarked as he surveyed the bloody scene: "Well, boys, you must have had a hot time of it, judging from appearances." There was silence among the men, who knew that an army was cosily reposing but four miles away, which could easily have averted the terrible bloodshed, but were so completely disheartened by the defeat at Chickamauga that they dare not venture from their stronghold to the relief of gallant "Corporal" Greene, who happily turned defeat into a heroic victory.

The following lines, composed by one of our command, fully relates the grand finale and

### CHARGE OF THE MULE BRIGADE.

Half a mile, half a mile,
Half a mile onward,
Right towards the Georgia troops
    Broke the two hundred.
"Forward the Mule Brigade,
Charge for the rebs !" they neighed,
Straight for the Georgia troops
    Broke the two hundred

"Forward the Mule Brigade!"
Was there a mule dismayed?
Not when the long ears felt
    All their ropes sundered
Theirs not to make reply;
Theirs not to reason why,
Theirs but to make them fly,
On to the Georgia troops
    Broke the two hundred

Mules to the right of them,
Mules to the left of them,
Mules behind them
    Pawed, neighed, and thundered.
Breaking their own confines,
Breaking through Longstreet's lines,

Into the Georgia troops
   Stormed the two hundred.

Wild all their eyes did glare,
Whisked all their tails in air,
Scatt'ring the chivalry there,
   While all the world wondered
Not a mule's back bestraddled,
Yet how they all skedaddled;
Fled every Georgian
Unsabred, unsaddled,
Scattered and sundered
How they were routed there
   By the two hundred

Mules to the right of them,
Mules to the left of them
Mules behind them
   Pawed, neighed, and thundered,
Followed by hoof and head
Full many a hero fled,
Fain in the last ditch dead,
Back from an "ass's jaw,"
All that was left of them—
   Left by the two hundred

When can their glory fade?
Oh! the wild charge they made!
   All the world wondered.
Honor the charge they made,
Honor the Mule Brigade—
   Long-eared two hundred

Major-general George H. Thomas issued an order
complimenting the column under Major-general Hooker,
which took possession of the line from Bridgeport to the
foot of Lookout Mountain, for their brilliant success in
driving the enemy from every position which they attacked The repulse by General Geary's command of
the greatly superior numbers who attempted to surprise
him, will rank among the most distinguished feats of
arms of the war.

We moved forward the next evening, and threw up a
line of works on the site of this night attack.

## CHAPTER XII

### Lookout Mountain—The Battle—The Regiment Re-enlist

The line of General Geary's division now extends along the foot of Lookout mountain, parallel with the rebel line, and only separated from it by the creek along its base. For nearly ten days the commissary stores intended for us have been largely forwarded to Chattanooga, leaving us with scarcely anything to eat. When on the skirmish line we often sent our reserves around to the right of the mountain to secure corn from a field in that location, held by the rebels, and quite lively little fights would result. Our boys always returned with corn, however, which we parched to allay in part the bitter pangs of hunger. As with everything earthly our long fast ended, rations came, and life began to seem almost worth living, exchanges of coffee and tobacco were almost hourly made between the Union and rebel soldiers, each forgetting for the time the hate engendered over the fight for corn. Our main line was being strongly fortified, the rebels meanwhile keeping up an almost continuous bombardmennt of our line from their batteries on the heights of Lookout. Strong details were employed in cutting away the forest on our front to enable our artillery to cover an hourly expected attack. The situation remained the same until November 23d, when, toward night, the beat of the "long roll" called Geary's division to arms. It at once moved promptly forward, formed line of battle, facing Lookout heights, and advanced to its base along the creek. Osterhaus' division of the Fifteenth corps, and Whittaker's brigade, of the Fourth corps, now advanced to the left of Geary's division. The rebels soon discovered this movement and promptly moved a strong force down the mountain side within easy musket range, where they strongly fortified during the night.

The morning of November 24th opened out a simultaneous discharge of our entire artillery, which was parked along the mountain's point, the infantry on our left advancing to the base of the mountain. The First brigade, led by Colonel Creighton, and followed by the Second and Third brigades, moved rapidly up the creek to the right under cover of the woods, then debouching to the left. The First brigade took the advance and began the ascent of Lookout heights, being favored by a friendly ravine extending toward the crest of the mountain. The brigade had advanced perhaps two-thirds of the distance before the enemy discovered its movements, and now the men renew their efforts, driving the enemy before them despite the terrible fire poured into our advance, and after a desperate struggle reach the rocky crest and disappear in a thick mist (referred to by most writers, we believe, as clouds, and which gave this engagement the title of the "battle above the clouds"). The line of the whole division is extended, and in a moment sweeps down in an impetuous charge on both the rebel flank and rear. Their batteries are reached, the cannoniers beaten back, and the guns captured. Onward, upward, with loud cheers our columns rush to victory, carrying everything before them. A whole brigade is captured, and Lookout mountain, since famous in song and story, is ours. This victory was won by Geary's men, assisted only by Whittaker's brigade acting as support. The troops below now came gallantly(?) up the mountain to claim, as usual, the honors won, as the voluminous reports subsequently written by their generals amply attest  Geary and his brigade commanders had no reports to make save that their division stormed the heights and  carried them, capturing the enemy's artillery and the entire rebel force occupying the main defenses of the mountain.   Some time after the capture the standard of the "white star" division was planted on the crest and the  stars and stripes was soon waving beside it.   No danger was incurred by this, as none of the enemy remained except the prisoners, yet it has been written and rewritten as if it were an event of some importance.

"The morning of November 25th revealed the white star standard of Geary and the glorious old stars and stripes to the army below, floating triumphantly side by side on Lookout's rocky crest.   Prolonged huzzas greeted the victors from below, and to confirm that 'to the victors belong the spoils,' a detachment from two regiments of Geary's command take charge of the prisoners, seven stand of colors, and a great number of cannon captured."

The rebels had burned the bridge across Lookout creek, which delayed our further advance a short time. A bridge was soon improvised, however, and a crossing was effected.   The command moved on to Rossville, where it engaged Braggs' left, while General Thomas, advancing from Chattanooga valley, moved up Missionary ridge, striking Bragg a crushing blow in the center, and Pap Sherman was making it warm for his right flank. About 2 o'clock P. M. the firing became general along the entire line, which continued until late in the afternoon, when the rebels were driven from  the field with great loss. The Union army advanced a short distance and bivouacked for the night.

November 26, we moved on after the retreating army, and at a small creek near Greysville, Georgia, had a skirmish, driving the enemy as far as Ringgold and Taylor's ridge, where they were in position behind breastwork in the narrow pass extending through the ridge in the direction of Dalton.

27th. Geary's division made a gallant charge upon the rebel works. The First brigade, commanded by Colonel William R. Creighton, made a direct assault on Taylor's ridge, while the Second and Third brigades engaged the rebels in the narrow defile. After a terrible struggle the Nationals were forced back a short distance. A battery was moved forward and placed in position, which opened with double shotted guns upon the enemy, soon driving them precipitately to the rear, leaving the Nationals in possession of the field. In this engagement the Union loss was quite heavy.

On the 28th the army moved back, Geary's division reaching Wauhatchie valley on the 29th. Resting a few days, when the Twenty-ninth Ohio regiment broke camp and on December 3d moved across Lookout creek, marched about two miles west of Summerville, on Lookout mountain, where it camped for the night. Returned to its old camp at Wauhatchie, Tennessee, on the 5th day of December, and the campaign of 1863 ended.

At Wauhatchie, on the 10th day of December, 1863, the Twenty-ninth Ohio, though now reduced to less than three hundred effective men for duty, almost to a man re-enlisted for three years more, should the war so long continue, and were given a thirty-days' furlough home for the purpose of recruiting. The headquarters of the regiment was established at Cleveland, Ohio.

It remained here some two months.  At last the decimated ranks were filled and, on the morning of February
8, 1864, the regiment bade a second good bye to friends,
and amidst their prayers for success and a safe return
departed for the front, determined to die for the flag if
necessary, and, after a tedious ride of many weary miles
arrived at Bridgeport, Alabama, via Louisville, Nashville,
and Murfreesboro, where it went into winter quarters and
remained until the opening of the spring campaign of
1864.

## CHAPTER XIII.

Shelmound—Wauhatchie Valley—Ringgold—Battle of Dug or Mill
Creek Gap or Buzzard's Roost—On the Move.

On the morning of May 3, 1864, at 10 o'clock, we broke camp, crossed the Tennessee river, and moved eastward along its south bank to Shelmound, where we encamped for the night  On the following day the march was resumed, the column halting for dinner in Wauhatchie valley. Crossing Lookout Creek and mountain, we encamped for the night on its east side and two miles distant from Chattanooga. The column resumed its line of march at 7 A M , on the 5th. Moving cautiously during the day, in the advance, it halted for the night a short distance west of Ringgold, Georgia. At daybreak on the following morning we moved forward, and about 9 o'clock formed line of battle, remaining here during the day and subsequent night. The beat of the "long roll" on the following morning called us to arms, and we immediately advanced in line of battle. When near Gordon's Springs General Kilpatrick passed to our right with his command. Our column came to a halt for the night near Tunnel hill

At about 11 A. M, on May 8th, we pushed forward in order of columns right in front, and at 3 o'clock arrived in front of John's Mountain at Rocky Face Ridge, on the summit of which the enemy were entrenched in force. The Twenty-ninth Ohio regiment and Twenty-eighth Pennsylvania of the First brigade, Colonel Candy commanding, with three regiments of Buschbeck's Second brigade, formed in line, the latter on the right, and in this order at once moved forward to storm the ridge. The position of the Twenty-ninth regiment in the assaulting column was on the extreme left, the Twenty-eighth Pennsylvania next on its right, connecting with the Second brigade. Our instructions were to make a strong demonstration, and to carry, if possible, the rebel position. While advancing to the assault, the brass bands in our rear indiscreetly commenced playing National airs, which attracted the attention of the rebel commander, who rapidly concentrated reinforcements in our front. The advance up the declivity was nearly as difficult as Lookout Mountain, and more completely fortified. Its summit was steep, precipitous, and covered with scraggy rocks and immense boulders From our position we commanded a fine view of Dug Gap, a narrow, artificial cut through the rocky summit, connecting with a road extending almost parallel with the ridge to the gap beyond, and by a zigzag course reaching the mountain's base. The rebels had so completely fortified themselves that it was next to impossible for our assaulting force to get nearer than their base. As we approached the rebel line, a regiment was moved by left flank across our front At this moment the rebel line opened a fire so deadly in effect that the regiment in our front became disordered and broke through our ranks to the rear, causing a momentary confusion in the ranks of the Twenty-ninth regiment. At this moment the order was given to advance, which was executed with a rush despite the deadly volleys that were cutting through our ranks. Up! up! we go to death or victory! and commenced to scale the obstructions close to their works; and now a storm of deadly missiles are hurled against us. Rocks, boulders, and even cart-wheels come crashing down upon us Yet we moved steadily in the deadly advance until ordered back by our officers, when we retired a few paces to reform our line, the fallen trees only separating us from the enemy.

Here we made a determined and bloody fight, but having no support to cover our flank we were subjected to a deadly cross-fire from the left, yet the regiment stubbornly stood its ground, returning shot for shot until its ammunition was exhausted. More was secured from the cartridge-boxes of the dead and wounded, and with this we fought on, determined to hold the position until reinforcements should reach us. Just before dusk an order came from the commanding general for the Twentyninth regiment to retire, all the other regiments having done so some time previous. To cover our retreat a line of skirmishers was thrown out, composed of men from each company who volunteered for this dangerous duty, and right nobly did they perform this work, firing with deadly precision as they retired from the field into the valley below, where the Twenty-ninth were already in bivouac, and comrades cheered lustily as the skirmishers came in, happy to know they had not met the fate of others

John Davis, of company B, a Scotchman by birth and one of the best shots in the regiment, fired the last shot in this day's action, and was the last to leave the field.

The Twenty-ninth regiment in this fight distinguished itself by brave conduct, though at last compelled to retire from lack of support. Our losses in killed and wounded was more than double that of any other regiment engaged: Killed, 26, wounded, 67, captured 1, total 94

General Geary highly complimented the regiment for its gallantry, remarking that he never saw men advance under such murderous fire, especially when unsupported

and where the chances of success were so desperate.
The Twenty-ninth regiment lost nearly one-third its
numbers during this three hours' engagement, and many
were the individual acts of heroism displayed, which it
would give the writer pleasure to record. As but few
are now remembered, the remainder would suffer an in-
justice were these given. It is, however, but simple justice to state that the regiment fully sustained its previous
reputation as a fighting organization, each individual
doing his full share in the terrible work. Subsequent
events proved that this assault was made to draw the
enemy to this point, thus giving McPherson's corps and'
Kilpatrick's cavalry an opportunity to possess Snake
Creek Gap, a desirable situation several miles in our
right rear, opening a flank movement directly on the enemy's rear.

On May 9th we encamp at Mill Creek, near Johns
Mountain, where we remain until 12 o'clock, midnight.
We then move to the right and throw up earthworks.
May 10th we are still at work. We receive the news of
General Grant's victory over General Lee at the Wilder-
ness, near Chancellorsville, Virginia, where our regiment
received such a baptism of blood a little more than a
year since. Alas! how many of our brave boys have
gone down to death since then.

May 11th. Still in the same position, hourly expecting orders to move; quartermasters remove all extra baggage to the rear, all men unable for active service sent to
hospital, and everything possible put into perfect fighting
order, and by the way it's ever so much nicer penning
these lines here in our cosy room in the far away Western
Reserve of the Buckeye State than was the actual experience in Secessia during those early May days of
1864.

On the 12th instant we moved forward to Snake Creek Gap, forming a junction with the Fifteenth and Sixteenth corps (McPherson's), where we remained during the night. At 2 o'clock P. M. on the following day we advanced toward Resaca, fully occupying Snake Creek Gap Our cavalry are sharply engaged with the enemy Here brave General Kilpatrick is wounded At 4 o'clock P. M. the battle is still raging fiercely, and the enemy are being slowly driven back. At last a hill is captured which covers the entire rebel line. Here we fortify and rest for the night

May 14th a severe engagement opens near Resaca; we advance by a circuitous route to the left, the Fourteenth corps is engaged, during the afternoon we joined our Twentieth corps and moving rapidly to the left, succeeded in rescuing a portion of the Fourth corps from disaster and defeat, and one of its batteries from certain capture, the infantry support having been driven back, leaving the battery at the mercy of the rebels. Robinson's brigade, of Williams' division, Twentieth corps, who were in the advance, fortunately reached the scene of action in time to prevent the capture of another battery by making a counter-charge on the advancing rebel legions We came up soon after this support, which soon ended in the complete repulse of the rebels, driving them beyond their fortifications. The Twentieth army corps received the compliments of the commanding general, Hooker, for their gallant work, which resulted in a loss to the enemy of some four hundred men killed and wounded.

## CHAPTER XIV.

### Battle of Resaca, Georgia—In Pursuit of the Fleeing Chivalry (?)

At an early hour on the morning of May 15th sharp skirmishing opened along our entire front.    General Geary's Second division moved a short distance to the left and halted for orders.    About 11 o'clock Generals Sherman, Hooker, and Thomas, with their respective staffs, reached the battlefield and immediately held a council of war    General Hooker is requested to assume command of selected troops to take the offensive, and is asked how large a force he required to capture a certain fort directly in our front, known to be the enemy's stronghold and the key to his position    Hooker astonished his superiors by replying :   " Geary's division can, I think, carry that position if it can be done by anyone." As this conversation was heard by our men we were prepared for what was to follow.

As soon as General Geary had received his instructions, the Second division moved to the attack in the following orders :   Second and Third brigades in the advance, with the First brigade closely massed in their rear, the latter advancing closely in support of the attacking column.   Our advance was met with obstinate resistance, yet we steadily pushed forward, driving the enemy back and gaining possession of three lines of hills in rapid succession, the last of which was in close proximity to the rebel fort, only a narrow ravine intervening.   The enemy are strongly entrenched in earthworks extending in the rear of the fort.    The First brigade commenced a rapid firing at short range to cover the sortie being made by regiments of the Second and Third brigades. These regiments rush gallantly forward to the assault. They are repulsed but quickly reform, and, with other regiments sent to their support, they again pass forward. The fort was captured and lost three times in succession, but at last the rebels are forced to flee before our furious charge. Leaving the guns they join the main line.

The Union forces prevented the rebels from again occupying the fort until dark, when detachments from the Twenty-ninth and other Ohio regiments of the First brigade were sent to open a trench through the earthworks of the fort through which to move the guns into the ravine below. The rebels discovering this charged down upon us to recapture the guns. Expecting such an attack the First brigade had moved forward into the ravine, and now waited the coming of the rebels. When close upon them a signal was given, which was followed by a sheet of flame along our whole line, dealing terrible destruction into the rebel ranks, immediately followed by a determined bayonet charge, which threw their lines into disorder and they fled panic-stricken over their fortifications, closely pursued by our command, whose loud huzzas sent Johnston's army in rapid retreat, abandoned all its cannon, hospital, and commissary stores, and with their usual savagery leaving their own dead and wounded upon the field. We also captured many prisoners.

This success was a grand victory for the "white star" division of the Twentieth corps, yet not unattended with losses, which were, however, light in comparison with those of the enemy. In fact, in the night attack we had so thoroughly surprised the enemy that but feeble resistance was made.

At an early hour on the morning of May 16th we pushed rapidly forward in pursuit of the retreating rebels. At 9 o'clock A. M. we came into line on the bank of the Coosa river, near the railroad bridge, which our cavalry had prevented the rebels from burning, though they had made repeated efforts to do so. The enemy's flight was so rapid that he had not even time to seriously impair the railroad track. Our locomotives, with trains of surplies, soon came in sight. We now advanced across the river and encamped for the night.

At 12 M. on May 17th, the general forward movement of our army was resumed. The Twenty-ninth regiment was the advance guard of its division, and assisted in driving the rebels from the little village of Calhoun, where we halt for the night. At 5 o'clock on the following morning we again moved forward in the direction of Rome, Georgia. At Rome cross-roads the rebels were met and promptly engaged by the Fourth corps; a lively fight ensued, resulting in slight losses on both sides. The enemy retreated, and we continued the pursuit until 9 o'clock P. M., when we encamped for the night.

On the next morning at early dawn we pushed forward, continuing until 3 o'clock P. M., when we halt and form line near Kingston, Georgia. The whole force of the enemy are immediately on our front, and the Fourth corps promptly open fire upon them, which resulted in a further movement of the chivalry to the rear.

We remain here until the morning of May 23d when we move about daylight via Cassville and Cass station to the Etowah river, which is crossed on pontoons, and a halt for the night made on its opposite bank. The next morning we resume the weary march, coming into line of battle at about 9 A. M. We advanced in this order up the Raccoon hills, or Alatoona range, until night, when we encamp at Burnt Hickory. The First brigade, as advance guard, moved ahead at daybreak, via the Burnt Hickory road.

7

## CHAPTER XV.

Pumpkin Vine Creek—Dallas, or New Hope Church—Slight Unpleasantness—Personal.

At Pumpkin Vine creek we discover the enemy and drive back his skirmishers, who are stationed on its opposite bank, recovering the bridge, which we cross and throw out skirmishers on the opposite side. While this was being accomplished, General Hooker and Staff, with a small body guard, pushed ahead to reconnoiter. He had not advanced far, however, when he was attacked by a force of rebel sharp shooters. He now came tearing back into our lines shouting to General Geary to move his First brigade into position to hold the enemy in check until the Second and Third brigades should come up, they being some four miles in our rear. We quickly formed line by columns to the right and left, the Twenty-ninth Ohio occupying position on the extreme left, Knapp's battery taking position immediately in our rear, to cover the bridge in case we were forced to retire before reinforcements should reach us. As the left company of the Twenty-ninth were completing the battle-line a rebel column was found marching in close proximity to our flank.

Ten paces to the front the skirmishers were hotly engaged, but our flank was uncovered. We immediately face to the left and prepare to fire, but are prevented by instructions not to draw on a general engagement but to hold the position at all hazards. The rebel column on our flank, however, slowly retired without firing a gun, and forming on their main line, which was massed in the

woods a short distance to our front.    During this time
we hastily changed front in form of a semi-circle to pro-
tect us from flank attack    This movement was executed
none too soon, as the enemy came immediately to the
attack, and a sharp engagement opened all along the
line, which was a hot one, yet it gallantly held its own
until the balance of its division came up   Forming in
bolumn with us, we advance on the rebel line and drive
them slowly back

The battle now became fierce and our assaults were
heroically met.   Generals Hooker and Geary were present
and ordered the attack, the plan of which was to advance
lines and fire, to be followed by bayonet charges, by
which the enemy was steadily driven back.    Our front
line was frequently relieved by columns from the rear,
thus keeping fresh men at the front.    Geary's division
alone had driven Hood's rebel corps back to the forks of
the road at New Hope church, when Butterfield's Third
division arrived and took position on our left.    Soon
after, Williams came up with the First division and
passed to the front, which allowed the Second division
to drop in the reserve long enough to clean our firearms
and replenish cartridge-boxes, when we again advance in
support of the First and Third divisions.

Just as the sun disappeared in the western horizon,
General Geary ordered the First brigade to charge the
enemy.    This movement was executed on the double-
quick, and as our columns passed in perfect alignment
to the front, Butterfield's and Williams' commands
greeted us with hearty cheers of genuine admiration.
Onward the column rushes, and closing with the enemy
delivers a terrible volley    The charge is continued, the
air resounding with defiant cheers as the enemy is driven
from the field and down a hill at a brisk run    It was

now beginning to grow dark, and the impetuous rush of the men soon brought them within a short distance of a line of brush-covered work which concealed the enemy's batteries, who at once opened a terrific and deadly fire of grape and canister into our ranks. Instantly falling on the ground, we deliver so destructive a fire on their cannoniers that their guns are soon silenced. Our left being without support, an attempt to carry their works was extremely hazardous. The regiment on our right had already retired some distance to our right rear, making the situation of the Twenty ninth regiment one of great danger, but owing to the darkness we knew nothing of it until an officer of Geary's staff came forward with an order to fall back, when we retired to a position some forty paces from the rebel line.

The enemy had now ceased firing, and perfect silence reigned, only broken by the groans of the wounded and dying. The Twenty-ninth regiment had suffered severe loss, and only the favorable depression in its front saved it from annihilation. W. F. Stevens, captain of company B, was wounded in this action.

The Fifth Ohio, on our right on higher ground, suffered fearfully from the masked batteries, one company being almost entirely decimated. This caused the regiment to retire to the knoll. Colonel Patrick, a most gallant officer of the Fifth, was killed, also seventy-five of his men killed and wounded. The loss of the Twenty-ninth Ohio in this charge was forty killed and wounded, shot down in almost the short space of time required to record it.

It was not long before we heard tremendous cheering in the distance on our right front, which was caused by Sherman moving a force in that direction, turning the rebel flank, which was soon in full retreat. Immediately

after, sounds were heard in the supposed deserted rebel
works, which we believed were our own men who had
recently occupied them, and by reason of this supposed
safety our whole command was soon in slumber deep
and heavy from exhaustion of the day's labor

At early dawn on May 26th the enemy discovered our
close proximity, and at once opened upon us with artillery, and at about the same time advanced its infantry
to attack us in our rear  This movement was discovered, however, in time to prevent its further progress.
After a hot fight the enemy retired to his fortifications.
During the day several attempts were made in the same
direction, but without effect  Near the close of the day
we were temporarily relieved and retired to a ravine a
few yards in our rear, where we received rations, the first
"square meal" in two days

At an early hour the following morning (May 27th)
our artillery took position at the breastworks and opened
a furious cannonading, which is replied to with spirit by
the rebel batteries  During the afternoon the enemy
made a sortie on our line, a general engagement ensued,
and the rebels were beaten back.  The Twenty-ninth
regiment loss was slight, we being well protected by rifle
pits.  The rebel loss in this attack was severe, their dead
and wounded being thickly strewn in front of our works.
During this attack General Sherman and staff took position in our rear.  General Hooker is generally where the
bullets fly thickest, and his utter disregard of danger has
won the love of the " boys," who call him " Uncle Joe,"
and who are all, at any time, ready to go through fire if
he so desires, knowing he will not ask them to go where
he fears to lead.

The battle continues throughout the following day,
with brisk infantry firing and heavy cannonading almost

incessantly.    As night again shrouds the bloody field the
Twenty-ninth regiment, with the exception of company
B, which was on the skirmish line, relieved the Seventh
Ohio, One Hundred and Ninth, and One Hundred and
Forty-seventh Pennsylvania.    The rebels were unusually
quiet during the night.    Company B remained on the
skirmish nearly all of the following day and was kept
hotly engaged.    The company's position was not more
than eight rods from the rebel outposts, who made it extremely hot for us as we went back and forth to the relief
of our comrades, and sometimes unsoldierly attitudes
were assumed to evade their deadly aim.    Late in the
day company B was relieved    Henry Brainard, Spencer
Atkin, and Henry Clark volunteered to go out and bring
in the bodies of Albert Atkin, C A Davis, and Jerome
Phinney, which they did, the enemy opening fire upon
them with musketry and artillery, the deadly missiles flying thick and fast about them.    Such was the treatment
of the "chivalry" to men bravely exposing themselves
to give Christian interment to the gallant men who had
fought their last battle.    However, none were injured.
While performing the last sad rites of burial, the rebels
came out in a sortie and made furious assaults along our
entire line.    Our men reserved their fire until the enemy
were close upon them, when, at a given signal, some
twenty cannon, double shotted with grape, opened fire,
which made the earth tremble with their awful thunder,
while the infantry sent deadly volleys into their ranks
The result of this fire was most terrible slaughter to the
enemy, who broke and ran anywhere to cover, leaving
several hundred dead and dying behind, the ground
between the two lines being literally covered with the
rebel dead    During the 30th there were several sharp
fights, our regiment having several men wounded.    May

31st the regiment was under fire, as usual, the greater part of the day, and at night was engaged in the construction of an advanced line of works, under a heavy fire from the entire rebel line. Before they were fully completed the rebels commenced an attack and we fell back on the main line. General Geary being present, exclaimed, "Get back to your command in readiness for an engagement." One ensued, which resulted in driving the enemy back with severe loss to them. We now resumed work and finally succeeded in completing the line, though continually annoyed by the enemy's firing.

On the morning of June 1st the regiment resumed its place on the front line and was soon furiously engaged, which continued during the fore part of the day. At noon the Twentieth corps was relieved by Logan's Fifteenth corps and moved to the left as support to the Fourth corps (General Howard). The following morning we moved towards the left and at 11 o'clock A. M. formed line and pushed forward in concert with Schofield's Twenty-third corps. We capture two lines of rebel works, the enemy falling back. That night we slept on our arms. At dawn on the 3d we advanced and were soon engaged with the enemy, the skirmishing along our whole line being very strong. During the day Sherman succeeded in turning the rebel right, causing him to retire with severe loss. Twenty-ninth loss : Killed, six, wounded, twenty-four ; captured, one ; total thirty-one. This is the tenth day we have been under fire. 4th.—Firing during all of last night. All quiet to-day.

## CHAPTER XVI.

Advance to Pine Knob—Battle at that Place—A Forward Movement.

At 5 o'clock on the morning of June 6th, the army pushed forward after the retreating enemy. When about two miles from Ackworth Station he makes a stand, and we wheel into line, the Twenty-ninth acting as skirmishers while the other troops were engaged in preparing rifle-pits. The Fourteenth corps now came up, forming on our left, and General Howard's Fourth corps on our right. The position remained the same until June 10th, when the Twenty-ninth Ohio is sent forward on a reconnoissance. A large force of rebels are found to be strongly entrenched on Pine mountain. At dark the regiment returned to the main line, where the situation remains unchanged until June 14th, when our entire force move forward. The Twentieth, with the Fourth corps on its left, take position immediately in front of the rebel army, on Pine mountain. At evening the Twenty-ninth was again advanced to the skirmish line, and was engaged, as was our artillery, throughout the greater part of the night. On the following day, June 15th, occurs the battle of Pine Knob, Georgia.

At early dawn our regiment pushed forward as the advance of a general flank movement on Pine mountain, which resulted in its capture without severe fighting. The Twentieth corps was changed from the front to the right. Moving rapidly in that direction it soon reached another strongly entrenched position of the enemy, when the column made a left half wheel, which brought

the first brigade of Geary's division directly in front of
Pine Knob.

This position of the enemy was found to be strongly
fortified. Twenty embrazures, from which as many cannon bristled, covered all the approaches to it. General
Hooker ordered General Geary to send two regiments in
a sortie against the rebel position, and the Twenty-ninth
Ohio and Twenty-eighth Pennsylvania regiments, the
latter on our left, were at once forwarded to the assault.
General Hooker, mounted on his famous gray charger,
advanced with us, immediately in rear of our line. The
general's presence greatly encouraged the men in this
desperate undertaking.

On the hill were the twenty cannon, which we knew
would soon belch forth destruction to our ranks. The
two regiments silently but rapidly cross a ravine where
they encounter two rebel regiments. These proved to
be the First and Twenty-ninth Georgia. We opened
fire briskly and charging upon them soon drove them in
disorder to the rear.

We pursued them so hotly that our standard-bearer
was at one time within a few paces of the rebel Twenty-
ninth Georgia colors, which we were making desperate
efforts to capture. The rebel color-bearer was shot,
but their flag was grasped again by another rebel who
escaped with it into their fortification. But the regiment
to which he belonged was nearly annihilated before it
succeeded in regaining its main line. Our regiment had
rushed upon them forcing them back step by step until
they were under cover, and we had succeeded in killing,
wounding, and taking prisoners all except the little handful who escaped with the flag. At the moment of their
escape we made a dash to carry their fortifications, but
were checked by abattis and a deep trench hidden by

brush. At this point their artillery opened with murderous discharges of grape and canister, which produced terrible destruction in our ranks. Still the line stands firm. Another instant and our men are laying flat upon the ground and the deadly missles go hissing harmlessly through the air over our heads. We now open a fire upon their cannoniers, so deadly in its character that the guns are soon silenced.

Night was fast coming on when our line was ordered to fall back to a more secure position. The men now engage in the erection of earthworks within a few rods of the rebel fort on the knob, which placed the Twenty-ninth Ohio in the extreme front, our flanking regiments assuming a circular position on our right and left rear. We were under fire all night, the rebel infantry and artillery keeping up an almost continuous rattle in their endeavors to drive our men from their labors on the fortifications. Despite this, however, we held our position, though suffering a constant loss in our ranks.

Just at daybreak on the 16th instant the Sixty-sixth Ohio, of our brigade from the reserve, relieved us ; we, however, left them well protected by the strong earthworks constructed during the night.

The Twenty-ninth Ohio regiment went into this action with two hundred members, of whom thirty-nine were killed and wounded. Among the killed was First Sergeant Joel E. Tanner, one of our bravest men. Soon after his death his commission reached us promoting him to a captaincy for bravery in action. God help that little wife of his in her far away northern home to bear his death bravely as the wife of a soldier should, even though all her hopes and bright anticipations seem shattered by the blow. Generals Joe Hooker and Geary announced in warm terms their admiration of the " gallant manner in which the Twenty-ninth Ohio and Twenty-eighth Pennsylvania regiments conducted themselves in the assault on Pine Knob." The former remarked that taking into consideration the deadly fire we were exposed to, we had accomplished that which he never saw so small a force attempt before. As he was present in the assault his opinion is of value.

Sharp skirmishing and artillery firing continued along the line during the day At night the Twenty-ninth regiment moved to the front, relieving the Sixty-sixth Ohio regiment It was nearly morning when we discovered that the enemy were withdrawing their artillery. We at once advanced and possessed the rebel fortifications on the hill with little trouble, as the artillery had already withdrawn and the infantry were rapidly following. After daylight we pushed forward, only to find the enemy in another strong position, which we at once attacked A rambling fire was kept up during the entire day.

During the following day (June 18th) the same state of affairs continued, the firing extending along our entire front. At an early hour next morning the enemy retreated, and we moved in pursuit, the Twenty-ninth Ohio regiment, as usual, in the advance as skirmishers. Why, I believe the "boys" would have rebelled had they not been put on the skirmish line whenever there was a prospect of somebody being killed on our side Rapidly we gained possession of two lines of hills, and soon found the enemy upon a third ridge, strongly fortified. A skirmish of two hours' duration ensues, and we are ordered to fall back to the main line, as support to Bundy's Thirteenth New York battery.

June 20th the Twenty-ninth regiment and its brigade are in line three miles southwest of Marietta, Georgia, and skirmished all day with the enemy. As night came on our division moved to the right, forming on the right of Butterfield's Third division. Our regiment was again on the skirmish line, and in active engagement during the greater part of the night. The next morning we formed line of battle near Culp's farm and to the right of Little Kenesaw mountain. At about 11 A. M. our regiment was withdrawn from the skirmish line, and at once began throwing up rifle-pits parallel with works of Williams' First division on our right and Butterfield's on our left. The Third brigade of the Second division now advanced and engaged the enemy, our single line affording feeble protection in the event of an attack on our position.

## CHAPTER XVII.

Battle of Culp's Farm or Kenesaw Mountain—The Glorious Fourth—
Advance to the Chattahoochie.

June 22d we move to the front, and occupy a ridge on Culp's farm, which covers the level on our front. We had been but a short time in this position when the rebel General Hood's corps was moved directly on our front, and immediately advanced in furious attack upon the divisions of Generals Geary and Williams. Our artillery was at once turned upon the advancing rebel columns, which, with the terrific volleys our infantry poured into their ranks, produced a sudden check to their further advance, and in less than one hour these two divisions succeeded in beating back and putting to total rout Hood's entire command, which suffered great loss, while ours was but slight. The enemy left on the field 2,100 killed, wounded, and prisoners, besides many wounded, removed from the field. The estimated rebel loss was 3,000 men. Eight hundred of the rebel dead were buried on the field.

At the close of this action a body of our skirmishers were deployed over the field, finding the enemy's dead and wounded scattered thickly about. In places they lay stretched across each other, literally heaped up, bloody, terrible—dead. Our skirmishers advanced rapidly, and were soon engaged with the enemy's rear, but this soon ceased, and we established a picket line for the night. We remained on the field until noon of the 23d, when we were retired and rejoined the main line.

At about 4 o'clock P. M., one hundred guns opened a

simultaneous fire on Little Kenesaw mountain. Directly in front of our regiment and across the creek, which flows along the base of the mountain, is level ground. At this point is situated a block-house and rifle-pits, the latter between the house and mountain, and both now held by rebel sharpshooters, who were continually picking off our cannoniers. General Geary, evidently contemplating an advance of his line, called for twenty volunteers from the Twenty-ninth regiment to dislodge these troublesome occupants of the block-house and rifle-pits. In response to this call two men from each company came quickly forward, and at once advanced across the creek and ravine. The rebels soon discovered the detachment, and opened fire upon it. Sergeant Griswold, of Company B, in command, rapidly advanced his men up the rise of open ground lying between him and the enemy, and with a rush amidst a perfect storm of bullets, closed on the rifle-pits, capturing all who remained in them.

We now approach the rear of the block-house and demand its surrender. The rebel lieutenant in command exclaimed from the window of the house: "You d—d yanks, take us if you can!" and immediately opened fire. The door of the house is soon battered down, and the rebels attempt to cut their way out. Finding themselves covered by nearly a score of rifles, aimed by determined men, all, with the exception of the rebel lieutenant and one other, threw down their arms and surrendered. The rebel·officer fired on the captors and lost his life by his rashness. We had now a total of twenty-one prisoners. Several others were killed or badly wounded. The former were sent at once to the rear, and the little force deployed along the road to hold the position until reinforcements should arrive. However, they were not furnished, and after holding the position some two hours a heavy body of rebels came upon us, stealing along under cover of the bushes on the opposite side of the road, suddenly arose and fired a volley at us. The speed we made across the level field with the rebels in hot pursuit, their bullets whistling past our ears in the most energetic manner, would have dismayed a professional pedestrian.

June 24th, skirmishing during the day. As night came on a detachment of the Twenty-ninth regiment was sent out on picket. Nothing occurred during the night, and at dawn we returned to our brigade, where orders were received to hold ourselves in readiness to move on notice, cannonading and skirmish fighting being kept up along the line.

The situation remained unchanged until June 27th. At an early hour this morning two men from each company of our regiment volunteered to advance to the relief of the Pennsylvania regiment on the outposts, and about 9 o'clock A. M. we moved forward. We were also to dislodge the rebel sharpshooters, who had been allowed to again possess the block-house and rifle-pits. Crossing the creek and ravine we made a quick dash toward the locality mentioned, amid a hot cross-fire from rebels along the fence before referred to. But as we close the rebels abandon the block-house and rifle-pits, yet dispute with the energy of desperation, every inch of our advance as they retire. We, however, gained possession of the road beyond the house, an important position covering the rebel left on Little Kenesaw.

They now opened fire on us from the mountain on our left and front. Making a flank movement to the left we came up in rear of some rebel rifle-pits, capturing eleven prisoners and holding the position until the

Fifth Ohio regiment came to our support. That regiment at once began to fortify, while we remained on the skirmish line under constant fire. The enemy discovered the work of the Fifth and trained their batteries from different directions on our position, and also advanced infantry, who made repeated attempts to dislodge us. Solid shot and shell came crashing through the block-house, the shells bursting amongst us in quick succession. Nor were their musketry behind in sending their death-dealing missiles upon us.

Knapp's battery soon came up the hill, and swinging into position, unlimbered and opened a rapid cross-fire on Little Kenesaw mountain. About this time the Fourteenth, with a portion of the Fourth corps, made a desperate assault on the mountain a short distance to our left. The engagement now became serious, one shell killing twelve and another six of our men. To hold the position we had captured was an arduous undertaking, and so severe was the fighting that those of us who had advanced early in the morning had fired nearly two hundred rounds. At dusk the fighting ceased, and we are recalled to our command.

June 28th.—This morning at sunrise we advance obliquely to the right, and, reaching an advanced position, throw up fortifications; rebel batteries open fire on us meanwhile. Our lookout, as he sees smoke issue from the rebel guns, calls out: "Lay down," "lay low," or "look out, she's coming," etc. Many laughable and other incidents occurred during this bombardment, such as attempts to dodge shells, etc. Charles Upton, of Company G, while carrying a rail, had it cut in two by a shell; he, however, escaped unhurt.

June 29th.—To-day the Fourteenth corps obtained a temporary truce under flag, during which they interred their dead. An assault is made on this corps during the early part of the night, but is repulsed, and we were not again disturbed.

June 30th.—During this afternoon the Twenty-ninth regiment received orders to move. About 10 o'clock at night our corps (the Twentieth) was relieved by the Fourteenth We at once marched several miles to the right in relief of the Twenty-third corps.

On July 1st our regiment was again engaged. The fighting ceased only with daylight. Sharp skirmishing and severe cannonading continued during the entire day of the 2d, and at night the Twenty-ninth regiment occupied its customary position—on the skirmish line This time, however, it was accompanied by the Twenty-eighth Pennsylvania. Just before daylight on the morning of July 3d, the enemy were found to be retreating, and we at once moved forward to find the works deserted, the troops having evacuated. The position, as supposed, was almost impregnable to direct assault, being constructed to enfilade an attack of infantry.

The army now push forward in pursuit of the retreating rebels, the Twenty-ninth Ohio and Twenty-eighth Pennsylvania taking the advance in the order of heavy skirmishers. We soon came upon Wheeler's rebel cavalry, and engaged his dismounted men so promptly that they fell precipitately back to where their horses were picketed The Twenty-ninth succeeded in capturing nearly one hundred of them in their hurried efforts to remount The Second division during the pursuit captured nearly nine hundred prisoners. The rebels were steadily falling back on the Chattahoochie river. It was late when we halted for the night. How sweet the wooing of the drowsy god after such long continued fatigue, only those who have been there can imagine, the soft side

of a rail on such occasions being more luxurious than
any patent spring contrivance of to-day.

July 4th. On this day, made glorious to all this good-
ly land by the forefathers of both the blue and gray, was
celebrated by the issue of full rations of hard-tack,
s——, bacon, and coffee, and wonderful feats of gor-
mandizing ensued. To make the day something of a
reminder of the Northern anniversary, with its tearing
headache of the 5th, General "Joe" ordered an issue
of liquor to the men, the first of the campaign. About
4 o'clock P. M. we broke camp and marched towards the
left, but soon came to a halt for the night.

At dawn on the following day we pushed forward and
took possession of a line of works the rebels had only
evacuated on our approach. They are now crossing
Chattahoochie river The advance is continued until
within about one and one-half miles of the river, where
we encounter a second line of rebel works, occupied by
the enemy to cover the retreat across the river

July 6th we occupy the position of yesterday. During the forenoon our regiment was support of Bundy's
New York battery, engaged in shelling the rebels from a
fort About 2 P M we returned with the battery to the
main line, and one hour later moved with our division to
the left and formed line of battle, in which position we
passed the night. On the day following we marched to
the left and assumed position in line between the Fourteenth and Fifteenth corps Sharp skirmishing was kept
up nearly all night. This position is maintained by our
regiment, with daily skirmishing, until the early dawn of
July 10th, when the Twenty-ninth Ohio is pushed forward on a reconnoissance. We discover that the enemy
have retreated across the Chattahoochie. On reaching
the river we deploy as skirmishers along the north bank,

the enemy being posted along the opposite side. Atlanta lies only nine miles to the south of us. The rebel army of General Joe E. Johnston is said to be strongly intrenched some four miles south of our position. A small number only of rebels remain on the opposite bank of the Chattahoochie. The Union and rebel pickets are on good terms, often meeting in the middle of the river, where they exchange coffee for tobacco, which, by the way, was a very scarce article with us. The Twenty-ninth Ohio regiment now musters only one hundred and fifty men for duty. The mustering officer tells us that we have lost more men killed and wounded in proportion to the number present at the beginning of this campaign than any regiment in the Western army.

July 6, we were in support of a battery during the forenoon. During the afternoon we moved to the left, camping in a beautiful grove of pines.

7th. Moved forward some three miles, to a ridge commanding a fine view of the country.

11th. The rebels have crossed Chattahoochie river. Our pickets are posted on its north bank.

17th Moved forward to the left, crossed the Chattahoochie river at Peace ferry about 9 o'clock P. M.

18th. Moved forward some two miles, skirmishing much of the distance

19th Advanced to Peach Tree creek, which we crossed, encountering the enemy and taking some prisoners.

## CHAPTER XVIII.

Battle of Peach Tree Creek—Some of the "boys" go to Andersonville.

On the morning of July 20th, just as old Sol was tinting the east with his rosy hue, our army began a general forward movement, the Twentieth corps in this advance being on the right centre, the Fourth corps left, resting on our right, and Newton's division (Fourth corps) connecting with our left. Slight skirmishing ensued early in the morning, but towards noon the enemy retired. The unbroken stillness which followed caused us to advance cautiously lest the rebels draw us into an ambush. On reaching Peach Tree creek, a narrow, sluggish stream, whose abrupt banks, covered with briars and a dense, almost impassable undergrowth, would be a fatal barrier to a routed army, especially as the stream was without bridges, the entire command came to a halt until crossings could be constructed. Previous to the crossing of the main line General Geary ordered forward a force in reconnoissance, consisting of the Twenty-ninth Ohio, Twenty-eighth Pennsylvania, a detachment of the Thirty-third New Jersey, and four pieces of Bundy's New York battery, Geary himself following and directing the movement. When once across we advanced over several rough sparsely wooded ravines until reaching an eminence overlooking a narrow, open valley on our front and left. Immediately on our right front was a piece of heavy timber, extending also on our rear. The ridge directly in our front was covered with a thick undergrowth, affording a fine position for an

ambuscade Our force was now brought to a halt·
Bundy's battery was hastily put into position on the ridge
to cover the valley. The Twenty-ninth Ohio assumed
position on the right, and the Twenty-eighth Pennsylvanfa
on the left of the battery. D. E. Hurlburt, captain of
company K, had charge of a detail from the Twenty-
ninth and Sixty-sixth Ohio regiments in the skirmish of
the timber, so he states.

The detachment of the Thirty-third New Jersey
deployed as skirmishers across the valley in our front,
General Geary and staff following closely in its rear.
While they were advancing, we hastily constructed a
light barricade of fence rails, and Bundy prepared his
battery for business We anxiously watched General
Geary and the skirmishers as they cautiously moved up
the ridge

When within a few yards of the underbrush a large
force of rebels came from cover, and with wild yells
rushed forward. Captain Bundy at once opened fire
upon them, which threw them into disorder, but did not
check their advance As Geary and staff passed over our
line his chief, Captain Elliott, fell from his horse, shot
dead Geary shouted to us, "A general engagement! a
general engagement! My brave men hold to your position. I will send support to you." He was answered
with rousing cheers. When the little remnant of the
skirmishing force had come in we commenced a rapid
fire in connection with Captain Bundy's double-shotted
guns, which speedily thinned the advancing columns of
rebels, but without avail, as the breaks were at once filled
with fresh troops As the rebels attempted to close with
us our men seemed to be endowed with the valor born
of desperation, and clubbed them back. Forward they
came, a dense mass of living fire, and bravely we sus-

tained the shock of twenty times our number. The sharp rattle of musketry, the loud roar of Bundy's guns, and the defiant shouts of the combatants, in close hand to hand conflict, can never be erased from the tablets of memory while life shall last. It was grandly, awfully terrible.

A dense smoke settled around the battery and enclosing the extreme left of the regiment, hid the position of our right. Suddenly firing begins on us from our rear. The cannoniers are disabled and the infantry are called upon to work the guns, which were instantly turned to the rear upon heavy masses of rebels advancing from the woods on our flank. The greater part of our regiment had discovered this movement in time to change front to rear, but were instantly forced back by the overwhelming numbers of the rebels, and those in charge of the battery were instantly surrounded by a powerful mob of yelling fiends. Still the double-shotted guns continue to belch forth fire and death, cutting great gaps in the ranks of the enemy at each discharge.

At the guns' front, with muskets clubbed, a hand to hand conflict was had, to allow the reloading of the guns. The situation was now most desperate. A cordon of the enemy hemmed in the brave band, now reduced to but seventy men, whose ammunition was exhausted, and at last they were forced to surrender the battery. Henry Rood, of company A, and Henry E. Clark, company B, are the only names the writer has been able to secure of those captured at this time.

General Geary came up soon after, charged the enemy and recovered the battery, which was instantly turned upon the rebels, causing great destruction. The prisoners were, however, too far in the rear for recapture. and they were conveyed to that loathsome earthly hell, Andersonville. What they endured, the cruelties of the studied starvation by express order of chivalric Jeff Davis, and the horrible atrocities accorded to defenseless prisoners by the Southern opponents in this unholy, ungodly conflict, the writer will not attempt to describe; language fails in the recital. Loss: Killed, two; wounded, seven; captured, five; total fourteen.

## CHAPTER XIX.

Siege of Atlanta—The Capitulation—General Sherman's Report.

July 21st, heavy skirmishing on our right. 22d, we moved forward in pursuit of the retreating rebels. 23d, we are now strongly intrenched, within two miles of Atlanta, Georgia ; lively skirmishing much of the time. 24th, shelling and picket firing to-day ; rebels charged our line but were repulsed. 25th, brisk firing all day. 26th, advanced our line forty rods. 27th, quiet along the lines 28th, heavy firing on our right, the rebels are repulsed. 29th and 30th, fighting continues.

August 2st to 3d, hot firing all the time. 4th, National Thanksgiving Day, fighting on our right, rebels driven back; skirmishing every day—all the time; getting monotonous. 25th, left our works and fell back to the Chattahoochie river, near Vining station ; marched all night. 27th, Major-general W. H. Slocum assumed command of the Twentieth army corps.

September 4th, moved forward to Atlanta, which we reached about 2 o'clock P. M ; marched through the city and went into camp about one and one-half miles west of the city. 6th, received an order from General Sherman that the campaign was ended, and that the troops are to have a full month's rest, that our task was not only done, but well done. 12th, the citizens of Atlanta were moved south to-day; from this date we lay in camp with little to mar our happiness till November 1st, when we received orders to send all our baggage to the rear and put ourselves in light marching order

November 5th, orders having been received for the troops to move, the Twenty-ninth struck tents and marched from Atlanta at 3:30 P. M. in the direction of Stone Mountain, some three miles, and camped for the night. At 1 o'clock P. M. on the following day, the regiment marched back to Atlanta, and again occupied its old camp.

During the afternoon of the 1st of September specific orders for the withdrawal of Stewart's rebel *corps de armee* and the militia were issued, and about sunset the latter were withdrawn from the trenches. When they were fairly on the road Stewart's corps followed, all being en route by midnight, except the cavalry, a brigade or two of infantry, and the pickets. These latter remained until the advance of the Twentieth corps neared the city on the morning of the 2d. The explosion of ammunition was of course heard at the position of the Twentieth corps, and though General Slocum (who it appears was in command of the Twentieth corps at the time) had received no intelligence of Sherman's great success at Jonesboro, he was not unprepared to find Hood gone any morning, and the explosions convinced him that the withdrawal was taking place. He instantly issued orders to his division commanders, Generals Ward, Williams, and Geary, to send out each a heavy reconnoissance at daybreak on the morning of the 2d.

About 1,000 men were detailed from each division, and at 5 A M. pushed forward on neighboring roads into Atlanta on the north and northwest, encountering no opposition. They pushed rapidly forward, and at 8 o'clock came in sight of the rebel intrenchments, so lately occupied with enemies but now silent and deserted.

Advancing rapidly, Colonel Coburn, commanding General Ward's reconnoissance, entered the enemy's works, encountering in the suburbs Mayor Calhoun, of Atlanta, and a deputation of the city council  The former nervously presented a paper surrendering the city and asking protection.  Colonel Coburn refused to receive the paper for informality, and directed that another should be drawn up.  Mayor Calhoun invited several of General Ward's staff to accompany him to the court-house, where the documents should be made *en regle*, promising at the same time to expel the drunken rebel stragglers, who were lingering in the streets and were disposed to skirmish with our advance.  He immediately took measures to effect the last, and accompanied by the officers whose names are offered in attest, he returned to the court-house, and the following document was drawn up :

" ATLANTA, GEORGIA,  
September 2, 1864.

"Brigadier-general Ward, Commanding Third Division Twentieth Corps.

"SIR :—The fortunes of war have placed the city of Atlanta in your hands, and as mayor of the city I ask protection to non-combatants and private property

"JAMES M. CALHOUN,  
Mayor of Atlanta. "

The preliminary formalities thus disposed of, our troops entered the city with music and flags, marching promptly and erect.  A fine flag-staff was found on the Franklin printing house, where the Memphis Appeal had been printed.  The stars and stripes were soon flung to the calm, sunny air amid the cheers of the brave men who had fought for so many weary, consuming days to place it there.

General Henry W. Slocum established his headquarters at the Trout house, the leading hotel of the city,

overlooking the public square. In the forts around Atlanta eleven heavy guns, mainly sixty-four pounders, were
left by the enemy; also about three thousand muskets, in
good order, stored in various parts of the city, were
found; also three locomotives in running order, and
large quantities of manufactured tobacco were discovered. Between one and two hundred stragglers, the
majority of them very drunk, were fished from their hid-
ing places and placed under guard at the court-house.

### GENERAL THOMAS' CONGRATULATORY ORDER.

ARMY HEADQUARTERS, July 26, 1864.

"The major-general commanding the army congratu-
lates the troops upon the brilliant success attending the
Union arms in the late battles. In the battle of the
20th instant, in which the Twentieth corps, one division
of the Fourth corps, and part of the Fourteenth corps
were engaged, the total union loss in killed, wounded,
and missing was 1,733. In front of the Twentieth corps
there were put out of the fight 6,000 rebels; 563 of the
enemy were buried by our own troops, and the rebels
were permitted to bury 250. The Second division of
the Fourth corps repulsed seven different assaults of the
enemy with light loss to themselves, and which must
have swelled the number of dead buried by the rebels to
beyond 300. We also captured seven stands of colors.
No official report has been received of the part taken in
the battle by the Fourteenth corps. In the battle of the
22d instant, the total Union loss in killed, wounded, and
missing was 3,500, and also 10 pieces of artillery. The
rebel loss in prisoners captured was 3,200. The known
dead of the enemy in front of the Fifteenth and Sixteenth corps and one division of the Seventeenth corps
was 2,142. The other divisions of the Seventeenth

corps repulsed six assaults of the enemy before they fell back, and which will swell the rebel loss in killed to at least 3,000. The latest reports state that we buried over 3,200 rebels killed in this fight. · There were captured from the enemy in this battle 18 stands of colors and 5,000 stands of arms.

"By command of

MAJOR-GENERAL GEORGE H THOMAS.

"W. D. WHIPPLE,
Assistant Adjutant-general."

GENERAL SHERMAN'S SPECIAL FIELD ORDER NO. 68.

"HEADQUARTERS MILITARY DIVISION, OF THE
MISSISSIPPI IN THE FIELD,
ATLANTA, GEORGIA, SEPT. 8, 1864.

"The officers and soldiers of the armies of the Cumberland, Ohio, and Tennessee have already received the thanks of the Nation through its President and commander in chief, and it remains now only for him who has been with you from the beginning, and who intends to stay all the time, to thank the officers and men for their intelligence, fidelity, and courage displayed in the campain of Atlanta. On the 1st day of May our armies were lying in garrison, seemingly quiet, from Knoxville to Huntsville, and our enemy lay behind his rocky-faced barrier at Dalton, proud, defiant, and exultant. He had time since Christmas to recover from his discomfiture on the Mission Ridge, with his ranks filled, and a new commander in chief, second to none of the Confederacy in reputation for skill, sagacity, and extreme popularity. All at once our armies assumed life and action and appeared before Dalton. Threatening Rocky Face, we threw ourselves upon Resaca, and the rebel army only escaped by the rapidity of its retreat, aided by the numerous roads with which he was familiar, and

which were strange to us. Again he took post, at Allatoona, but we gave him no rest, and by a circuit toward
Dallas and a subsequent movement to Ackworth, we
gained the Allatoona pass. Then followed the eventful
battles about Kenesaw and the escape of the enemy
across the Chattahoochie river. The crossing of the
Chattahoochie and breaking of the Augusta road was
most handsomely executed by us, and will be studied as
an example in the art of war. At this stage of our game
our enemies became dissatisfied with their old and skil-
ful commander and selected one more bold and rash.
New tactics were adopted. Hood first boldly and
rapidly on the 20th of July fell on our right at Peach
Tree creek, and lost again. On the 22d he struck our
extreme left and was severely punished; and finally again
on the 28th he repeated the attempt on our right, and
that time must have been satisfied, for since that date he
has remained on the defensive. We slowly and gradually drew our lines about Atlanta, feeling for the railroads
which supplied the rebel army and made Atlanta a place
of importance. We must concede to our enemy that
he met these efforts patiently and skilfully, but at last he
made the mistake we had waited for so long and sent
his cavalry to our rear, far beyond the reach of recall.
Instantly our cavalry was on his only remaining road,
and we followed quickly with our principal army, and
Atlanta fell into our possession as the fruit of well-con-
certed measures, backed by a brave and competent army.
This completed the grand task which had been assigned
us by our Government, and your general again repeats
his personal and official thanks to all the officers and
men composing this army for the indomitable courage
and perseverance which alone could give success. We
have beaten our enemy on every ground he has chosen,

and have wrested from him his own Gate city, where were located his foundries, arsenals, and workshops, deemed secure on account of their distance from our base and the seeming impregnable obstacles intervening. Nothing is impossible to an army like this, determined to vindicate a government wherever our flag has once floated, and resolved to maintain them at any and all cost.

"In our campaign many, yea very many of our noble and gallant comrades have preceded us to our common destination, the grave, but they have left the memory of deeds on which a Nation can build a proud history. McPherson, Harker, McCook, and others dear to us all, are now the binding links in our minds that should attach more closely together the living, who have to complete the task which still lies before us in the dim future.

"I ask all to continue as they have so well begun, the cultivation of the soldierly virtues that have ennobled our own and other countries,—courage, patience, obedience to the laws and constituted authorities of our Government, fidelity to our trusts, and good feeling among each other; each trying to excel the other in the practice of those high qualities, and it will then require no prophet to foretell that our country will, in time, emerge from this war purified by the fires of war and worthy its great founder, Washington.

"W. T. SHERMAN,
Major-general commanding "

## CHAPTER XX.

With Sherman to the Sea—Colonel Schoonover's Journal—Siege of Savannah

Tuesday, the 8th instant, the Twenty-ninth was very busy holding election. Detachments from other organizations were permitted to vote at the Twenty-ninth headquarters. The Twenty-ninth regiment cast three hundred and eighty-four votes. Of these Lincoln received three hundred and fifty and McClellan thirty-four. During the day the regiment was wide awake and enthusiastic, and gave every soldier a chance to vote. At 6:30 A. M. on the following day, while the regiment was in tents eating breakfast, the rebels opened a lively fire with artillery, at short range. The enemy approached our picket, which was posted west of camp, covering the Sandtown road, who were surprised and fell back without firing a shot; hence the first intimation that we had that the enemy was near was the report of their artillery and the bursting of shells in our midst The Twenty-ninth fell in and took position behind the fortification which the regiment had constructed. In the meantime a line of skirmishers was sent out and soon the enemy were driven back. A portion of the brigade was sent out on the Sandtown road, marched a few miles, but the Confederates had flown, and late in the afternoon the scouting party returned to camp.

November 10th. Remained in camp occupied in the usual camp and picket duties, and the inspection of amunition, arms, and accoutrements, and all was quiet, and at 8 o'clock in the evening the city of Atlanta took fire and was nearly annihilated  Saturday, the 12th, in camp, and all is quiet  Sunday, November 13th, the Twenty-ninth was detailed to tear up and destroy the railroad, and 7:30 marched out on the railroad leading to Chattanooga, and was engaged until 10 at night in burning the ties and bending the rails  At night the regiment returned to its old camp at Atlanta   14th instant, in camp; all quiet.  A man in company I was injured by falling from a building  15th instant, marched at 6:30 A. M. on the road leading to Stone mountain in a southeast direction from Atlanta, and at 6 P. M. halted and went into camp (marched fifteen miles).  16th instant, marched at 7 30 A. M., and at 5:15 P. M. halted and camped for the night (marched twelve miles).  17th instant, marched at 5 o'clock A. M., and after marching twelve miles halted for dinner, and at 2 P. M. fell in and marched until 5 P. M , when the regiment halted and went into camp  18th instant, moved at 4:30 A. M ; marched ten miles, and at 12 M. halted for dinner; fell in at 1 o'clock and at 6 P. M. halted and camped for the night (marched twenty miles during the day).  19th instant, marched at 6:30 A M.

Twentieth instant, moved fourteen miles and camped for the night near Edenton  21st, marched through Edenton in the direction of Milledgeville, a distance of sixteen miles, and went into camp.  22d, marched at 5:30 A. M., halted at 12 M. one hour for dinner, and at 1:15 P M fell in and marched until 8 o'clock P M., passed through Milledgeville and crossed the Oconee river and camped for the night.  23d, Twenty-ninth regiment detailed for picket ; fell in and moved east about three-fourths of a mile, passing through the woods and advancing into an open country ; during its stay on

picket duty some of the boys went out on a foraging expedition, and it is not necessary to state that they were
successful, and that honey, sweet potatoes, and some
fine chickens (which the quartermaster had left), made a
very pleasant repast. 24th, received orders to join the
brigade; marched at 7 o'clock A. M., and halted at 1:30
for dinner, fell in at 2:15 P. M., halted at 7:30, camped
for the night, marched fifteen miles. 25th, moved at 7
A. M., passing through a low country covered with heavy
timber and thick undergrowth ; the Twenty-ninth was
train guard, halted at 12 M., at Buffalo creek, for dinner;
found the bridge destroyed, parked the train, and late in
the afternoon the bridge was repaired and the regiment
with the train crossed, passed through Buffalo swamp
and camped for the night, marched twelve miles. 26th,
the regiment was ordered up at 3:30 A. M., remained on
arms until 7:30, when it marched with the brigade; halted
at 1:30 P. M. at Sandersville for dinner, and in the afternoon marched to the Georgia Central railroad, tore up
about two miles of track, and at 8:30 went into camp;
drew rations of honey for supper. 27th, marched at 5
A. M., reached the railroad at 8:50, tore up the track,
and at 2:30 P. M. marched to Davisboro, which it
reached at 9 o'clock, and camped here ; marched nine
miles. 28th, in the forenoon marched back to the railroad, and tore up track until 5 o'clock P. M., then
marched back to Davisboro, and camped for the night ;
nothing special transpired during the night except the
burning of a house, which accidentally (?) took fire ;
search was made in the regiments of the brigade by the
staff officers to find out if possible the cause of the fire,
but "not guilty" was the response. 29th, marched at
6:30 A. M., halted at 11:30, at Bartlows station, for dinner, and in the afternoon marched through Bostwick and

went into camp; marched 14 miles. 30th, marched at 6 A. M., halted at Daniel Blake's plantation for dinner, and in the afternoon marched four miles and camped for the night

December 1, 1864, marched at 7:30 A. M , the Second division in the advance, passed through a low, wet country, almost impassable to the ordnance train ; halted at 8:15 and camped for the night, marched fifteen miles. 2d, marched at 6 A M , First brigade in advance, moved about ten miles, halted at 12 M for dinner, at a creek where the rebels had destroyed the bridge, and while preparing dinner, the Twenty-ninth regiment was ordered to fall in, which it did without delay, and marched to the creek, the enemy was found on its opposite bank in considerable force ; the regiment was ordered to drive the enemy out of the timber, force them back and hold them while the bridge was being rebuilt; we loaded our guns, and crossing the bank four companies under Captain Schoonover advanced to the right up the road, through the timber (which was a thick undergrowth) driving the enemy out of the woods and into an open field about one mile from the bridge, barricaded the road with rails, and the other six companies under Major Wright, advanced direct to the point through the woods about one mile, the enemy falling back . the regiment held its position until the bridge was rebuilt, and a crossing effected, and late in the P. M. the brigade moved through the swamp and camped for the night 3d, remained in camp until after dinner, then moved forward the remainder of the day and all night; had no supper, halted at 7 A M for breakfast, near Millen ; the old stockade was empty, the prisoners having been removed the day before; after breakfast on the 4th, we moved forward, marched all day, and at 8 P. M. halted and camped for the night. 5th, marched at 7 A. M., halted at 2:30 P. M for dinner, moved three miles in the afternoon, and at 6 went into camp for the night. 6th, marched ten miles and camped for the night. 7th, marched at 7 A. M., halted at 12.30 for dinner, rained all the forenoon, had no dinner; marched in the afternoon, halted at 7 P. M. and camped for the night, near Springfield ; marched twelve miles. 8th, marched at 6:30 A M and camped at 4 30 P M near Eden.

9th instant at 9 A M , moved six miles and halted thirty minutes for dinner at Wallhower Swamp, where the Confederates were found in force The fallen timber which obstructed the road was soon removed by the Pioneer corps, and in the meantime with the Third brigade, of Geary s division in the advance, had a sharp skirmish with the rebels. While the road was being cleared the Second division were resting on their arms, except the Third brigade, which had advanced nearly through the swamp While engaged with the enemy the train was ordered forward, and the Twenty-ninth regiment advanced on double-quick in support of the brigade thus engaged. Passing the train it reached the Third brigade, which had advanced about one mile and a half The Twenty-ninth immediately formed line on the left of the road in rear of the Third brigade, and skirmished until dark, when the firing ceased During the night the rebels fell back. 10th instant, moved at 7 A M. and marched through the swamp where we found small earth works and two small field pieces masked to cover the road through the swamp, but when the boys in blue were discovered the rebels moved to the rear. The regiment marched thirteen miles with some skirmishing and artillery firing during the day and night.

When about four miles from the city of Savannah, Georgia, rebel artillery was found to be in the road behind earthworks to impede our progress. The Twenty-ninth regiment, with the brigade, filed to the left of the road and took position in the timber, where it bivouacked for the night. After leaving Atlanta, Georgia, on the 15th day of November, 1864, the army was designated as the Army of Georgia, the Twelfth and Fourteenth corps, known as the left wing, commanded by Major-general H. W. Slocum, and the Fifteenth and Seventeenth corps, known as the right wing, commanded by Major-general O. O. Howard, Major-general William T. Sherman in command of the Army of Georgia.

On this march the army cut loose from the base of supplies at Atlanta, and lived mostly from forage on the country. On reaching the enemy within four miles of Savannah, on the 10th day or December, the division had accumulated several hundred head of cattle. Sunday, December 11th, moved in the morning about one mile, and took a position near the rebel lines, the Twenty-ninth regiment, on the extreme left of the line, with its left reaching the Savannah river. While in this position the rebels opened fire with artillery from a fort immediately in our front, and the infantry from their strong line of works, kept up a continual fire. The brigade remained in line until late in the afternoon, sustaining slight loss, when it fell back through the open field into the woods and laid on arms all night. On the 12th inst., at 2.30 A. M., fell in and advanced to the front about one-half mile to the old levee, and thence filed to the left. Marched about three-fourths of a mile, halted, and prepared to charge the rebels. To do so the right had to pass a dike or canal with four or five feet of water, and assault the fort and breastworks in

open field. The charge was abandoned, and at 4 30 A.
M. the regiment returned to camp, where we remained
skirmishing and artillery firing during the day. On the
13th inst. the Twenty-ninth was on skirmish line all day.
During the night we advanced our line through a woods,
which was heavy pine, mixed with live oak, within two
hundred yards of the rebel line, where they were strongly
intrenched. Between the contending armies was no
timber except scattering undergrowth, and a canal near
the rebel line of works. In this advanced position the
regiment dug rifle-pits, which were strongly barricaded
with timber.

In the lines of rifle-pits our pickets were stationed and
performed the duty of skirmishers, being relieved
every twenty-four hours, which was done under cover of
night. In the meantime the regiment fell back about
one-fourth of a mile, and constructed works of heavy
timber, in the rear of which the men put up their shelter
tents. Here they could partake of the scanty rations (but
dare not sleep), as the artillery firing and skirmishing
was kept up continually day and night on the 14th, 15th,
16th and 17th, and Sunday, the 18th, skirmishing and
artillery duelling all along the line. On the 19th skirmishing all day. In the evening a detail was made from our
brigade under the command of Major Myron T. Wright,
to construct new lines of works. While engaged in the
work at 7 o'clock P M., he received a severe wound in the
left foot (at which time Captain Jonas Schoonover took
command), the ball entering the foot a little below the
instep, and lodged into the center of the heel about one
inch from the bottom of the foot. On the 20th, firing
all along the line. This ceased at 11 o'clock P. M. The
Twenty-ninth regiment, with its brigade and division,
has been in position on the left of the road leading

from Springfield to the city of Savannah, with its main line in the timber, its right resting on the river. During the ten days the command remained in front of Savannah it took charge of large rice mills on the river, and supplied the men with rice. The quartermaster used large quantities for the train teams. At one time rice sold for fifty cents per quart (before the capture of Fort McAllister, on December 13th, 1864). The rebels in our front were behind a heavy line of works, which was surmounted with large timber called head logs, with port holes in their front. At their rear was a large body of timber, their right rested on the river, where they had constructed two forts, one near the river, and the other a short distance west along their line, where they had a strong position behind sand bags. But our lines were advancing nearer every day, and during the night of December 20th they evacuated their works, and fell back to Savannah, crossing the river into South Carolina. At 4 A. M., on the 21st day of December, the Twenty-ninth fell in, and moved in the advance of the brigade to the front. Passing the rifle-pits, it filed to the left. across the canal near the rebel fort, finding their works and entire line evacuated. We moved on in the direction of Savannah. On reaching the city, the Twenty-ninth Ohio and Twenty-eighth Pennsylvania regiments moved down the river to Fort Jackson, which had been evacuated and set on fire. The regiments reached the fort at 9 A. M., and at 12 o'clock at night the rebels blew up their gunboat Beauregard. We remained at the fort until December 24th, with the usual routine of camp and garrison duty. In the meantime the Twenty-ninth took an inventory of the ordnance and ordnance stores captured by the Twenty-ninth regiment and the Twenty-eighth Pennsylvania in Fort Jackson and other forts along the Savannah river. On the 24th instant the regiment was ordered to move at 9 A. M. The Twenty-ninth, in rear of the Twenty-eighth Pennsylvania volunteers, marched to the city of Savannah, passing through it, and encamping on the west side.

On the 25th, 26th, 27th, 28th and 29th, fixing company quarters, and attending to the usual routine of camp and guard duty. Friday, the 30th, the army reviewed. The Twenty-ninth regiment moved from camp at 8:30 A. M., and marched to Liberty street in the city of Savannah, where it joined the brigade formed on the left, in prolongation with the Sixty-sixth regiment of Ohio volunteers. After review it returned to its old camp at 2 o'clock P. M. Saturday, the 31st, inspection and muster for pay at 10 A. M.

January 1, 1865, monthly inspection at 2 o'clock P. M. 2d, 3d, 4th and 5th, nothing occurred except the usual camp duty. 6th, 7th, 8th and 9th, in camp, and up to the 18th the Twenty-ninth was doing camp duty, and on the 18th received news of the fall of Fort Fisher. From the 19th to the 25th engaged in camp duty and regimental drill.

----

### CAPTAIN SCHOONOVER'S REPORT.

HEADQUARTERS TWENTY-NINTH OHIO
VETERAN VOLUNTEER INFANTRY.
SAVANNAH, Georgia, Dec. 28, 1864

A. H. W. Creigh, first lieutenant, and acting assistant adjutant-general First brigade, Second division, Twentieth corps:

" LIEUTENANT :—In compliance with circular from headquarters First brigade, Second division, Twentieth corps, dated Savannah, Georgia, December 23, 1864, I have the honor most respectfully to make the following report :

"I took command of the regiment in front of Savannah, Georgia, on December 20, 1864. Nothing worthy of note transpired during the day. At 4 o'clock A. M. of the 21st instant the Twenty-ninth in advance of the First brigade, took up a line of march to the city of Savannah, and from there to Fort Jackson, when I reported to Colonel Flinn, Twenty-eighth Pennsylvania volunteers, for duty, and performed garrison duty until December 24th, when the regiment was ordered to march at 9:30 A M The Twenty-ninth in rear of Twenty-eighth Pennsylvania volunteers, marched to the city, and through it to the west side, where we are now encamped

"I am very respectfully, your obedient servant,

JONAS SCHOONOVER,

Captain commanding Twenty-ninth Ohio Veteran Volunteer Infantry

"HEADQUARTERS FIRST BRIGADE,
SECOND DIVISION, TWENTIETH ARMY CORPS.
SAVANNAH, Georgia, December 25, 1864.

"Captain W. T. Forbes, assistant adjutant general ·

"In compliance with circular order No. 144, I have the honor to submit the following report of the operations of this brigade, from the capture of Atlanta, September 2, 1864, to the occupation of Savannah, Georgia, December 21, 1864, etc., etc .   .   .   .   .
December 2d, the march was resumed at daybreak and was uninterrupted until Buckhead creek was reached The bridge over this place was partially destroyed, and a few of the enemy's cavalry were on the opposite side of the swamp. Major Wright, commanding the Twenty-ninth Ohio volunteers, was ordered to cross the creek

with his regiment and drive and keep away this force, which was accomplished without loss. The command camped for the night near Buckhead church.    .    .

December 12th to December 20th inclusive, a substantial line of works was thrown up for the protection of the command from the artillery of the enemy, and in addition to this two forts, with thirteen embrasures in the aggregate, were constructed by the command. The working parties on Fort No. 2 were under the command of Captain Kreicler, One Hundred and Forty-seventh Pennsylvania volunteers, and those on Fort No. 3 under command of Captain E. B. Woodbury, Twenty-ninth Ohio volunteers. Both these officers and the men under their command are deserving of praise for the energy and perseverance manifested in the prosecution of the duty assigned them.

"December 21st, the enemy having evacuated their position the night previous, their works were occupied at an early hour by the skirmishers of the division, and by sunrise the city of Savannah was entered and occupied, this brigade being in line in the advance into the city. Soon after reaching the city, the Twenty-eighth Pennsylvania and Twenty-ninth Ohio volunteers, under command of Colonel John Flynn, were, by order of the commanding-general of division, through Captain Veale, aide-de-camp, dispatched to occupy Fort Jackson and the smaller forts and batteries near it. The possession of the forts and other works was gained with but slight resistance.

"Inventory of ordnance and ordnance stores captured by the Twenty-ninth Ohio volunteers and the Twenty-eighth Pennsylvania in Fort Jackson and other forts on the Savannah river: Forty-four thirty-two-pounders, two ten-inch Columbiads, twenty eight-inch Columbiads, two rifled thirty-two-pounders, twelve twenty-four-pounder howitzers, one eight-inch mortar, three three-inch rifled field-pieces, etc., etc. Of the ninety-one guns captured, fourteen only were found to have been spiked and shotted. The gun-carriages were broken and temporarily disabled, and all the implements were broken and destroyed.

"To the regimental commanders I tender my thanks for the strict obedience to orders, and the enforcement of the regulation prescribed in regard to the conduct of the march, and especially are they due to Major M. T. Wright, Twenty-ninth Ohio volunteers, who was seriously wounded while supervising the working parties on the forts, for the promptitude exhibited by him in the execution of all orders, and his strict attention to the duties incumbent on him throughout the entire campaign.

"Respectfully submitted,

"ARIO PARDEE,
Commanding Brigade "

EXTRACT—OFFICIAL REPORT OF GENERAL GEARY.

" December 29th, a conference of the division and' brigade commanders with the general commanding the corps, was held at 10 A. M. to-day, with the view to the adoption of a plan for storming the enemy's works, as soon as the heavy guns should be in readiness to open fire. Fort No. 1 was finished this evening The details from the First and Third brigades continued work on the other forts during the night, under a heavy artillery fire from the enemy. Several casualties occurred, among them Major Wright, a most valuable officer, commanding the Twenty-ninth Ohio volunteers, who was severely wounded by a shell. Sloan's battery of three-inch rifled guns had already taken position in a work thrown up to the right of Fort 3, and in the open field.

"December 20th The usual artillery firing and sharp shooting to-day. By this evening we had constructed and in readiness for use in the contemplated assault, two hundred large straw fascines, to fill up ditches in front of the enemy's works; also a large number of fascines made of bamboo-cane. The latter were to be used for bridging the canal by laying them across baulks, which were furnished from the pontoon train for that purpose. The work on Forts 2 and 3 was well advanced to-day, and would probably be completed to-night. Three siege-guns (thirty-pounder Parrotts) were brought down this evening and mounted in Fort No. 2. I ascertained this morning that the enemy had completed a pontoon bridge from Savannah across to the South Carolina shore, and notified the general commanding corps of the discovery. This bridge was about two and a half miles from my left The usual artillery firing was kept up by the enemy during the day and night. During the night I heard the movement of troops and wagons across the poontoon bridge before mentioned, and sent a report of the fact to the general commanding corps. Leaving one of my staff to watch the sounds in that direction, I notified my officer of the day and brigade commanders to keep a vigilant watch upon the enemy, as they were probably evacuating. The details on Forts 2 and 3 continued working through the night, the enemy shelling them heavily.

" December 21st. After 3 o'clock this morning the firing ceased, and my pickets advancing to the enemy's line, found them hastily retreating. Having possession of their line of works with all their cannon in front of my own and the other division of the corps, I immediately sent a staff officer to notify the general commanding, and at the same time pushed forward rapidly in the direction of Savannah, hoping to overtake and capture a part of the enemy's force. My skirmishers deployed and swept over all the ground between the evacuated works and the Ogeechee canal, from the river to the Augusta road, while my main body of troops marched rapidly by the flank through McAlpin's plantation to the Augusta road, and on into the city. Just outside of the city limits near the junction of the Louisville and Augusta roads, I met the mayor of Savannah and a delegation from the board of alderman, bearing a flag of truce. From them I received in the name of my commanding general the surrender of the city. This was at 4:30 A. M., and I sent immediately another staff officer to announce the surrender to the general commanding the corps He had considerable difficulty in passing the line of another division of this corps on the Augusta road, but finally convinced them that he belonged to the Twentieth corps and not to the enemy. In the meantime my entire division entered the city of Savannah at early dawn, and before the sun first gilded the morning clouds, our National colors, side by side with those of my own division, were unfurled from the dome of the exchange, and over the United States custom house. The brigade which led on entering the city, was at once ordered to patrol it, reduce it to order and quiet, and prevent any pillaging or lawlessness on the part either of soldiers or citizens My orders on the subject were very strict, and within a few hours this city, in which I had found a lawless mob of low whites and negroes pillaging and setting fire to property, was reduced to order. Many millions of dollars worth of cotton, ordnance and commissary stores, etc., which would have been otherwise destroyed, were saved to the United States Government, and the citizens once more enjoyed security under the protection of that flag which again waved over them, exactly four years since the passage by the State of South Carolina of the Secession Act.

"Two regiments from Pardee's brigade, the Twenty-eighth Pennsylvania and Twenty-ninth Ohio veteran volunteers, were sent down to Fort Jackson, and early in the morning had possession of it and all the intermediate and surrounding works. The iron-plated ram, Savannah, which lay in the river below the city, threw shells at these two regiments as they flung the stars and stripes to the breeze from the walls of Fort Jackson. All the other gun-boats of the enemy had been fired by them and burned to the water's edge

"On the arrival of the major-general commanding the left wing, I was, by his order, placed in command of the city. Until nearly 10 A. M. continued firing was heard in the direction of Beaulieu, and supposing that a portion of the enemy might still be south of us, I kept one brigade under arms during the forenoon. Three rebel flags were captured by my command, which will be duly forwarded.

"I am, Colonel, very-respectfully

Your obedient servant,

JOHN W GEARY,

Brigadier-general commanding Second division Twentieth corps."

## CHAPTER XXI.

The Carolina Campaign—Washington—Grand Review—The New Flag—Westward, and Home again

On the 27th day of January, after the order to march was issued, the Twenty-ninth broke camp and marched at 8 A. M., in rear of the Sixty-sixth Ohio regiment; halted at 2 P. M. and encamped for the night (marched twelve miles) 28th instant, marched at 7 A. M. in rear of the Sixty-sixth Ohio regiment and brigade train; at 7 P. M. camped for the night (marched ten miles) 29th instant, marched at 6.30 A. M., Twenty-ninth in rear of Sixty-sixth Ohio, and passed through Springfield; halted at 2 P. M. and camped for the night. 30th instant, in camp, three companies of the Twenty-ninth regiment went on picket 31st instant, in camp

February 1st The Twenty-ninth regiment inspected by General Ario Pardee at 9 A. M. 2d instant, the ordinary camp and picket duty was the order of the day. The 3d instant, ordered to march at 6 P M ; the order was countermanded, and we went into camp for the night. 4th, marched at 6 A. M., the Twenty-ninth in advance of the brigade; crossed the Savannah river at Sisters' Ferry at 10 A M , marched five miles and camped for the night, Twenty ninth detailed for picket 5th, relieved at 2 P. M , marched in rear of brigade, and at 9 30 P M , went into camp for the night (marched six miles). 6th, marched at 7 A M , halted at 11:30 for dinner, fell in at 12 M., halted at 5 P. M. and camped for the night (marched fifteen miles) 7th, marched at 7 A M., ; at 6:30 P M went into camp for the night. 8th instant, marched at 6 A. M., halted at 11:30 for dinner; in seven minutes fell in and marched five miles, halted at 3.15 and camped for the night near Buford Bridge. 9th, marched at 6 A. M., Twenty-ninth in advance of brigade and with ordnance train; marched eighteen miles, and at 5 P. M. camped for the night near Blackville, South Carolina. 10th, marched at 7 A. M., halted near Blackville, and at 2 P. M. crossed the Edisto river, and at 10 P. M. camped for the night (marched eight miles) 11th instant in camp. 12th marched at 6 A. M., arrived at the North Edisto river this afternoon (a distance of ten miles), engaged in a skirmish in which the Fifth Ohio had one man killed and three wounded. Company G of the Twenty-ninth had one man killed, Jack Rape. Went into camp for the night. 13th, marched at 6 A. M., crossed the North Edisto and skirmished with the enemy. Halted and remained until 9 P. M., when the regiment fell in, marched four and one-half miles and halted for the night. The Twenty-ninth went on picket. Tuesday, 14th, marched at 8 A. M. some six miles and halted. Our regiment went on picket as usual. 15th instant, marched at 7 A. M. in rear of brigade, skirmishing; marched ten miles; went into camp at Lexington at 3 P. M.; at 5 o'clock moved to the left of the Sixty-sixth Ohio. Thursday, 16th, marched at 8 A. M. one mile to the rear and went on picket; at 6:30 fell in and marched six miles as rear guard to the Twentieth army corps; halted and went into camp at 4 P. M. 17th, marched at 9 A. M. 18th, marched at 6:30 A. M., crossed the Seluda river at 1:30 P. M., halted for dinner: at 2:15 fell in and marched four miles; halted at 5 P. M. and camped for the night. Sunday in camp until 3:30 P. M. when "fall in" was sounded by the bugler. The Twenty-ninth fell in and took the advance of brigade,

marched four miles, and at 11:30 P. M. halted for the
night near Bush river. The Twenty-ninth was again
fortunate and went on picket. 20th, marched at 1 P. M.
in rear of brigade and at 7 P. M. went into camp for the
night (marched six miles, crossing Broad river near
Frost's Mill) 21st instant, marched at 6 A. M. and
entered Winsboro at 11 30 A. M. Five companies of the
Twenty-ninth detailed for picket. The other companies
camped for the night. 22d, Left Winnsboro at 3:45 P.
M., marched six miles and camped for the night. 23d,
marched at 6:30 A. M., six miles, halted at 10:20 A. M. an
hour for dinner; at 11·30 fell in and marched forward,
crossed the Catawba river and went into camp at midnight. Friday, 24, marched at 9.30 (we were the division train guard), halted at 1 P. M. for dinner ; at 2 P.
M. fell in and marched five miles · at 4:30 halted and
camped for the night; rainy. Saturday, 25th, rainy ;
remained in camp Sunday, 26th, marched at 7 A. M.,
with Twenty-ninth Ohio in advance of brigade ; halted
at 3 P. M and camped for the night (marched ten miles).
27th, marched one and one-half miles, crossed Hanging
Rock creek and went into camp. 28th, marched at 6:30
A. M., Twenty-ninth in rear of brigade (marched eight
miles), and went into camp at 1 P. M. Mustered for pay
for January and February.

Wednesday, March 1st, marched at 1 P. M., and at
9 P. M. halted and went into camp for the night near Big
Clinch creek (marched twelve miles). 2d, marched
at 8 A. M., at 12 M. halting for dinner. In the afternoon
moved one-eighth of a mile and camped for the night.
3d, marched at 6:30 A. M.; moved with wagon train;
reached Chesterfield at 11·30 P. M. and went into camp
for the night (marched thirteen miles), March 4th,
moved at 7 A. M., Twenty-ninth in advance of brigade;

halted at 4 P. M. and camped for the night (marched nine miles). 5th, remain in camp all day; detailed Charles Galpin, company C, and J. Bennett Powers, company E, as escort at Twentieth corps headquarters. 6th, marched at 8 30 A. M, Twenty-ninth in rear of brigade; reached Cheraw at 1.15 P. M ; halted for dinner, and at 4 fell in and crossed the river, marched four miles and camped for the night (marched sixteen miles). 7th, marched at 7 A. M.; halted at 2:30 P. M.; went into camp for the night, marched on the Fayetteville road (fourteen miles). 8th, marched at 11.30 A. M., halted at 1:30 for dinner; at 4:30 fell in, and at 10:15 P. M. halted and camped for the night (marched eight miles). 9th, marched at 6:30 A. M., and at 2 P. M, halted for dinner; at 3 fell in, and at 6 halted and went into camp for the night (marched thirteen miles). 10th, marched at 3:30 P. M.; Twenty-ninth in advance of brigade, marched four miles and camped for the night. 11th, marched at 6:30 A. M., Twenty-ninth in rear of brigade, halted at 7:30 P. M. for supper, and at 10:30 fell in and marched until 2:20 A. M.; went into camp for the night (marched thirteen miles). 12th, marched at 8 A. M ; reached Fayetteville at 4 P. M., and camped for the night (marched thirteen miles). 13th, marched at 2:30 P. M.; passed through Fayetteville and camped for the night. 14th, marched at 4:30 A. M.; crossed Cape Fear river; marched two miles; halted for breakfast, and remained in camp for the day. 15th, marched at 12 M., eight miles, and at 11 P. M. camped for the night. 16th, marched at 9 A. M., Twenty-ninth in advance of brigade, and at 7 P. M. halted; Twenty-ninth were fortunate enough to remain a detail for picket (marched seven miles). 17th, on picket. 18th, marched at 7 A. M., Twenty-ninth in rear of brigade; halted at 7 P. M., and went into camp for the night (marched eight miles). 19th, marched at 11 A. M., with division train (marched eleven miles); halted at 6:30, and camped at 9:30 P. M.; packed up and marched with train on Goldsboro road, joined First and Third divisions of the Twentieth army corps; marched all night, and in the morning arrived at the battlefield of Bentonville. 20th, in camp all day with constant artillery firing during the day. 21st, in camp and the artillery is steadily firing. 22d, marched at 8 A. M., Twenty-ninth Ohio in advance of brigade; halted at 12 M. for dinner; at 1 P. M. fell in and marched on the Goldsboro road; halted at 12 M. at night, and went into camp (marched fifteen miles). 23d, marched at 6 A M , Twenty-ninth Ohio in rear of division train; halted at 11:30 for dinner, at 12:30 P. M. fell in, crossed the Neuse river (marched twelve miles), and went into camp for the night Corporal Exceen, company A, was wounded by a rebel while on picket. 24th, marched at 7 A. M. and entered Goldsboro, North Carolina, at 12 M.; passed through town and went into camp; at 4:30 P. M. orders were received detailing the Twenty-ninth Ohio to guard a wagon train for the Second division, reached the point of destination at 7 P. M., near the Wilmington railroad, and camped for the night (marched eight miles). 25th, marched at 8 A. M., and arrived at Goldsboro at 12 M. (noon); passed through town about two miles and went into camp.

From March 25th to April 9th we were doing the usual duty in and around camp and on picket. On the 10th inst. marched at 6 A. M., moved up the river and went in camp for the night at 11 o'clock. 11th, marched at 6 A. M., reached Smithfield at 3 P M., camped for the night. 12th, received the news of the surrender of General R. E. Lee and his army at 8 A. M. and marched at

9 A. M.; halted at 6.30 P. M. and camped for the night (marched seventeen miles). 13th, marched at 5:30 A. M , Twenty-ninth Ohio in advance; passed through Raleigh, North Carolina, and at 2:30 P. M halted and went into camp (marched fifteen miles). Remained in camp until the 25th. On the 20th reviewed by General John W. Geary, and on the 22d the Twentieth army corps was reviewed by General W. T. Sherman. Sunday, 23d. inspection. 25th, arched at 9 A. M., Twenty-ninth Ohio in rear of brigade; halted for dinner, and at 3 P. M. fell in and marched fifteen miles; halted at 8 P. M. and camped for the night. 26th and 27th, in camp 28th, returned to our old camp near Raleigh, North Carolina. 29th, in camp 30th, marched at 7 A. M.; passed through Raleigh, and at 6 P. M. halted and camped for the night (marched fifteen miles).

May 1st, marched at 5 A. M ; at 12 M. halted for dinner; at 1 P. M. fell in, crossed Tar river, and at 6 P. M. camped for the night (marched twenty-three miles). 2d, marched at 5 A. M.; halted at 11:45 for dinner; at 1 P. M fell in, marched twenty miles, and at 5 P. M. camped for the night (Twenty-ninth Ohio in advance of brigade). 3d, marched at 4 30 A. M ; marched to the State line of Virginia, a distance of eleven miles, and camped for the night. 4th, marched at 6 A. M.; crossed the Roanoke river, at 2 P. M. halted for dinner; at 5 fell in and moved forward; halted at 6:30, and camped for the night (marched twenty miles). 5th, marched at 5.30 A. M.ʳ at 2.15 P. M. halted for dinner; marched at 4; halted at 6:30 and camped for the night (marched twenty miles). 6th, marched at 5 A. M ; halted at 10.45 for dinner, fell in at 1 P. M.; passed Black and White station on the south side railroad, and at 6:30 P.

M. camped for the night (marched eleven miles). 7th, marched at 6 A. M.; at 11 45 halted for dinner; fell in at 1:30 P. M., and crossed the Appomatox river; at 6.15 camped for the night, Twenty-ninth Ohio in advance of brigade (marched twenty miles). 8th, marched at 6 A. M.; passed Clover Hill coal mines, halted at 12 M. for dinner, at 1 P. M. fell in and marched to Falling creek, and at 7 P. M. camped for the night, Twenty-ninth Ohio in rear of brigade (marched twenty miles). 9th, moved our camp two miles. 10th, in camp all day. 11th, marched at 10 A. M., passed through Manchester and Richmond in the afternoon, and at 5.30 camped near Brook's creek for the night (marched twelve miles). 12th, marched, at 6 A. M., on Brooks pike; halted at 10 A. M. for dinner; at 12 M. fell in and marched to Ashland, and at 6.30 camped for the night (marched 12 miles). 13th, marched at 5.30 A. M.; crossed the South Anna, halted at 11.30 for dinner; at 1 P. M. fell in, crossed the Little river, and at 3.30 went into camp (marched sixteen miles). Sunday, 14th, marched at 5 A. M., Twenty-ninth Ohio in advance of brigade; crossed the North Anna river, and at 12 M. halted for dinner; fell in at 2 P. M.; marched on the Spottsylvania Court House road, halted at 5.30 and camped (marched eighteen miles). 15th, marched at 5 A. M., Twenty-ninth Ohio in rear of brigade and division train, halted at 11:45 for dinner, fell in; passed through Chancellorsville, crossed the Rappahannock and at 10 P. M. camped for the night (marched twenty miles). 16th, marched at 4.30 A. M.; halted at 12 M. for dinner; at 1:30 P. M. fell in and marched on the road that leads to Warrenton junction via Hartwood church, and camped for the night (marched, eighteen miles). 17th, marched at 5 A. M., reached Brentsville at 2 P. M., a distance of twelve miles, and camped for the night. 18th, marched at 6 A. M.; halted at 12 M. for dinner; fell in at 2:30 P. M, marched until 9 P. M , and camped for the night, William Lutz, company H, injured by the falling of a tree (marched fifteen miles). 19th, marched at 6 A. M., halted at 12 M for dinner, at 1:30 fell in, moved forward; at 6·30 P. M. reached Clouds Mills, Twenty-Ninth Ohio in advance of brigade (marched fifteen miles) 20th, 21st, 22d, 23d, and 24th, in camp.

25th, moved forward to Washington, District of Columbia, where it attended the grand review, the grandest spectacle the world has ever seen, and thence to Bladensburg, where it received the new colors, which the following matter, furnished by comrade G. W. Holloway, will sufficiently explain.

The new flag for the Twenty-ninth regiment, contributed by the citizens of Summit and Ashtabula counties, was accompanied by the following letter from Colonels Buckley and Fitch. The receipt of the new flag is gracefully acknowledged by the letter of Mr. G. W. Holloway, appended thereto, which letter was accompanied by the old flag, which had been borne by this gallant regiment in so many bloody battles

AKRON, May, 1865.

COL. JONAS SCHOONOVER DEAR SIR :—We have the honor and pleasure of forwarding to the gallant old Twenty-ninth another national flag, the gift of its old friends in Ashtabula and Summit counties This is the third national flag given the regiment from the same source. It is certainly a strong proof that its friends still believe it to be one of the bravest of the brave of the many noble regiments Ohio has given to fight this great battle. If the regiment had no other proof than s old and tattered flags, that alone would show that it had been in the thickest of the fight, ever ready to breast the fury of the battle storm; but its history tells us that it has borne an honorable part in nearly a score of the hardest fought battles of the war. Citizen soldiers, take this flag and bear it aloft wherever duty calls, and your friends will take your past record as a guarantee that it will never be dishonored by the Twenty-ninth Ohio Veteran Volunteer Infantry. Colonel, please remember us to the dear old Twenty-ninth, and accept for yourself our best wishes

LEWIS P. BUCKLEY,
WILLIAM T. FITCH,
Old Cols. of the Twenty-ninth Ohio.

HEADQUARTERS TWENTY-NINTH OHIO, ⎫
BLADENSBURG, MARYLAND, June 5, 1865. ⎰

Colonels Buckley and Fitch, and S. A. Lane, Esq.:

GENTLEMEN:—In the name of the officers and men of the Twenty-ninth Ohio veteran volunteer infantry, I herewith acknowledge the receipt of the beautiful flag presented the regiment, and in return I present to you the old one, which it has been our proud honor to carry victoriously over many hard-fought battle-fields. That dear "old flag" which has been our companion through years of fearful war and carnage, and which symbolizes our glorious nationality, tells its own story. We return it to you, but not so beautiful in form and color as when presented to us eighteen months ago. But whilst its external beauty has been defaced, yet the great life-giving principles of which it is the exponent, are all the more deeply enshrined in the hearts of its defenders, and Liberty receives through this standard another bright and shining star to her beautiful constellation. Take it, then, and place it among the archives of the nation, that it may be preserved as a sacred memorial, and handed down to latest posterity as a glorious legacy and standard that was borne, as by angel hands, in opposition to oppression and rebellion. Be assured that it is with a renewed national pride that we look upon this beautiful flag presented to the Twenty-ninth Ohio, by the patriotic and loyal citizens of Summit and Ashtabula counties. The past history of almost four years in war, speaks for our conduct as soldiers and patriots for the future. We promise never to desert this flag, nor will we permit traitors or rebels to wrest it from our hands. We will always be willing and ready to unfurl it in defense of the principles of our glorious, free Republic. Truly our country's faith has learned a new interpretation of her standard. The white typifies the purity of purpose which belongs to her true ruler; the red points to the crimson tide in which life flows forth a willing offering; the blue reminds her of her home in heaven, to which all the good are gathered; the stars in her banner tell of light in darkness, and she shall learn to range them in a new and beautiful order, as the constellation of the cross. It is that flag which has solved most conclusively the long disputed problem of a free republican form of government. It was that flag which was so bravely and triumphantly carried through the ordeal of war by our Revolutionary sires, and encircled them with a halo of glory that shall be handed down untarnished to millions of unborn freemen It was that flag which, under God, enabled our forefathers to gain our glorious independence, and here, in this beautiful land of lakes and rivers, rear a temple of liberty which stands first among the nations of the earth, the envy and admiration of all. It is the flag which we have learned to love and to defend, and which we cherish in our hearts as the guardian angel of our country.

May that same God who has given so many brave hearts to defend it, continue to preserve it, and may it give light and liberty to millions who are yet groaning under tyranny and oppression. But we would not pass by unnoticed the many noble brave men who offered themselves a willing sacrifice upon our country's altar in defense of that national banner. The voices of our fallen comrades are borne to us in solemn silence by every breeze that fans our brow The South is billowed with the graves where sleep the patriot martyrs of constitutional liberty, until the resurrection morn. We hold them dear to our hearts, for may it never be forgotten that their deeds of valor facilitated the consummation of the glorious results which have just been achieved. Though they be dead, they yet speak, and will continue to speak to the end of all time, and dear to each patriot heart will ever be the memory of those who died in defense of the Union.

> "There are many
> Patriots have toiled in their country's cause,
> Bled nobly, and their deeds, as they deserve,
> Receive proud recompense. We give in charge
> Their names to the sweet lyre The historic muse
> Proud of her charge, marches with it down
> To latest time and sculpture, in her turn,
> Gives bond, in stone and ever-during brass,
> To guard and immortalize her trust "

At Bladensburg we went into camp, and remained until June 10. Marched to Washington at 8 P. M., and embarked on the cars of the Baltimore & Ohio railroad and steamed away homeward, bound to Parkersburg by way of Grafton, West Virginia, thence by boat to Louisville, Kentucky; moved five miles into the country, where we remained until the 13th day of July, when we were mustered out. Repairing to Camp Taylor, near Cleveland, Ohio, we were paid off and formally discharged from the service on the 22d and 23d days of July, 1865

We have now followed the regiment through nearly four years of the most arduous service which ever fell to the lot of any organization of this character, marching and fighting through most of the States in rebellion, its pathway marked by the graves of our comrades who fell. In the interim, hundreds of the brave 1540 who were upon its rolls, pass under the charge of the worse than fiends of hell, who presided at Libby, Belle Isle, Andersonville, and other courts of death, by courtesy called rebel prisons, where, after being robbed of all they possessed, and even stripped of necessary clothing, they were subjected to a systematic course of starvation (and that, too, under the immediate supervision of that foul blot upon humanity, Jeff Davis) until their brave spirits went out to the God who gave them. In the army of the East, with the army of the West, with Sherman in the glorious march to the sea, and the brilliant campaign of the Carolinas—where there was danger and death—shone the "white star" of the Twenty-ninth. The skirmish line and the advance became so nearly the normal condition of the regiment that assignment to positions less dangerous elicited exclamations of surprise from the "boys."

At length the last ditch, so frequently referred to by the braggart rebels, was reached—chivalrous Jeff Davis in hoc and crinoline begged that mercy be shown to "woman and children." The bubble secessia burst, and the command, now reduced to a mere handful, turn sadly northward, its columns " gaping from the havoc of shot and shell, and the disease of the camp, and prison pen, its colors ragged and torn, but proud and defiant as ever —one grand ovation to the living, a sad wailing requiem for the dead," and "good byes" are said in the beautiful Forest city, as each departed for their homes to assume the peaceful avocations of four years before.

Gradually they have drifted away—some to a quiet nook in the country church yard, and others to the east, west, and south, until now they may be found in nearly every State and Territory in this vast Union. Annually they come together in re-union at some convenient point in Puritan Western Reserve, and

> " Fight their battles o'er again."

Each year a committee is appointed whose duty it is to draft resolutions of condolence to the memory of the comrades whose "final statements" have been called for since the last meeting, and this committee *always have something to do* Each yearly roll call is shorter than its predecessor, and it does not require a long look into the future to find only the roll—no one to call it, and none to answer to their names if called.

> Absent "comrades, gone before us
> In the 'great review' to pass—
> Never more to earthly chieftain
> Dipping colors as ye pass—
> Heaven accord ye gentle judgment
> As before the throne ye pass."

While almost within gun shot of the site of the canvass covered field of 1861, busily engaged in well nigh vain endeavors to retain his grip upon the "ragged edge" of a somewhat precarious existence, and but a few laps in advance of the grim gentleman with the hour glass and scythe, abides

THE DRUMMER BOY(?) OF COMPANY B.

## GENERAL REVIEW.

The following review of the battles, sieges, marches, and campaigns in which the Twenty-ninth regiment was engaged, is from the pen of Colonel Jonas Schoonover. It gives in brief the important work of the regiment during its nearly four years' service, and should the "gentle reader" find the descriptive portion of the history too voluminous, she has but to turn to this review to find consolation.

Beginning with the service in the winter of 1861–2, along the waters of the Potomac and its tributaries, and in the mountain regions of Hampshire county, the Romney expedition in West Virginia, the advance to Winchester via Little mountain and Martinsburg, thence into the Shenandoah valley. The Strasburg march, which ended in the battle of Winchester, where the Federal army, under General Shields, and the rebels, commanded by General T. J. Jackson, at Kernstown, engaged in a sanguinary battle on March 23d, 1862, in which the Union army gained a victory. The Twenty-ninth Ohio done its full share, suffering slight loss in killed and wounded. The march up the valley to Madisonburg; the long march to Fredericksburg, leaving the Shenandoah valley at New Market on the 12th day of May, 1862, and reaching Fredericsburg May 22, 1862, a day or two later returning to Luray via Warrenton and Front Royal, up the Luray valley to Port Republic, where, on the 9th day of June, it engaged in battle with heavy loss in killed and wounded. 'One hundred and ten were made prisoners. The Twenty-ninth was engaged at short range in the open field against three times its number over four hours. During the time the struggle was desperate on both sides. The battle of Cedar mountain, seven miles from Culpepper Courthouse, on August 9th, the Union army under Banks, the rebels under Longstreet, the Twenty-ninth was engaged in the open field without cover, and sustained considerable loss. Then followed the retrograde move to Culpepper; the campaign of General Pope, including the second battle of Bull Run; and the march to Frederick City, the winter and spring campaign of 1862 and 1863, under Major-general Joseph Hooker, at Dumfries, was memorable for its intense suffering, then came the march to Chancellorsville, and the battle there, which began May 1st, and ended on the 3d, in which the Twenty-ninth suffered heavy loss and was the last to leave the field. May 5th we crossed the Rappahannock on our way to Gettysburg via Aqua creek, Dumfries, Fairfax Court House, Leesburg, Edward's Ferry, Harper's Ferry, Frederick, and Littletown, where we fought one of the most determined battles of the war, commencing on the 1st and ending on the 4th day of July, 1863.

We returned to Virginia, moved to New York to quell riots, returned again, advanced to the Rapidan, reported to the Department of the Cumberland, via the Baltimore & Ohio railroad, crossing the Ohio river at Bellaire. On September 30th, we passed through Columbus, Ohio; Indianapolis, Indiana, and Louisville, Kentucky, and halted at Murfreesboro, Tennessee. In October we passed down to Stevenson and Bridgeport, Alabama, and up the Tennessee river to Wauhatchie valley.

On November 24th and 25th, we were engaged in the battle of Lookout mountain; Missionary Ridge on November 24th and 25th, and Taylor's Ridge and Ringgold, Georgia, on November 26th and 27th, 1863.

In December of the same year we re-enlisted, and during the winter we prepared for a vigorous and active campaign in the early spring of 1864. On May 3d, we left Bridgeport, Alabama, on the Georgia campaign, passing around Lookout Mountain, Rossville, and Crawfish springs. On May 8th, the Twenty-ninth regiment took an active part in the battle of Dug Gap, Georgia, where it distinguished itself for bravery unparalleled in modern history ; every fourth man was killed or wounded. We moved on to Resaca, and in the fight of the 14th our loss was light. We moved on to Calhoun, Adairsville, Kingston, and Cassville on May 21st. In the battle of Pumpkin Vine Creek (or Dallas) from May 25th to the 28th, we met with some loss. In the battle of Pine Knob on June 15th, the Twenty-ninth suffered severe loss. Many of its brave heroes, whose valor will ever be held in memory by every survivor of the Twenty-ninth regiment, were killed. The battles of Lost and Kenesaw Mountain were on June 20th and 27th, and we advanced to the Chattahoochie river, via Marietta, Georgia, and then to the battle of Peach Tree Creek.

The Georgia campaign, from May 8th until the evacuation of Atlanta on September 2, 1864, a period of four months, was one continuous battle. The marching through Georgia was a glorious achievement, and will ever be recorded as one of the most brilliant feats in this or any other war. In Sherman's grand march to the sea and the siege and capture of Savannah, Georgia, the Twenty-ninth did its full share. It was engaged from December 10th to the 21st, when it entered the city of Savannah. On January 27, 1865, we moved on the campaign through the Carolinas, and were engaged in the following battles, and skirmishes of this campaign ;

Averysboro, North Carolina, on March 16th; Bentonville, North Carolina, on March 19, 1865, and marching to Goldsboro on March 24th. After Johnston's army at Raleigh, North Carolina, and the final march through Virginia to Washington in May, 1865, we took part in the grand review, thence to Louisville, Kentucky, on to Camp Taylor at Cleveland, Ohio, and home. The regiment was in the service nearly four years, and it is but justice to state that during its entire term it was *never driven from its position by direct assault.*

## OFFICIAL ROSTER.

The writer of the volume visited the office of the adjutant-general at Columbus, Ohio, and prepared a verbatim copy of the rolls of the Twenty-ninth regiment as transcribed in that office, which was published and issued with the proof copies. The following roster is largely from the pen of Colonel Jonas Schoonover, who is responsible for its correctness.

### FIELD AND STAFF.

Colonel Lewis P. Buckley, mustered into service December 28, 1861, honorably discharged, for disability, January 26, 1863.

Colonel William T. Fitch, mustered into service July 17, 1863; promoted to major January 28, 1864; wounded at Dug Gap, Georgia, May 8, 1864; discharged for wounds received in action, October 13, 1864.

Colonel Jonas Schoonover, mustered out with regiment, entered service as captain October 15, 1861; promoted to major January 18, 1865; to lieutenant-colonel April 1, 1865; to colonel July 12, 1865; the only officer of the regiment commissioned before leaving the State, who served through the war; commanded company H from November 1, 1864, to January 31, 1865.

Lieutenant-colonel Thomas Clark, mustered into service as major August 15, 1861, promoted to lieutenant-colonel November 28, 1861; honorably discharged, for disability, June 19, 1863.

Lieutenant-colonel Edward Hayes, discharged, for disability, November 17, 1864; entered the service as captain August 26, 1861; promoted to major August 16, 1863; to lieutenant-colonel October 17, 1863; wounded at Dug Gap, Georgia, May 8, 1864.

Major John S. Clemmer, mustered into service December 25, 1861; honorably discharged, for wounds received at Port Republic, Virginia, December 12, 1862.

Major Myron T. Wright, died January 7, 1865, from wounds received in action at Savannah, Georgia, December 19, 1864; wounded at Peach Tree creek, Georgia, July 20, 1864; entered service as first lieutenant; promoted to captain March 13, 1862, to major October 29, 1864, to lieutenant-colonel January 18, 1865.

Major Everson J. Hurlburt, mustered out with regiment; entered the veteran service as captain; promoted to major April 24, 1865; lieutenant-colonel July 12, 1865; mustered out with regiment ; wounded in battles of Port Republic, Virginia, Cedar Mountain, Virginia, and Gettysburg, Pennsylvania.

Surgeon Amos K. Fifield, mustered into service August 23, 1861; discharged, for disability, August 12, 1864.

Surgeon Ellwood P. Haines, resigned June 26, 1865; promoted assistant surgeon March 31, 1863 ; promoted to surgeon August 29, 1864.

Surgeon Thomas B. Miser, mustered out with regiment; entered service as assistant surgeon August 24, 1864; promoted to surgeon June 26, 1865.

Assistant Surgeon Sylvester S. Burrows, mustered into service September 10, 1861; honorably discharged January 26, 1863.

Assistant Surgeon Cyrus Hosack, mustered into service August 22, 1862, discharged, for disability, August 7, 1863.

Adjutant Comfort T. Chaffee, mustered into service August 27, 1861; honorably discharged, no reason assigned, April 13, 1862

Adjutant Theron S. Winship, mustered into service September 16, 1861, honorably discharged, for disability, January 26, 1863.

Adjutant James B. Storer, discharged by reason of wounds received in action, November 30, 1864; entered the service as sergeant, promoted to sergeant-major March 14, 1862; to adjutant January 20, 1863, wounded at Dug Gap, Georgia, May 8, 1864.

Adjutant Thomas Folger, mustered out with regiment July 13, 1865; transferred to field and staff as adjutant April 6, 1865; promoted captain July 12, 1865

Regimental-quartermaster Oscar F. Gibbs, promoted to captain May 25, 1864; honorably discharged for disability April 3, 1865; mustered into service October 21, 1861

Chaplain Russell H. Hurlburt, mustered into service December 10, 1861; honorably discharged, for disability, August 4, 1862.

Chaplain Lyman D. Ames, mustered into service February 19, 1863; resigned June 26, 1865.

### TRANSFERRED

Sergeant-major Palmer Williamson, mustered into service August 25, 1861; transferred to company G; promoted to second lieutenant December 21, 1861.

Sergeant-major James B. Storer, mustered into service October 17, 1861, transferred to company F, promoted to second lieutenant April 13, 1862.

Sergeant-major Benjamin W. Smith, mustered into service August 19, 1861, transferred to company K; promoted to second lieutenant August 9, 1862; see company K.

Sergeant-major Cary H. Russell, mustered into service September 30, 1861; transferred to company G; promoted to second lieutenant March 1, 1862; see company G.

Sergeant-major Charles W Kellogg, mustered into service August 26, 1861, transferred to company C, promoted to second lieutenant December 1, 1863; see company C.

Sergeant-major Henry M. Ryder, mustered into service August 26, 1861; transferred to company C; promoted to second lieutenant January 26, 1863, see company C.

Sergeant-major Jacob Buck, mustered out with regiment, re-enlisted as sergeant December 21, 1863, promoted sergeant-major June 19, 1865, first lieutenant July 12, 1865.

Quartermaster-sergeant Martin D Norris, mustered into service August 14, 1861, transferred to company A; promoted to second lieutenant April 13, 1862; see company A

Quartermaster-sergeant Caius C Lord, mustered out with regiment, promoted to quartermaster-sergeant June 17, 1865

Hospital Steward Ellwood P. Haines, mustered into service September 16, 1861 ; transferred to field and staff; promoted to assistant surgeon March 31, 1863.

Hospital Steward John Heffelfinger, mustered out with regiment.

Commissary-sergeant Nathan L. Parmeter, mustered out with regiment, promoted to commissary-sergeant June 16, 1865.

Principal Musician Gurley G. Crane, mustered into

service September 10, 1861; transferred to company F; promoted to second lieutenant March 13, 1863, see company F.

Principal Musician Richard Noonan, mustered into service September 10, 1861, transferred to veteran reserve corps, date unknown.

Principal Musician Andrew J. Ream, absent since July 9, 1865.

Principal Musician Richard Lewis, no discharge furnished on muster-out roll

### DISCHARGED

Quartermaster-sergeant George W. Beckwith, discharged August 8, 1864.

Sergeant-major Lyman H. McAdams, discharged to accept promotion as first lieutenant in company D (see company D) December 18, 1864.

Sergeant-major David W. Thomas, promoted to sergeant-major December 18, 1864, discharged to accept promotion as first lieutenant in company H January 21, 1865 (see company H).

Sergeant-major George McNutt, promoted to sergeant-major March 1, 1865, discharged to accept promotion as first lieutenant in company H (see company H) June 19, 1865

Quartermaster-sergeant Giles R. Leonard, promoted quartermaster-sergeant August 8, 1864; discharged to accept promotion as first lieutenant in company C (see company C) June 18, 1865.

Commissary-sergeant Marcus F. Roberts, promoted commissary-sergeant April 1, 1865; discharged to accept promotion as first lieutenant in company K (see company K) June 16, 1865.

Commissary-sergeant William H. Wright, discharged

to accept promotion as captain in company H (see company H) April 9, 1865.

### REGIMENTAL BAND.

Mustered out and discharged by General Order July 2, 1862.

Leader Chauncy Brainard, mustered into service August 26, 1861.

Albert E. Brainard, mustered into service August 26, 1861.

George B. Mason, mustered into service September 10, 1861.

William Meeker, mustered into service September 10, 1861.

Albert Walker, mustered into service September 10, 1861.

Calvin Crane, mustered into service September 10, 1861.

Erastus Brainard, mustered into service September 10, 1861.

Walter St. John, mustered into service August 14, 1861.

John Price, mustered into service August 19, 1861.

William H. Rawdon, mustered into service September 16, 1861.

Lucius K. Woodbury, mustered into service September 10, 1861.

Buel W. Brainard, mustered into service August 26, 1861.

Henry Beach, mustered into service September 10, 1861.

Moses C. Rist, mustered into service September 10, 1861.

Corwin Spencer, mustered into service September 10, 1861.

Lewis Price, mustered into service August 19, 1861.

Johnson W. Mattison, mustered into service August 26, 1861.

Luther H. Canfield, mustered into service August 14, 1861.

Henry H. Ray, mustered into service October 15, 1861.

The following names appear upon the original roster but do not again occur: Rufus Daniels, Edward B. Fitts, Charles N. Bancroft, E. P. Hall, S. H. Kent, and E. B. Woodbury.

———

## COMPANY A.

Mustered into service September 7, 1861. Mustered out by reason of expiration of term of service.

Captain William T. Fitch, promoted colonel July 17, 1864.

Captain Everson J. Hurlburt, promoted second lieutenant February 28, 1862, first lieutenant May 1, 1862; captain June 28, 1863; major April 10, 1865; lieutenant-colonel July 12, 1865.

Captain David W. Thomas, promoted first lieutenant company H January 6, 1864 (see company H); captain company A April 19, 1865.

First Lieutenant Leverett Grover, resigned January 28, 1862.

First Lieutenant William S. Crowell, resigned April 13, 1862

First Lieutenant Winthrop H. Grant, promoted second lieutenant May 15, 1863; to first lieutenant July 18, 1863; killed in battle at Dug Gap, Georgia, May 8, 1864

First Lieutenant Silas G. Elliott, promoted second lieutenant June 18, 1863; first lieutenant May 25, 1864; captain company E January 6, 1865 (see company E).

First Lieutenant Thaddeus E. Hoyt, promoted first sergeant June 12, 1864; first lieutenant January 21, 1865.

Second Lieutenant Martin D Norris, resigned October 28, 1862.

### NON-COMMISSIONED OFFICERS.

Sergeant Everson J. Hurlburt, promoted

Sergeant Chauncy H. Coon, promoted first sergeant February 28, 1862, discharged September 30, 1864.

Sergeant Winthrop H. Grant, promoted to first lieutenant July 18, 1863; killed at Dug Gap, May 8, 1864.

Sergeant Silas G. Elliott, promoted

Sergeant Wallace B. Hoyt, died in Andersonville prison October 20, 1864.

Corporal Newton B. Adams, transferred to company I December 17, 1861.

Corporal Andrew L. Rickard, killed in battle, Pine Knob, Georgia, June 15, 1864.

Corporal Roderick M. Gates, died at Alexandria, Virginia, August 27, 1863.

Corporal Thaddeus E. Hoyt, promoted.

Corporal Marcus F. Robert, promoted

Corporal Joseph B Dalrymple, mustered out with company.

Corporal James M. Loomis, discharged April 17, 1863.

Corporal Henry C. Rood, mustered out with company.

Drummer Richard Lewsi, transferred to non-commissioned staff November 1, 1863.

Wagoner William Daniels, discharged June 28, 1862.

## PRIVATES.

James M. Bronson, mustered out with company.

Marshall A Brown, died at Winchester, Virginia, March 10, 1862

Pulaski B. Broughton, mustered out by reason of expiration of term of service September 9, 1864.

Henry E Clafflin, mustered out with company.

Francis M. Canfield, discharged July 23, 1862.

Charles Covert, transferred to Veteran Reserve corps August 14, 1863.

Mortimer M. Canfield, transferred to Veteran Reserve corps September 1, 1863

Loren M Coon, promoted to corporal January 1, 1864.

Emory G. Clark, transferred to Veteran Reserve corps February 15, 1864.

Julius Coleburn, discharged April 3, 1862.

Henry Decker, discharged July 30, 1862.

Perry A. Decker, discharged October 4, 1862.

Alma L. Dalrymple, died at Winchester, Virginia, May 2, 1862

George H. Dudley, discharged January 30, 1863

Henry Turner, discharged October 18, 1864.

Daniel Thatcher, mustered out with company.

Horace E. Woodin, mustered out with company.

W. B. Shearer, discharged June 20, 1865.

Abram Exceen, discharged October 9, 1862.

John A. Exceen, promoted to corporal January 1, 1864.

John Ellis, transferred to Veteran Reserve corps March 30, 1865.

Alpheus A Fenton, transferred to Veteran Reserve corps August 1, 1863.

Joseph M. Sober, discharged February 6, 1863.

William A. Thompson, discharged October 9, 1862.

Eli P. Young, discharged April 5, 1863

Charles H. Broughton, discharged June 28, 1862.

George Birch, discharged June 28, 1862.

Edwin O. Brown, died from wounds received at Gettysburg, Pennsylvania, July 20, 1863.

William A. Frisbie, discharged November 8, 1864

Leonard Grover, discharged February 18, 1863

Rosalva W. Graham, discharged November 1, 1862.

John W. Henry, discharged July 10, 1862.

Sylvester Hyde, discharged July 20, 1862.

Cyrus Hendrick, discharged for wounds received at Gettysburg July 3, 1863, October 17, 1863

Edwin W. Herrick, mustered out with company.

Eli M. Holcomb, discharged November 22, 1862.

John Hague, promoted to first sergeant.

Addison Harley, discharged July 25, 1862.

William C. Ives, died at Cumberland, Maryland, March 5, 1862.

Eli C. Joles, discharged July 2, 1862.

George W. Jones, mustered out with company.

Lafayette M. Johnson, promoted to first sergeant March 1, 1865

Adrian M. Knowlton, killed in battle at Dug Gap, Georgia, May 8, 1864

Henry Bolster, discharged November 30, 1862

Almond O. Hungerford, discharged November 1, 1861.

Wallace R. Williams, discharged June 13, 1865.

Elizer Wilder, discharged July 22, 1862.

William L. Wood, promoted to corporal January 1, 1864.

Montezuma St John, discharged August 5, 1862.

Robert E. Woodbury, discharged June 25, 1865.

Augustus Thompson, discharged July 20, 1862.

John W. Bartlett, discharged July 28, 1862.

Sylvester C. Buck, discharged June 13, 1862.

Ammi B Benjamin, promoted to corporal June 1, 1865.

Christopher C. Bugbee, discharged June 28, 1862.

Emory J. Maltby, promoted to first sergeant June 15, 1864.

Albert H. Frayer, promoted to corporal June 1, 1865.

Orlin B Laskey, discharged September 9, 1864

Starr O. Latimer, discharged March 14, 1863.

James E. March, discharged February 4, 1863.

Abram W. McNaughton, died at Cumberland, Maryland, January 28, 1862

Gillispie B. Mowry, discharged June 5, 1865.

Franklin B Mowry, mustered out with company.

Franklin Potter, killed in battle of Dug Gap, Georgia, May 8, 1864.

Emerson Richerson, died at Cumberland, Maryland, March 10, 1862

Cyrus Roath, killed in battle at Pine Knob, Georgia, June 15, 1864.

Burdette L. Roberts, discharged August 4, 1862.

Nelson W. Simmons, discharged July 17, 1862.

John Sylvester, discharged February 18, 1863.

Wilber Sloat, mustered out with company.

Theodore Smith, died at Bridgewater, Alabama, March 25, 1864.

John Shears, discharged September 12, 1862.

Alonzo Squires, discharged May 18, 1862.

Pickering P. Smith, promoted to sergeant.

Silas R. Thompson, discharged April 5, 1863.

Corporal Seth N Hubbard, died at Martinsburg, Virginia, April 12, 1862.

Volney Wilson, mustered out with company.

Thaddeus W. Simmons, discharged June 20, 1862.

Abram B. Durfee, mustered out with company.

Nathaniel Wilder, mustered out with company.

George De Wolf, discharged October 9, 1861.

David Fox, discharged November 1, 1861.

Ferdinand Burt, transferred to company K November, 1, 1861.

Washington I. Dutcher, transferred to Veteran Reserve corps, September 1, 1863.

Almoner Woodruff, transferred to company I, December 17, 1861.

Almond O. Hungerford, discharged November 1, 1861.

RECRUITS OF 1862.

George Root, died at Dumfries, Virginia, March 16, 1863

William Monger, absent without leave.

Robert Monger, absent without leave.

Stephen H. Crane, discharged January 11, 1863.

Diodate Ensign, discharged February 15, 1863.

Reuben Smith, discharged August 3, 1863.

Gaius St. John, discharged February 15, 1863.

Charles Babb, discharged June 5, 1865

L. H. Dalrymple, discharged June 5, 1865.

James O. Latimer, discharged March 30, 1863

Isaac Monger, discharged June 5, 1865.

Oscar Parkill, discharged April 10, 1865.

Samuel Ray, discharged June 1, 1865.

RECRUITS OF 1864.

Daniel B. Alderman, mustered out with company.

Isaac E. Haggett, wounded near Marietta, Georgia, July 1, 1864, mustered out with company.

Alonzo LeBlanc, mustered out with company.

Francis Wilbur, mustered out with company.

Thomas Bonner, substitute, captured March 11, 1865.

Isaac Brian, substitute, mustered out with company.

Daniel Brook, substitute, mustered out with company.

Jacob Critten, substitute, mustered out with company.

Peter B. Covert, substitute, mustered out with company.

John Carey, substitute, mustered out with company.

Jesse Freel, drafted, discharged July 7, 1865.

Jacob Kramp, drafted, discharged July 12, 1865.

James Mitchell, drafted, mustered out with company.

George McKammin, drafted, mustered out with company.

Charles Blake, substitute, died at Savannah, Georgia, December 31, 1864.

Robert McKee, drafted, died in North Carolina, April 6, 1865.

Henry Miller, drafted, died at Savannah, Georgia, March 31, 1865.

Jacob Ballenbach, drafted, discharged June 5, 1865.

Jacob Cunningham, substitute, discharged June 5, 1865

Gottleib Fell, drafted, discharged June 5, 1865.

Franklin Hawkins, substitute, discharged June 5, 1865

Jacob Kanauf, substitute, discharged June 5, 1865.

Ferdinand Kable, drafted, discharged June 5, 1865.

Henry Oswald, drafted, discharged June 5, 1865.

James O. Parker, substitute, discharged June 5, 1865.

Isaac Samms, drafted, discharged June 5, 1865.

William Smalley, drafted, discharged June 5, 1865.

Joseph Sockwell, drafted, discharged June 5, 1865.

Walter St John, transferred to regimental band September 20, 1861.

Seth E. Wilson, transferred to company I, December 17, 1861.

---

## COMPANY B.

Mustered into service September 7, 1861.

Captain Wilbur F Stevens, discharged at expiration of term of service, September 9, 1864

Captain Thomas W. Nash, promoted second lieutenant October 30, 1862; first lieutenant June 29, 1864; captain October 12, 1864; mustered out with company.

Captain Andrew Wilson, promoted first lieutenant November 26, 1862; promoted captain May 25, 1864, discharged by expiration of term of service October 31, 1864.

First Lieutenant Alfred Bishop, resigned February 13, 1863.

Second Lieutenant John J Hoyt, joined for service in 1862, resigned November 1, 1862.

Second Lieutenant Edward T Curtis, joined company as second lieutenant October 1, 1862; detached in Veteran Reserve corps March 20, 1864; promoted first lieutenant May 25, 1864; mustered out with company.

Sergeant Benjamin N. Smith, transferred to non-commissioned staff May 1, 1862.

Sergeant Joel E. Tanner, promoted second lieutenant June 25, 1864; killed at Pine Knob, Georgia, June 15, 1864.

Sergeant Francis M. Hewitt, discharged June 19, 1862

Sergeant Perry O. Warren, discharged September 24, 1862.

Sergeant Byron A. Isham, discharge not furnished.

Sergeant Nathan A. Germond, mustered out with company.

Sergeant Lewis Montgomery, mustered out with company.

Sergeant A. J. Langworthy, mustered out with company

Sergeant Henry F. Brainard, mustered out with company.

Sergeant Henry E. Clark, mustered out with company.

Sergeant Rush Griswold, promoted first lieutenant company F, May 26, 1865.

Sergeant George McNutt, transferred to non-commissioned staff, April 6, 1865.

Corporal Orville Fairbrothers, died May 27, 1862.

Corporal Levi K. Bean, died of wounds April 2, 1862.

Corporal Darius B. Peck, discharged August 5, 1862.

Corporal Frank A. Chapman, discharged January 3, 1863.

Corporal Elbridge Potter, discharged for wounds, November 27, 1864.

Corporal Albert Bishop, transferred to company I, December 30, 1861.

Corporal Edwin Furman, discharged June 1, 1862.

Corporal Spencer Atkin, mustered out with company.

Corporal Albert H. Benham, mustered out with company.

Corporal John Davis, mustered out with company.

Corporal Vanness Jordan, mustered out with company.

Corporal Henry Hicks, mustered out with company.

Musician George W. Miles, died June 20, 1862.

Musician Hamilton SeCheverell, captured at Winchester, May 14, 1862; discharged July 3, 1862, by reason of General Order No. 65, A. G. O.

Musician John Price, transferred to regimental band, September 10, 1861.

Musician Lewis Price, transferred to regimental band, September 10, 1861.

Musician Henry Cedar, captured; discharged June 15, 1865.

Isaiah Brainard, discharged September 9, 1864.

Newell Hicks, discharged September 9, 1864.

Milton B. Hoskins, discharged September 9, 1864.

Manley A. Rowe, discharge not furnished.

Robert Stewart, discharge not furnished.

Harvey Beckwith, killed at Winchester, Virginia, March 23, 1862.

Alvinson A. Kinney, killed at Cedar Mountain, August 9, 1862

John Baur, captured June 9, 1862, died in rebel prison.

Conant Brainard, died April 30, 1862.

Charles F. Baur, died April 19, 1862.

Andrew Bright, recruit of 1862, died June 2, 1864.

George Gale, recruit of 1862, died April 14, 1863.

Herman O. Holmes, died April 6, 1862.

Clark Hull, died July 14, 1862

Jacob Kohler, died May 4, 1862.

Newcomb Knapp, died April 23, 1862.

John Marvin, died February 7, 1862.

Robert McFall, died June 27, 1862.

Jonas Newman, died April 5, 1862.

Dyer Newcomb, died January 29, 1863.

William Potter, died of wounds, July 8, 1864.

Albert Rogers, died January 7, 1862.

Jesse Rockwell, died February 25, 1862.

Robert Sills, died in Libby Prison, no date.

William H. Vanscoit, died April 5, 1862.

Rufus Wilson, died June 1, 1862.

Cassius Giddings, claimed as minor September 9, 1861

Jerome Doe, absent without leave.

Benson L. Haskins, absent without leave.

Frank Leonard, absent without leave.

Walter Nelson, recruit of 1862, discharged November 11, 1862.

Gilbert Rowe, absent without leave.

Hannibal Smith, absent without leave.

Darius Ames, discharged September 25, 1863.

Elmer T. Allen, discharged June 2, 1862.

Samuel S. Andrews, discharged June 18, 1862.

Leslie P. Allen, discharged May 30, 1862.

Franklin B. Ackley, discharged June 12, 1862.

Monroe Burgett, discharged September 14, 1862.

Lewis Baur (1862), discharged November 5, 1862.

Oscar J. Burbank, discharged February 15, 1863.

Thomas Beckwith, discharged June 26, 1862.

William R. Carr, discharged August 6, 1862.

Sterling Chapman, discharged January 30, 1862.

Andrew J. Curtiss (1862), discharged December 20, 1863.

Frederick Case, discharged February 13, 1863.

Benjamin H. Durfee, discharged October 25, 1862.

Holce Durfee, discharged March 3, 1863.

Joseph C. DeWolf, discharged February 13, 1863.

Mortimer DeWolf, discharged December 31, 1862.

John W. Ingersoll, discharged October 16, 1862.

Joseph H. Failer, discharged October 12, 1862.

Edwin C. Holmes discharged June 18, 1862.

Ralph Hartwell, (1862), discharged October 29, 1862.

Nelson Hendrick, discharged December 15, 1862

Frank Hartwell (1862), discharged December 10, 1862.

David Knapp (1862), discharged November 1, 1863

Alfred Lewis (1862), discharged March 5, 1863.

Earl P. McArthur, discharged April 12, 1862.

Charles W Matthews, discharged September 15, 1862

Robert McKee, discharged February 13, 1862

Daniel Potter, discharged October 25, 1862.

Seth C. Pierce, discharged October 20, 1862

Reuben Pitney (1862), discharged November 1, 1862.

Edward Phillips, discharged April 5, 1863.

Stephen A. Stanley, discharged February 13, 1863.

Lamson Wright, discharged February 13, 1863.

Sidney B. Wilder, discharged February 13, 1863.

Samuel R. Emmes (1862), transferred to Invalid corps February 16, 1864.

Albert Grate, transferred to Veteran Reserve corps June 15, 1864

Finley Hollett, transferred to Veteran Reserve corps March 20, 1864.

Byron A. McArthur, transferred to company I, December 30, 1861

Stephen Sturdevant, transferred to company I, December 15, 1861

George W Atkin, mustered out with company.

Job Brazee, mustered out with company

Daniel J. Baur, mustered out with company

Dudly Brown, mustered out with company.

William P Johnson, mustered out with compauy.

James Rounds, mustered out with company.

George Wright, mustered out with company.

Peter Dennis, mustered out with company.

John Edwards (1863), wounded at Mill Creek, Georgia, mustered out with company

Jeremiah Hennesy (1863), mustered out with company.

James Ryan (1863), discharged July 10, 1865.

Daniel A Smith, no record of discharged.

George Barne, substitute, mustered out with company.

Michael R. Godfrey, substitute, mustered out with company.

John Mason, substitute, mustered out with company.

Samuel S McDonald, substitute, mustered out with company

Joseph Pearce, drafted, sick in hospital

Martin V. Rudolph, drafted, discharged July 5, 1865.

Adam Rymond, substitute, mustered out with company.

John A. Trackler, substitute, mustered out with company.

Robert Stewart, substitute, sick in hospital.

John Tester, substitute, sick in hospital

Albert W. Atkins, killed at Dallas, Georgia, May 29, 1864.

Jerome Phinney, killed at Dallas, Georgia, May 29, 1864

Cornelius A. Davis, killed at Dallas, Georgia, May 29, 1864

Melancthon Poe, substitute, died at Savannah, Georgia, February 15, 1865.

Jacob Scott, drafted, died at Savannah, Georgia, December 22, 1864

George W. Warden, 1863, died at Marietta, Georgia, October 29, 1864.

George W. Wright, died at Chattanooga, Tennessee, May 31, 1864.

Samuel S Andrews, discharged June 5, 1865.

John Burns, discharged November 17, 1864.

Peter Dancoe, 1863, discharged June 19, 1865.

Thomas B. Dustin, substitute, discharged June 5, 1865.

Andrew J Folk, drafted, discharged June 5, 1865.

Cyrus Grubb, drafted, discharged June 5, 1865.

Henry H Harder, 1862, discharged June 5, 1865.

Andrew Hogan, 1863, discharged May 6, 1865.

Leonard Hammond, drafted, discharged June 5, 1865.

Daniel Heck, drafted, discharged June 5, 1865.

Harrison Hay, substitute, discharged May 26, 1865.

William Julien, substitute, discharged June 5, 1865.

Joseph S. Lewis, substitute, discharged June 5, 1865.

Byron Moffett, substitute, discharged June 5, 1865.

Samuel Myres, drafted, discharged June 5, 1865.

Ely Oaks, drafted, discharged June 5, 1865.

George W. Stocking, 1862, discharged June 5, 1865.

William H. Stratton, substitute, discharged June 5, 1865.

Rees Hickey, substitute, discharged June 5, 1865.

Leroy Sill, substitute, discharged June 5, 1865.

John C. Shaw, substitute, discharged June 5, 1865.

Avery Turner, 1862, discharged June 5, 1865.

William Thornton, drafted, discharged June 17, 1865.

Charles Wilson, substitute, discharged June 5, 1865.

Jacob W. Yohe, drafted, discharged June 12, 1865.

## COMPANY C.

Mustered into service September 7, 1861.

Captain Edward Hayes, promoted to signed to staff July 17, 1863.

Captain Rollin L. Jones, promoted from first sergeant to captain January 6, 1865 ; captured at Port Republic June 9, 1862; wounded at Pine Knob, Georgia, June 9, 1864; mustered out with company.

First Lieutenant Benjamin F. Perry, resigned, by reason of disability, June 20, 1862.

First Lieutenant Frank T. Stewart, promoted and assigned to duty at Alexandria, Virginia, April 3, 1863

First Lieutenant Almor B. Paine, promoted from private to first lieutenant January 6, 1865; captain January 29, 1865, and assigned to company F (see company F).

Second Lieutenant Henry M. Ryder, promoted from sergeant-major April 10, 1863; died at Georgetown, District of Columbia, September 25, 1863.

Second Lieutenant Charles W. Kellogg, promoted to second lieutenant June 20, 1862; first lieutenant April 3, 1863; to captain October 12, 1864; transferred to company F (see company F).

Second Lieutenant Giles R. Leonard, transferred to non-commissioned staff as quartermaster-sergeant August 8, 1864, promoted first lieutenant May 31, 1865; mustered out with company

Sergeant George W. Britton, killed at Port Republic, Virginia, June 9, 1862

Sergeant Daniel W. Rolph, discharged, date unknown.

Sergeant George W. Beckwith, transferred to non-commissioned staff, May 1st, 1862.

Sergeant Nelson H. Bailey, mustered out with company.

Sergeant Warren A. Baker, mustered out with company.

Sergeant Charles C. Fitts, mustered out with company.

Sergeant Obed. K. Phelps, mustered out with company.

Sergeant Eli Britton, mustered out with company.

Sergeant Charles W. Kellogg, promoted June 20, 1862.

Sergeant Rollin L. Jones, promoted January 6, 1865.

Corporal William A. Burwell, killed at Port Republic, June 9, 1862.

Corporal Henry M. Ryder, promoted to sergean major, and transferred to non-commissioned staff.

Corporal John Chapell, discharged November 11, 1862.

Corporal Algernon Kingsley, discharged November 11, 1862.

Corporal Hiram Laughlin, mustered out with company.

Corporal Joel W. Lee, mustered out with company.

Corporal William N. Runyon, mustered out with company.

Corporal John Warren, mustered out with company.

Corporal Henry C. Lord, mustered out with company

Corporal James Wenham, mustered out with company.

Corporal Michael Maloney, mustered out with company.

Corporal Charles J. Galpin, mustered out with company.

Corporal Joseph Winby, mustered out with company.

Henry C. Carey, served three years, discharged.

Edgar O. Miller served three years; discharged.

Beneville Miller served three years; discharged.

John Gray, killed at Dug Gap, Georgia, May 8, 1864.

Julius Lavelle, killed at Chancellorsville, Virginia, May 3, 1863.

Allen L. Monty, killed at Port Republic, Virginia, June 9, 1862.

John Williams, killed at Gettysburg, Pennsylvania, July 3, 1863.

John Yokes, killed at Cedar Mountain, Virginia, August 9, 1862.

Willis Sisley, killed at Port Republic, Virginia, June 9, 1862.

Albert H. Beardsley, died at Cumberland, Maryland, February 17, 1862.

Oliver P. Crosby, died at Edinburg, Virginia, April 23, 1862.

Romeo Churchill, died at Harper's Ferry, Virginia, January 13, 1863.

Charles E. Dudley, died at Cumberland, Maryland, February 4, 1862.

Wellington G. Gillett, died at Mount Jackson, Virginia, May 20, 1862.

David B. Parker, died from wounds received, August 12, 1862.

James Thomas, died at Cumberland, Maryland, March 9, 1862.

Aaron Warner (1862), died at Bridgeport, Alabama, June 3, 1864.

William P. Dady, absent without leave.

Asa J. Dibble (1862), absent without leave.

James C. Griffin (1862), absent without leave.

Floyd D. Lane, mustered out with company.

John Leslie, absent without leave.

William H. Shires, absent without leave.

Stephen Warren, discharged April 21, 1863.

Loren B. Brainard, discharged August 5, 1862.

Sherman W. Bronson, discharged July 15, 1863.

Thaddeus R. Brown, discharged November 26, 1862.

Daniel V. Chaffee, discharged, date unknown.

Luther Clark, discharged April 15, 1862.

Robert A. Cunningham, discharged February 18, 1863.

James Clark (1862), discharged May 14, 1863.

Charles W. DeWitt, discharged, date unknown.

Edwin M. Devan, discharged November 13, 1863.

George Eastlick, discharged for wounds, June 9, 1862.

George Enos, discharged August 5, 1862.

Marvin E. Forbes, discharged October 29, 1862.

John A. Frazier, discharged June 27, 1864.

Edwin Gibbs, discharged April 3, 1863.

Joseph Hall, discharged for wounds November 6, 1862.

Daniel S. Halstead, discharged July 21, 1862.

Hiram Lyons, discharged August 15, 1862.

Lester W. Leavitt (1862), ditcharged October 29, 1862.

Lucius O. Linsley, discharged October 30, 1862.

Norman Morrill, discharged, date unknown.

Erwin F. Mason, discharged for wounds received at Gettysburg, Pennsylvania, July 3, 1863.

Byron Philps (drummer), discharged April 3, 1863.

Wellington Palmer, discharged, date unknown.

John D. Rea, discharged July 8, 1862.

David Ryckman, discharged October 30, 1862.

James F. Rowley, discharged July 8, 1862.

William Yokes, discharged for wounds received September 1, 1864.

Chauncy Brainard (musician), transferred to regimental band September 10, 1861.

Sylvester Strickland, discharged February 18, 1863.

Buel W. Brainard (musician), transferred to regimental band September 10, 1861.

Albert E Brainard (musician), transferred to regimental band September 10, 1861.

Russell W Cross, transferred to Invalid corps August 1, 1863.

William J. Chambers, transferred to Invalid corps August 1, 1863

William Eldred, transferred to company I December 13, 1861.

James Fleming, transferred to company F, November 1, 1861.

Thomas F. Henderson, transferred to company I December 13, 1861.

Ransom S. Krahl, transferred to company I December 13, 1861.

Johnson W Mattison, transferred to regimentrl band September 10, 1861.

Thomas J. Merrill, transferred to Invalid corps, December 1, 1863.

Martin Owen, transferred to company I December 13, 1861.

John R. Polley, transferred to company I December 15, 1861.

Euclid M. Supplee, transferred to company I December 15. 1861.

John Sage, transferred to company I December 15, 1861.

John Scofield, transferred to company F November 1, 1861.

Henry Strale (1862), transferred to invalid corps.

Orlando Wakeman, transferred to company I December 15. 1861.

Truman A. Kellogg (wagoner), mustered out with company.

Warren Algers, mustered out with company.

George D. Brockett, wounded May 8, 1864, discharged July 22, 1865.

Johnson Noble, captured, mustered out with company.

Charles E. Parkill, wounded, mustered out with company.

Henry C. Price, captured, mustered out with company.

Benjamin F. Sperry, captured, mustered out with company.

John C. Shaw, missing in action at Peach Tree Creek, Georgia July 20, 1864.

James Turton, captured, mustered out with company.

David Thomas, wounded, mustered out with company.

David Clark (1862), discharged July 12, 1865.

Obed Knapp (1862), mustered out with company.

Christe Arnold, drafted, mustered out with company.

Frederick Blench, substitute, mustered out with company.

Aus. Bowman, drafted, mustered out with company.

Charles Clause, substitute, mustered out with company.

Andrew Goff, drafted, mustered out with company.

John Humbell, drafted, mustered out with company.

Albert Kunerd, substitute, mustered out with company.

Eibs Lemmers, substitute, mustered out with company.

Lorenz Paul, drafted, mustered out with company.

John Ritter, drafted, mustered out with company.

Andrew Reser, drafted, mustered out with company.

Abraham Schivenforth, drafted, mustered out with company.

Frank Slomp, drafted, mustered out with company.

Henry Lunnemen, substitute, mustered out with company.

Frank S. Faller, substitute, mustered out with company.

John Kepler, joined the company at Camp Chase, Ohio, January, 1862; killed at Dug Gap, Georgia, May 8, 1864.

Jacob Dunkell, drafted, died April 17, 1865.

Allen Mason, died from wounds May 29, 1864.

Charles F. W. Marshall, substitute, absent without leave.

John Ald, substitute, discharged June 5, 1865.

Israel Bech (1862), discharged June 5, 1865.

William H. Clark, substitute, discharged June 5, 1865.

Sidney O. Crosby (1861), discharged June 9, 1865.

Fred Deffinger, substitute, discharged June 5, 1865.

Aaron Everly (1862), discharged June 5, 1865.

Samuel E. Fay (1862), discharged May 26, 1865.

Michael Fisher, drafted, June 5, 1865.

William Hawk (1862), discharged June 5, 1865

William Hettishimer, substitute, discharged June 5, 1865.

William Helmholz, drafted, discharged June 5, 1865.

William Hollis, drafted, discharged June 5, 1865.

John E. Kelk, drafted, discharged June 5, 1865.

Christian Kah, drafted, discharged June 5, 1865.

Dryden Lindsley (1861), wounded May 8, 1864; leg amputated; discharged January 9, 1865.

John L. Myer, drafted, discharged June 5, 1865.

Hiram O. Morgan (1862), discharged June 5, 1865.

Jacob Buck, drafted, discharged June 5, 1865.

George Roesch, substitute, discharged June 7, 1865.

Daniel Schaunn, drafted, discharged June 5, 1865.

James Fleming, wounded at Dug Gap, Georgia, May 8, 1864; transferred to Veteran Reserve corps.

Martin Winkel, drafted, discharged June 10, 1865.

Andrew Main, transferred to naval service, no date.

Micajah J. Rice, transferred to company D July 31, 1865.

---

## COMPANY D.

Mustered into service September 27, 1861.

Captain Pulaski C. Hard, resigned March 13, 1862.

Captain Myron T Wright, promoted to captain November 26, 1862; promoted to major January 5, 1864.

Captain Lyman H. McAdams, promoted to first lieutenant November 12, 1864; promoted to captain January 6, 1865; mustered out with company.

Captain George W. Dice, promoted to first lieutenant April 13, 1862; promoted to captain May 25, 1864; killed in action at Pine Knob, Georgia, June 17, 1864.

First Lieutenant Joshua Hile, promoted to first lieuteant January 6, 1865; mustered out with company.

Second Lieutenant James H. Grinnell, honorably discharged April 10, 1864.

Sergeant George W. Dice, promoted.

Sergeant John H Knox, died at Strasburg, Virginia, May 22, 1862.

Sergeant William E Dockery, transferred to company I, December 23, 1861.

Sergeant Joseph C. Ewart, discharged April 20, 1862.

Sergeant Lyman H McAdams, promoted·and transferred to non-commissioned staff, May 18, 1863.

Sergeant Charles G. Talcott, veteran, mustered out with company.

Sergeant Joseph Parks, veteran, sick in hospital.

Sergeant Jacob Rodenbaugh, veteran, mustered out with company.

Sergeant Jacob Replogle, veteran, mustered out with company.

Sergeant John G Wait, veteran, mustered out with company.

Sergeant Samuel Wooldridge, veteran, killed at Dug Gap, Georgia, May 8, 1864.

Corporal Lewis B. Starks (1861), served three years.

Corporal George Welsh (1861), served three years.

Corporal Frederick C. Remley, killed at Port Republic, Virginia, June 9, 1862.

Corporal Laben Robinson, discharged April 4, 1863.

Corporal William A. Hart, discharged December 22, 1862.

Corporal James S. Alexander, discharged September 27, 1864.

Corporal Leonard E. Gaylord, mustered out with company.

Corporal Jacob C. Glass, mustered out with company.

Corporal Norman Cochran, mustered out with company.

Corporal Edy Randall, mustered out with company.

Corporal Walter Randall (1863), mustered out with company.

Corporal George Faust, killed at Dug Gag, Georgia, May 8, 1864.

Corporal George J. Young, died from wounds, July 1, 1865.

Corporal Charles Steese (1862), discharged, G. O. No 77, June 5, 1865

Corporal Norman J. Smith, transferred to Veteran Reserve corps, March 8, 1865.

Hiram Harring (1861), served three years.

George Montenyohl (1861), served three years.

Washington Shanfelt (1862), served three years.

Henry A. Thompson (1861), served three years.

John B. Yohey (1861), served three years.

William H. Alexander (1861), no record.

Eber Bennett (1862), killed at Pine Knob, Georgia, June 16, 1864.

Thomas J. Bare (1862), killed at Dug Gap, Georgia, May 8, 1864.

Benjamin F. Pontious killed at Gettysburg, Pennsylvania, July 3, 1863.

Samuel Shanafelt (1862), killed at Chancellorsville, Virginia, May 3, 1863.

Charles A. Clapp, died at Jefferson, Ohio, December 5, 1861.

Elisha Hamilton, died at Luray, Virginia, June 24, 1862.

William H. Jones, died at Lynchburg, Virginia, July 21, 1862.

Leonard Squires, died from wounds at Alexander, Virginia, September 4, 1862.

Andrew Wolcott, died at Alexandria, Virginia, September 4, 1862.

Elias Walters (1862), died at Dumfrees, Virginia, April 10, 1863.

Evan H. Wright (1862), died at Frederick, Maryland, December 7, 1862.

Alvin W. Niman, died at Cumberland, Maryland, March 14, 1862.

George W. McCormick, absent without leave.

Warren B. Crane, musician, discharged October 22, 1862.

Bennett H. Wadsworth, musician, discharged September 26, 1863.

Andrew Hunsicker, wagoner, discharged November 9, 1863

William H. Bloomfield, discharged August 22, 1862.
Lewis Ball (1862), discharged July 17, 1863.
John G. Caskey (1862), discharged July 17, 1864.
Rufus T. Chapman, discharged September 27, 1864.
William C. Finney, discharged June 8, 1863.
Marshal Hoagland, discharged September 27, 1864.
Enoch Hastings, discharged August 2, 1862.
John H. Hue, discharged June 4, 1863.
William Hile (1862), discharged December 3, 1862
Phineas B. Jones, discharged August 22, 1862.
John A. Jones, discharged July 25, 1862.
John Lamberson, discharged June 15, 1863.
Noah Leohrer, discharged February 18, 1863.
Lauren Merrian, discharged July 22, 1862.
William Midisker, discharged January 19, 1863.
William Mendleson, discharged December 20, 1862.
Henry W. Morrill, discharged December 20, 1862.
Almon Nimon, discharged August 17, 1862.
Richard Partridge, discharged November 4, 1862.
Isaac Powlus, discharged October 23, 1862.
Hiram Ream, discharged February 18, 1863.
Lewis Richardson, discharged December 10, 1862.
William C. Stoughton, discharged August 3, 1862.
John G. Stinhour, discharged August 17, 1862.
Solomon Streeker, discharged June 5, 1862.
Edwin E. Skinner, discharged August 17, 1862.
Lansing D. Standish, discharged January 18, 1863.
John H. Steese, discharged November 16, 1862.
Merwin Shaw (1862), discharged November 14, 1862.
John H. Snyder, discharged April 7, 1865.
Presley Thomas (1862), discharged October 3, 1863.
George Fordt (1862), discharged May 20, 1863.
Valentine Viers, discharged April 4, 1863.
Henry F. Waters, discharged August 15, 1862.

Gurley G. Crane, musician, promoted.

Charles Dudley, transferred to company I December 23, 1861.

Horace H. Heath, transferred to company I December 22. 1861.

Stephen Kissinger, transferred to company I December 27, 1861.

Richard Noonan, musician, transferred to veteran reserve corps.

Andrew J. Ream, musician, transferred to company I December 30, 1861.

Micajah J. Rice (1862), transferred to veteran reserve corps.

William P. Williamson, promoted.

William H. Wright, promoted to commissary sergeant Septemper 15, 1861.

Oscar Brewster, transferred to company F, Seventh Ohio regiment; volunteer by re-enlisting December 22, 1863.

Joseph Chalfant, discharged June 14, 1865.

George Ellis, mustered out with company.

Aaron W. Golden, mustered out with company.

William D. Haynes, prisoner of war.

Martin M. Hutchinson, mustered out with company.

David Hartigan, sick in hospital.

Luther Lindsley, mustered out with company.

Samuel W. Parks, transferred to naval service.

Charles Sherboney, sick in hospital.

Daniel Schaaf, mustered out with company.

Jacob Winters, mustered out with company.

Ezra Spidle (1862), prisoner of war.

Everett T. Shaw, mustered out with company.

Montgomery Alexander (1864), mustered out with company.

John H. Becktold (1864), mustered out with company.

John A Burkert (1864), mustered out with company.

David M. Brown (1864), sick in hospital.

William E. Dales (1863), mustered out with company.

Noah W. Taylor (1863), mustered out with company

John H. Hue (1863), mustered out with company.

John C. Hawley (1864), mnstered out with company.

Nicholas Long (1864), sick in hospital.

Robert Lutz (1863), mustered out with company.

Isaac Medisker (1863), mustered out with company.

David W Powell (1863), sick in hospital

James W. H. Snyder (1864), no record of discharge

Lorenzo McVallen (1863), mustered out with company.

John J. White (1863), mustered out with company.

Patrick Cox, substitute, mustered out with company.

James Daily, substitute, mustered out with company.

William Monroe. drafted, mustered out with company.

Robert Maryhagh, substitute, mustered out with company

John McArty, substitute, no record of discharge

Samuel McCarren, substitute, mustered out with company.

William D. Bogan, substitute, mustered out with company.

Alfred Hilbert, substitute, mustered out with company.

Martin Lowrcy, substitute, mustered out with company.

Henry Reck, substitute, mustered out with company.

Jacob Snyder, substitute, mustered out with company.

Benjamin Switzer, substitute, mustered out with company.

Simon Shenk, substitute, mustered out with company

Holmes J. White, drafted, mustered out with company.

Henry A. Hane (1864), killed at Dug Gap, Georgia, May 8, 1864.

William Hastings (1864), killed at Dallas, Georgia, May 25, 1864.

John W. Stuer (1864), killed at Dug Gap, Georgia, May 8, 1864.

Charles A. Downey (1861), wounded at Dug Gap, and died at Ringgold, Georgia, May 15, 1864

Jacob Gardner (1861), killed at Dug Gap, Georgia, May 8, 1864.

Christopher Beck (1861), died of wounds September 16, 1864.

Stephen J. Iles (1861), died March 8, 1864

Theron W Smith, died July 8, 1864

Levi Baughman, died September 2, 1864

John H. Montgomery, died June 2, 1864.

Simon J. Peters, died June 27, 1864.

John Demland, substitute, died December 8, 1864

Charles Mullett, died July 1, 1865

Levi Rank, drafted, died June 7, 1865.

Henry E Bryan, discharged, no date

Archey C. Ferguson (1862), discharged June 5, 1865.

Francis Huffman (1862), discharged June 5, 1865.

George W. Holloway (1862) discharged June 5, 1865.

Sylvanus Hile, mustered out with company.

Jacob Koplin, mustered out with company.

Benjamin Snyder, mustered out with company.

Edward Spicer, mustered out with company

George Shaw, mustered out with company.

David C. Winkler, 1862, discharged, G O. No. 77, June 5, 1865.

Franklin J. Waltz, mustered out with company.

Thomas Duny, discharged March 27, 1865.

Elias Shatt, discharged May 26, 1865.

Seth M. Thomas, discharged May 28, 1865.

James Bowles, discharged, G. O. No. 77, June 5, 1865.

Daniel D Luke, discharged June 24, 1865.

Duncan McKenzie, mustered out with company.

Peter C McEvery, mustered out with company.

Barney Gockey, mustered out with company.

James H. Scott, mustered out with company.

Thomas Sanders, mustered out with company.

Benjamin Showles, discharged, G. O. No 77, June 5, 1865.

William G. Buss, mustered out with company.

## COMPANY E.

Mustered into service September 27, 1861.

Captain Horacio Luce, killed in battle of Port Republic, Virginia, June 8, 1862.

Captain Ebenezer B. Howard, 1862, promoted from second to first lieutenant April 13, 1862; captain June 9, 1862, resigned March 6, 1863.

Captain Silas G. Elliott, promoted first sergeant December 12, 1863; first lieutenant June 12, 1864; captain, January 21, 1865; transferred from A to E; mustered out with company.

First Lieutenant Theron S. Winship, transferred to regimental staff as adjutant, April 13, 1862.

First Lieutenant Addison J. Andrews, promoted first sergeant December 22, 1863; first lieutenant, January 21, 1865; mustered out with company.

First Lieutenant William Neil, 1862, promoted to first lieutenant April 13, 1862; resigned January 30, 1863.

First Lieutenant Thomas W. Nash, promoted to captain, and transferred to company B January 1, 1865.

Second Lieutenant Albert Durkee, 1862, promoted from corporal to second lieutenant April 13, 1862, resigned July 9, 1862.

Second Lieutenant William B. Quirk, joined for duty September 19, 1862; resigned October 17, 1862.

Second Lieutenant Theodore L. Gould, 1862, promoted from first sergeant October 27, 1862, discharged for disability at Georgetown, District of Columbia, no date

Second Lieutenant George Hayward, killed at Gettysburg, Pennsylvania, July 3, 1863.

First Sergeant Nathan L. Parmeter, promoted to commissary sergeant, transferred to non-commissioned staff, June 16, 1865.

First Sergeant Charles Howard, mustered out with company.

Sergeant Addison E. Tracy, mustered out with company.

Sergeant William Sterling, mustered out with company.

Sergeant Francis Culver, mustered out with company.

Sergeant Alonzo H. Sterrett, transferred to United States infantry November 22, 1864

Sergeant William Colburn, promoted to sergeant June 16, 1865; mustered out with company.

Corporal Hiram Dalrymple, mustered out with company.

Corporal Hiram Thornton, paroled prisoner of war.

Corporal Lewis Harper, mustered out with company.

Corporal Charles W. Cary, mustered out with company.

Corporal Heman Dewey, mustered out with company.

Corporal Lucius Deane, discharged February 16, 1863.

Corporal Rufus H. Hulburt, 1862, paroled prisoner of war.

Corporal Jacob V. D. Clark (1862), mustered out with company.

Corporal Isaac Dalrymple, killed at Port Republic, Virginia, June 9, 1862.

Corporal George A. Sinclair, discharged July 24, 1862.

Corporal Daniel Platt, Sr., discharged July 22, 1862.

Corporal Albert Doty (1862), discharged June 5, 1865.

Musician Charles Luce, mustered out with company.

Musician John S. Bellows, discharged April 3, 1863.

Wagoner William H. Holden, mustered out with company.

### PRIVATES.

Albert Blanchard, served three years.

John C. Greenlee, served three years.

George J. Putney, served three years.

Daniel W. Platt, Jr., served three years.

Edward Byron, served three years.

James B. Bagley, killed in battle at Cedar Mountain, Virginia, August 9, 1862.

Orrin Brewer, died at Strasburg, Virginia, May 14, 1862.

Andrew Beardsley, died at Alexandria, Virginia, July 29, 1862.

G. W. Batchelor, died at Dumfries, Virginia, March 8, 1863.

Ethan Davis, died at Cumberland, Maryland, March 8, 1862.

Nelson Gillett, died at Pierpont, Ohio, July 15, 1864.

William Johnson, died at Cumberland, Maryland, April 10, 1862.

James S. Pike, died at Jefferson, Ohio, January 14, 1862.

Harvey A. Reaves, died at Winchester, Virginia, June 26, 1862.

Hiram Sly, died in rebel prison in June, 1862.

Thomas Schultz, died of wounds at Stafford Court House, Virginia, May 12, 1863.

Truman H. Williams, died at Bridgeport, Alabama, February 29, 1864.

Daniel Berringer, absent without leave.

Washington Ellsworth, absent without leave.

John S. Haddock, absent without leave.

Orenus Jones, absent without leave.

West Roberts, absent without leave.

Isaac Roberts, absent without leave.

John Sammon, absent without leave.

Walter Woodward, absent without leave.

Herman Benson, discharged July 25, 1862.

Edward J. Brewer, discharged October 25, 1862.

Charles Blake, discharged February 18, 1863.

Wilder H. Crawford, discharged June 26, 1862.

Albert Crouch, discharged June 6, 1862.

Elijah Curtis, discharged for wounds July 12, 1862.

Loren Culver, discharged July 3, 1862.

Isaac Conklin, discharged August 29, 1862.

John A. Ford, discharged February 18, 1863.

David B. Franklin, discharged September 5, 1863.

David Goodwill, discharged August 3, 1862.

Wallace W. Hill, discharged August 30, 1862.

Steven B. Hopkins, discharged March 10, 1863.

Emery Hopkins, discharged April 3, 1863.

Charles H. Hawkins, discharged November 27, 1863.

George A. Lillie, discharged July 24, 1863.

Marshal Morse, discharged November 24, 1862.

Isaac A Meeker, discharged July 26, 1862.

Daniel M. Morley, discharged February 18, 1863.

Calvin Pier, discharged August 14, 1862.

James O Phillips, discharged July 29, 1862.

Peter Proctor, discharged December 2, 1862.

Henry Rhoades, discharged July 24, 1862.

George Ryan, discharged October 25, 1862.

Stedman J. Rockwell, discharged November 20, 1862.

William Robinson, discharged November 3, 1862.

Peter Vanskoik, discharged August 19, 1862.

Lewis Webber, discharged for wounds September 9, 1862.

L. J. Woodward, discharged February 18, 1863.

Ancil O. Benjamin, transferred to company K December 13, 1861

Frederick Brown, transferred to Sixth United States cavalry October 31, 1862.

LeGrand Bivius, transferred to Invalid corps, September 17, 1863.

George M. Cowgill, transferred to company K, December 13, 1861.

Elias H. Durfee, transferred to company K December 13, 1861

Luther Fowler, transferred to company K December 13, 1861

Hiram Griggs, transferred to company K December 13, 1861.

Charles P. Rhoades, transferred to Invalid corps September 1, 1863

Cornelius Hinkle, transferred to company K, December 13, 1861.

Joseph Hammond, transferred to company K, December 13, 1861.

Elwood P. Haines, transferred to non-commissioned staff hospital steward, September 16, 1861.

Levant Hill, transferred to Sixth United States cavalry, October 31, 1863.

Franklin Lovejoy, transferred to Sixth United States cavalry, October 31, 1863.

Thaddeus Marsh, transferred to company K, December 29, 1861.

Lorenzo B. Norton (1862), transferred to invalid corps January 12, 1864.

William Pond, transferred to company K, December 13, 1861.

Lewis Shores (1862), transferred to invalid corps, September 1, 1863.

William L. Cary, mustered out with company.

Roby Dewey, mustered out with company

Orlando Gunn, mustered out with company.

David W. Hall, paroled prisoner

Hamilton Hill, on detached service.

James Jones, mustered out with company.

Robert Vanskoyt, mustered out with company.

Henry Warren, mustered out with company.

Calvin Wilson, mustered out with company

Alvah B. Cole (1862), in hospital.

Thomas G. Franklin (1862), in hospital.

Joseph R. Lynn (1862), on detached duty.

Chauncey Mason (1862), in hospital

RECRUITS OF 1864.

Carlisle W. Kinnear, mustered out with company

James B. Powers, mustered out with company.

John P. Benjamin, drafted in hospital.

James E. Browning, drafted, in hospital.

William C. Chatman, substitute, mustered out with company

John Cooper, drafted, mustered out with company.

Isaac N. Elsea, substitnte, mustered out with company.

Erastus F. Francis, drafted, mustered out with company.

Ezra Isham, substitute, in hospital.

John A. Loach, substitute, mustered out with company.

Jesse Lake, drafted, in hospital.

William C Ramsey, substitute, mustered out with company.

William Stiner, substitute, in hospital.

Riley Toland, drafted in hospital.

Joseph White, drafted, mustered out with company.

Albert N Atwater, died at Monroe, Ohio, July 4, 1864.

William F. Boal, drafted, died at New York City, April 5, 1865.

Barney Brick, veteran, died at Atlanta, Georgia, September 8, 1864.

Thomas S. McCartney, veteran, died of wounds, Chattanooga, Tennessee, July 16, 1864.

Samuel Perry, substitute, died at New York City April 8, 1865.

Adison E. Way, drafted, died at New York City April 19, 1865

James Braiden, substitute, absent without leave.

Cyrus B. Boal, drafted, discharged June 5, 1865.

Richard Cash, substitute, discharged June 5, 1865.

John Cowen, substitute, discharged June 5, 1865.

Morton M. Cook, drafted, discharged June 5, 1865.

Charles Hermandaffer, substitute, discharged June 5, 1865

Lewis Jacobs, drafted, discharged June 5, 1865.

Benjamin Holton (1862), discharged December 9, 1864.

Peter Jacobs, drafted, discharged June 5, 1865.

Henry Johnson, drafted, discharged June 5, 1865.

John W. Kinner (1862), discharged June 5, 1865.

John Kuner, drafted, discharged June 5, 1865.

Michael Mayhew, veteran, discharged May 26, 1865

Ephraim Oman, drafted, discharged June 5, 1865.

Simon Riley, drafted, discharged June 5, 1865.

Joseph Sucre, drafted, discharged June 5, 1865

Sherman Tuttle, veteran, discharged June 5, 1865

Charles Beckworth, transferred to Veteran Reserve Corps April 21, 1865

---

## COMPANY F

Mustered into service September, October, November, and December, 1861.

Captain John T. Morse, resigned April 15, 1862.

Captain Eleazer Burridge, promoted first lieutenant April 13, 1862; captain May 1, 1862; discharged February 3, 1863, for wounds received in battle of Port Republic June 9, 1862.

Captain Roland H. Baldwin, promoted first sergeant September 16, 1862; promoted to captain February 3, 1863; resigned November 1, 1864.

Captain Almer B Paine, promoted from private to sergeant July 1, 1862; first sergeant March 1, 1863; first lieutenant January 6, 1865, captain June 28, 1865; mustered out with company

First Lieutenant Hamblin Gregory, resigned January 26, 1863, disability.

First Lieutenant Rush Griswold, promoted to corporal

January 1, 1862, sergeant May 1, 1862; first sergeant June 16, 1864; first lieutenant January 6, 1865, mustered out with company

First Lieutenant Charles W. Kellogg, promoted to second lieutenant June 20, 1862, first lieutenant January 26, 1863; captain company K April 24, 1865.

Second Lieutenant James B Storer, promoted second lieutenant April 13, 1862, first lieutenant and adjutant January 26, 1863, to captain October 12, 1864.

Second Lieutenant Gurley G. Crane, promoted second lieutenant March 1, 1863; first lieutenant May 25, 1864; discharged July 10, 1864.

Sergeant Harrison L. Martindale, discharged for disability May 10, 1862.

Sergeant Joseph Jerome, discharged for wounds September 16, 1862.

Sergeant Marcus E. Gregory, discharged Aug. 1, 1862.

Sergeant George Gray, discharged February 18, 1863.

Sergeant Solon Hall, discharged November 10, 1862.

Sergeant Edwin Williams, died May 23, 1862.

Sergeant Charles F. Waldron, transferred to Invalid corps March 27, 1863.

Sergeant Almer B Paine, promoted.

Sergeant Absalom Case, promoted to first sergeant, mustered out with company.

Sergeant Cornelius Woodford, mustered out with company.

Sergeant Isaac J. Houghkirk, mustered out with company

Sergeant Orlando Wilson, mustered out with company

Sergeant Charles M. Dustin, mustered out with company.

Sergeant R. H. Baldwin, promoted February 3, 1863.

Corporal Simpson McLean, mustered out November 2, 1864.

Corporal Nathan Harvey, discharged December 13, 1862.

Corporal Hugh Macumber, discharged October 8, 1862.

Corporal Naaman B Noyes, discharged November 25, 1862.

Corporal Cyrenus Van Volkenburg, discharged November 8, 1862.

Corporal Burton Pickett, died from wounds August 14, 1862.

Corporal William Lindsley, transferred to Invalid corps March 22, 1864.

Corporal Spencer E. Balch, mustered out with company.

Corporal Cornelius V. Clark (1864), mustered out with company.

Corporal Iremus M Foot (1862), discharged June 5, 1865.

Corporal C. N. Hayes, discharged April 18, 1863.

Charles Cain, served three years; discharged October 18, 1864.

Jason Manley, served three years; discharged October 18, 1864.

Jesse B. Pickett, served three years, discharged October 18, 1864.

Oscar F. Stetson, served three years; discharged October 18, 1864.

John Schofield (musician), discharged February 18, 1863.

Daniel Ansinger, discharged February 18, 1863.

Corwin Broughton, discharged May 10, 1862.

Job Broughton, discharged June 23, 1862.

Jason Brigg, discharged October 9, 1862.

John W. Buele (1862), discharged December 11, 1862.

Caleb S. Buele (1862), discharged March 4, 1863.

Miles Chadwick, claimed as minor, no date.

Cornelius V. Clark, discharged November 12, 1862.

William L. Crosby (1862), discharged March 6, 1863.

Robert Cannon, discharged October 20, 1862.

Martin P. Durkee, discharged August 28, 1863.

Elmer Ewer, discharged November 1, 1862.

James Flood, discharged April 25, 1863.

Youngs E. Gregory, discharged February 24, 1863.

Andrew Harroun, discharged June 10, 1862.

Alexander D. Harroun, discharged February 18, 1863.

Luther C. Hawley (1862), discharged November 22, 1862.

Daniel D. Hill, discharged April 1, 1863.

Parish Joice, discharged May 10, 1862.

John C. McLean, discharged November 14, 1862.

Melvin Malone, discharged November 12, 1862.

Jehiel Maltby (1862), discharged April 10, 1863.

Frederick Meno, discharged August 12, 1862.

Eliphalet S. Outis, discharged November 12, 1862.

George A. Patcher, discharged December 12, 1862.

Louis Rynd, discharged June 30, 1863.

Thomas Ryne, discharged April 14, 1863.

Chester Smith, discharged November 16, 1862.

Ambrose Sperry, discharged February 8, 1863.

Peter Shelby, discharged February 8, 1863.

Pomeroy Smith, discharged April 4, 1863.

James Thorp, discharged August 12, 1862.

Ellsworth W. Taylor, discharged October 1, 1862.

George Wick, discharged April 3, 1863.

Frederick R. Johnson, killed at Port Republic, Virginia, June 9, 1862.

Josiah D. Johnson, killed at Gettysburg, Pennsylvania, July 3, 1863.

Sidney M. Smith, killed at Port Republic, June 9, 1862.

Oscar Stickney (musician), died April 28, 1863.

John A. Austin, died April 2, 1862.

Hiram E. Balch, died February 18, 1862.

John J. Belnap, wounded, died June 17, 1864.

Franklin Dimock, died February 18, 1862.

Michael Dowling, died May 18, 1862.

Alexander Neal, died from wounds March 29, 1862.

George Meno, died from wounds August 12, 1862.

Ellison Reed, Jr., died November 1, 1862.

James H. Whitney, died in Libby prison June 3, 1862.

Perry H. Chapin, absent without leave.

John Dodge, absent without leave.

Robert Davidson, absent without leave.

Russell Goodrich, absent without leave.

James Shelby, captured at Fredericksburg May 24, 1862.

Peter Smith, absent without leave.

Henry M. Babcock, held by Sixth Ohio cavalry in previous enlistment.

John Blodgett, transferred to company K, December 11, 1861.

John Carson, transferred to invalid corps, August 1, 1863.

Michael Flinn, transferred to invalid corps December 9, 1863.

James Fleming, transferred to company C November 2, 1861.

Loren Frisby (1862) transferred to invalid corps January 22, 1864.

Ellery W. Gray, transferred to company K December 14, 1861.

William Knox, transferred to company K December 14, 1861.

James King, transferred to Invalid corps August 1, 1863.

John Sarsfield, transferred to company K December 14, 1861.

Jonathan Taylor, transferred to company K December 14, 1861.

Alonzo Cole, discharged June 5, 1865.

William Call, mustered out with company.

James Foss, mustered out with company.

Ellery L. Gray, mustered out with company.

Asa E. Sanford, honorably discharged, no date.

Luther Walker, mustered out with company.

Albert Parker, musician (1864), mustered out with company.

Richard Adams, substitute, sick in hospital.

Horace Bradley, substitute, discharged May 25, 1865.

Howard Bell, drafted, mustered out with company.

Trenton R. Capus, substitute, mustered out with company.

John H. Castello, substitute, mustered out with company.

Andrew P. Debs, substitute, mustered out with company.

William Freeman, substitute, discharged July 6, 1865.

Miron S. Giles, substitute, mustered out with company.

Augustus Howell, substitute, mustered out with company.

David Nichols, substitute, mustered out with company.

Columbus Shoemaker, substitute, mustered out with company.

William P. Vins, substitute, mustered out with company.

Joseph Weaver, substitute, mustered out with company.

Jabin S. Dustin, killed at Pine Knob, Georgia, June 15, 1865.

John L. Best, substitute, died December 5, 1864.

Richard Conn, drafted, died December 8, 1864.

Thomas Clifford, drafted, died March 2, 1865.

Joseph Datson, substitute, died March 2, 1865.

George Hautworth, drafted, died May 26, 1865.

Lysander T King (1864), died May 6, 1865.

Ephraim Odell, substitute, died February 1, 1865.

Elmore Stevens (1864), died July 10, 1864.

George Williams (1864), died of wounds June 27, 1864.  ·

Franklin A. Helwig (1864), discharged May 27, 1865.

William Batchelder (1864), discharged June 17, 1864.

William F. Babcock, substitute, discharged June 5, 1865.

George W. Brenfield, substitute, discharged May 27, 1865.

Henry C. Canfield, veteran, discharged August 10, 1864.

Jacob Cramer, drafted, discharged June 5, 1865.

Thomas Dowling, veteran, discharged May 15, 1865.

Matthew Dickey, substitute, discharged June 5, 1865.

Joseph Dixon, substitute, discharged May 27, 1865.

Franklin Flood, veteran, discharged March 8, 1865.

Samuel Ferguson, substitute, discharged May 27, 1865.

Martin Freshcorn, substitute, discharged June 5, 1865.

Jacob Histend, drafted, discharged June 5, 1865.

Decatur Humphrey (1862), discharged May 22, 1862.

Alpheus W. Hardy (1862), discharged June 5, 1865.

Cassius N. Rixford, substitute, discharged June 5, 1865.

Charles Riley, drafted, discharged June 15, 1865.

Samuel J. Rodman, drafted, discharged June 5, 1865.

Henry Stero (1862), discharged June 5, 1865.

William Sober (1862), discharged June 5, 1865.

George S. Scott, substitute, discharged June 5, 1865.

Sheridan B. Smith, discharged January 18, 1865

Syrenus VanVolkenburg (1864), discharged May 26, 1865.

Peter Dowling, veteran, transferred to First United States Pioneer brigade, Army of Cumberland, August 24, 1864

---

## COMPANY G.

Mustered into service September 30, 1861.

Captain John S. Clemmer, commissioned captain September 30, 1861; promoted December 21, 1861.

Captain Josiah J. Wright, commissioned first lieutenant September 30, 1861; promoted captain December 21, 1861, resigned October 1, 1862.

Captain James Treen, commissioned second lieutenant September 30, 1861; promoted to Captain October 21, 1862; resigned May 25, 1863.

Captain Wilbur F. Chamberlain, promoted first sergeant December 22, 1863; first lieutenant May 25, 1864; captain October 12, 1864; mustered out with company.

First Lieutenant Benjamin F. Manderbach, promoted corporal December 22, 1863; sergeant May 9, 1864;

first sergeant July 1, 1864; first lieutenant January 6, 1865; mustered out with company.

First Lieutenant Cary H. Russell (1863), served three years; promoted captain October 12, 1864.

Second Lieutenant W. P. Williamson, Winchester, Virginia, March 23, 1862, the first in the regiment to die by rebel bullets.

Sergeant George Strohl, captured June 9, 1862; mustered out October 18, 1864.

Sergeant Albert W. Hall, discharged December 22, 1864.

Sergeant Alexander C French, killed at Cedar Mountain, Virginia, August 9, 1862.

Sergeant Edward F. Smith, killed at Chancellorsville, Virginia, May 3, 1863.

Sergeant George Sherbondy, died at Aqua Creek, Virginia, April 25, 1863.

Sergeant George Treen, discharged June 20, 1862.

Sergeant Adam Hart, transferred to Veteran Reserve corps, August 8, 1863.

Sergeant David Y. Cook, mustered out with company.

Sergeant Charles W. Martin, mustered out with company.

Sergeant Isaac Madlem, mustered out with company.

Sergeant Roswell B. Hoffman, mustered out with company

Sergeant George Hammontree (1863), mustered out with company.

Sergeant Ellis T. Green, killed at Dug Gap, Georgia, May 8, 1864.

Sergeant Christian F. Remley, killed at Dug Gap, Georgia, May 8, 1864.

Sergeant Lewis Crocker (1862), discharged June 5, 1865.

Sergeant Stephen W. Griffith (1862), discharged June 5, 1865.

Sergeant C. N. Russell, promoted.

Sergeant W. F. Chamberlain, promoted.

Sergeant B. F. Manderbach, promoted.

Corporal John D. Treen, mustered out December 22, 1864.

Corporal Augustus Belden, killed by guerrillas, May 30, 1862.

Corporal Charles Robinson, killed at Port Republic, Virginia, June 9, 1862.

Corporal John W. Ewell, died at Cumberland, Maryland, March 6, 1862.

Corporal Alfred P. Atchinson, discharged July 10, 1862

Corporal Conrad Zittle, transferred to Veteran Reserve corps, September 30, 1863.

Corporal George C. Guest (1862), mustered out with company.

Corporal Gustavus A. Monroe, mustered out with company.

Corporal Thomas White (1862), discharged May 1, 1865.

Corporal Hammond W. Geer (veteran), discharged May 23, 1865.

Corporal Andrew Thompson, drafted, discharged May 1, 1865.

Corporal William Wirt, died at Nashville, Tennessee, June 30, 1864.

Corporal Franklin Wirt, no record.

Corporal Martin M. Mills, absent without leave.

Corporal E. B. Hubbard, absent without leave.

Corporal A. C. French, promoted to sergeant.

Corporal T. Caldwell, absent without leave.

Corporal G. F. Hewett (veteran), mustered out with company.

## PRIVATES.

William Fisher, served three years.

John Gross, served three years.

Eli Harrington, served three years.

Frank Metzler, served three years.

James M. McCormick, served three years.

John W. Wise, served three years.

John A. Kummer (1861) in hospital.

Hiram C. Hill, killed at Gettysburg, Pennsylvania, July 3, 1863.

William F. Harrington, killed at Peach Tree creek, Georgia, July 20, 1864.

John Rowland, killed byguerrillas, May 3, 1862.

Jacob Rosenbaum, killed at Port Republic, Virginia, June 9, 1862.

George F. Brayenton, died of wounds May 17, 1864.

Lewis D. Clemmens, died at Providence, Rhode Island, September 7, 1862.

Robert W. Hall, died at Frederick, Maryland, January 15, 1863.

Charles D. Hine (1862), died at Middlebury, Ohio, March 31, 1863.

William H. Hartley (1862), died of wounds July 15, 1864.

Newton P. Humison, died in rebel prison July 28, 1862.

Joseph Loomis, died at Cumberland, Maryland, February 26, 1862.

Tallio E. McCain, died of wounds, August 8, 1863.

James L. Smith (1862), died at Dumfries, Virginia, March 3, 1863.

Urias Reifschneider, absent without leave.

Inman Lewis (1862), absent without leave.

Daniel Wise, absent without leave.

Oscar C. Andrews, claimed as a minor.

Lester P. Burke, discharged July 16, 1862.

Albert Bentley, claimed as a minor.

John Cephus, discharged October 9, 1862.

Noah Downey discharged June 29, 1864.

Henry Edson (1862), discharged September 12, 1864.

Henry H. Ewell, discharged July 21, 1864.

William A. Haze, discharged June 7, 1862.

Dudley W. Fisher, discharged June 17, 1862.

Jacob Gates (1862), discharged November 3, 1862.

John Huggett, discharged February 1, 1863.

Joseph Limerick, discharged July 16, 1862.

Jehiel Lane, Jr., discharged October 11, 1862.

John A. Lower, discharged July 16, 1862.

Oliver Lee, discharged November 1, 1861.

William H. Moore, discharged August 15, 1862.

James H. McDonald, discharged August 10, 1862.

George F. West, discharged July 19, 1862.

John B. Nowling, discharged November 20, 1862.

Richard D. Riley (1862), discharged April 25, 1863.

Ernest S. Smith, discharged November 3, 1862.

James W. Smith, discharged June 12, 1863.

Ferris Townsend, discharged November 15, 1862.

Mortimer Vanhyning, discharged October 22, 1861.

Carroll W. Wright, discharged July 30, 1862.

Franklin Winkleman, discharged December 22, 1861.

John Watson, discharged December 19, 1862.

Charles Young, discharged October 11, 1862.

John Barnes (1862), transferred to Veteran Reserve corps September 30, 1863.

Edward Curtiss (1862), promoted.

Jehiel Lane, discharged October 24, 1862.

Christian Conrad, transferred to company K, December 14, 1861.

George W. Deane, transferred to company K, December 14, 1861.

Charles Downey, transferred to company D, December 18, 1863.

Michael Greenwall, transferred to company I, December 13, 1861.

William L. Low, transferred to company K, December 14, 1861.

William Luce (1862), transferred to company K, January 15, 1862.

David McIntyre, transferred to company K, January 1, 1862.

Louis Pegg, transferred to company I, December 14, 1861

John Randall, transferred to company K, December 14, 1861.

De Witt C. Stevens, transferred to company I, December 14, 1861.

William F. Waterman, transferred to company I, December 14, 1861.

Edward Alley (veteran), mustered out with company.

William Cline (veteran), mustered out with company.

Thomas Cummins (veteran) mustered out with company

James B. Treen (veteran), prisoner of war.

Charles Upham (veteran), prisoner of war.

Samuel Winkleman (veteran), mustered out with company.

James Gaule (1862), missing in action May 8, 1864.

Charles E. Griffin (1862), mustered out with company.

Justice Townsley (1862), in hospital May 25, 1865.

Andrew B. Holman (1862), in hospital March 1, 1865

Erick Osborn (1862), mustered out with company.

Frank O. Weary (musician), mustered out with company.

George W. Gibson (1864), in hospital July 24, 1864.

Francis D. Leeds (1864), substitute, mustered out with company.

Norman Bateman (1864), substitute, mustered out with company.

Absalom Brooks (1864), in hospital January 25, 1865.

Calvin G. Brown (1864), in hospital April 28, 1865.

William Davis (1864), substitute, mustered out with company.

Patrick Dignen (1864), drafted, mustered out with company.

David Foley (1864), substitute, mustered out with company.

James McPeck (1864), substitute, mustered out with company.

Anderson Montague (1864), drafted, in hospital April 28, 1865.

James Suies (1864), substitute, in hospital December 21, 1864.

John L. Shipman (1864), substitute, in hospital April 25, 1865.

Francis Tucker (1864), absent without leave July 5, 1865.

John C. Kendrick, mustered out company.

William C. Lantz (veteran), killed at Dug Gap, Georgia, May 8, 1864

John S. Rape (1864), killed at North Edisto River, South Carolina, February 12, 1865.

Jacob D Foster (veteran), died March 29, 1864.

Mitchell Bubbington (1864), substitute, died December 11, 1864

Adam Hulbert (1864), substitute, died March 25, 1865.

Morgan Johnson (1864), died February 26, 1864.

James A. Lane (1864), drafted, died November 25, 1864.

George Murray (1863), died of wounds, May 9, 1864.

John A. Stewart (1864), substitute, died November 29, 1864

John Woodard (1864), died of wounds, May 11, 1864.

Martin Yingling (1864), absent without leave.

Ransom J. Fisher (1864), substitute, discharged January 1, 1865.

Joseph B. Arbach (1864), drafted, discharged June 5, 1865.

Vincent C. Brown (1864), drafted, discharged June 1, 1865.

Simon P. Eversole (1864), drafted, discharged June 5, 1865.

Christopher C. Garrison (1864), drafted, discharged June 5, 1865.

John Campbell (1862), discharged May 25, 1865.

Daniel S. Hardman (1864), drafted, discharged June 5, 1865.

Cornelius Horrigan (1864), drafted, discharged June 5, 1865.

Byron Law (1864), discharged May 4, 1865.

George J. McCormick (veteran), discharged June 1, 1865

William Rush (1864), drafted, discharged June 5, 1865.

William H. Stillwell (1864), drafted, discharged June 5, 1865.

John F. Weidle (veteran), discharged September 29, 1864.

William Woodard (1864), discharged September 12, 1864.

Thomas Bolton (1864), discharged May 4, 1865.

---

## COMPANY H.

Mustered into service in October and November, 1861.

Captain William H. Wright, promoted captain April 9, 1865; mustered out with company.

Captain Jonas Schoonover, discharged to accept promotion, April 1, 1865.

Captain Andrew J. Fulkerson, promoted to captain May 25, 1864; mustered out August 15, 1864.

First Lieutenant George McNutt, promoted to sergeant December 22, 1863; sergeant-major March 1, 1865; first lieutenant June 19, 1865; mustered out with company.

First Lieutenant David W. Thomas, discharged to accept promotion, April 1, 1865.

Second Lieutenant Henry Mack, resigned May 2, 1862.

Second Lieutenant Thomas W. Nash, discharged to accept promotion June 28, 1864.

Sergeant Thomas W. Nash, promoted.

Sergeant O. H. Remington, discharged September 26, 1863.

Sergeant James B Storer, promoted to non-commissioned staff February 15, 1862.

Sergeant James L. Ferguson, discharged June 18, 1862.

Sergeant Henry L. Curtiss, discharged October 10, 1862.

Sergeant Charles Fairchilds, died at Alexandria, Virginia, September 11, 1862.

Sergeant Alphonzo Hazzen, mustered out with company.

Sergeant Reuben Farnam, mustered out with company.

Sergeant John Davis, mustered out with company.

Sergeant Floyd Morris, mustered out with company.

Sergeant Thomas Davis, killed at Pine Knob, Geergia, June 15, 1864.

Sergeant Thomas Folger, promoted.

Sergeant Jacob Buck, transferred to non-commissioned staff.

Sergeant D. W. Thomas, promoted.

Corporal Lewis Wagoner, discharged September 24, 1862.

Corporal Warren H. Connell, killed at Dug Gap. Georgia, May 8, 1864.

Corporal C. H. Edgerly, discharged 1862.

Corporal William Liggett, died at Middletown, Virginia, May 26, 1862.

Corporal George B. Myers, discharged May 26, 1862,

Corporal Marcus Humphrey, discharged November 3, 1864.

Corporal Charles H. King, discharged July 17, 1865.

Corporal Lewis Rogers, mustered out with company.

Corporal Lester Bruno, mustered out with company.

Corporal George Nichols, mustered out with company.

Corporal George Manning (1862), mustered out with company.

Henry Murgan (musician), discharged July 19, 1862.

Corporal John Bissell (1862), mustered out with company.

John C. Hart (musician), discharged 1863.

John Ardis, absent without leave. January 11, 1862.

John D. Hall, absent without leave, December 22, 1861.

Reuben Wagoner, absent without leave November 30, 1861.

Isaac Wells, absent without leave May 21, 1862.

Merick Q Smith, absent without leave.

John Wilson, absent without leave June 22, 1862.

Eli Raudebush, discharged March 7, 1862.

Jacob Baird, discharged April 3, 1862.

G. T. Boak, mustered out with company.

Frank H. Boyer, served three years, discharged November 3, 1864.

John Best, discharged January 28, 1862.

William Dennings, transferred to Veteran Reserve corps December 16, 1863.

Willard Dennison, discharged October 10, 1862.

Joseph Ernsparger, discharged November 3, 1864.

Jacob Fritz, discharged November 3, 1864.

O. C. Field, mustered out with company.

David Harbaugh, discharged November 3, 1864.

John Heffelfinger, transferred to non-commissioned staff March 3, 1863.

Lewis Harris, killed in action at Winchester, Virginia, March 23, 1862.

John Harris, discharged September 26, 1862.

Henry Hazzen, discharged July 15, 1862.

Samuel W. Hart, discharged July 10. 1865.

O. W. Hale, discharged by special order number —, 1861

George C. Kellogg, discharged May 29, 1862.

Theodore Jones, transferred to Veteran Reserve corps April 16, 1864.

A. A. Kellogg, musician, mustered out with company.

David Kittinger, served three years, discharged November 3, 1864.

Eli Oberholtz, discharged.

C. H. Paine, discharged, served three years, November 3, 1864.

Lauren L. Porter, discharged, no date.

Silas Payne, discharged, July 12, 1862

Joseph Pierson, died at Mt. Jackson, Virginia, May 3, 1862.

Alfred A. Palmer, mustered out with company.

William Peet, discharged July 21, 1862.

Charles Rotart, served three years, discharged November 3, 1864.

Herman Ridder, discharged July 25, 1862.

George Youells, served three years, discharged November 3, 1864.

Andrew Robinson, transferred to Veteran Reserve corps May 7, 1864.

Hiram Root, discharged August 4, 1862.

William Robinson, discharged, July 22, 1862.

Jacob Snowberger, mustered out with company.

George Slusser, served three years, discharged November 3, 1864.

John Smith, died at Chattanooga, Tennessee, May 25, 1864, of wounds received in action at Dug Gap, Georgia, May 8, 1864.

Frank J. Smith, transferred to naval service May 18, 1864.

Norman Saulsbury, died at Frederick, Maryland, April 3, 1862.

Henry H. Scott, discharged December 3, 1862.

Jesse C. Stall (1862), mustered out with company.

William Spear, discharged, by reason of wounds, May 3, 1865.

C. C. Tooker, discharged December 9, 1862.

Evander Turner, discharged to accept promotion, April 13, 1865.

Henry Wolf, discharged, by reason of wounds—no date.

Oliver O. Wright, transferred to Veteran Reserve corps December, 1863.

William H. Tooker, mustered out with company.

Robert M. Wilkins, killed at Cedar Mountain, August 9, 1862.

Alexander Wallace, discharged December 4, 1862.

William Davis, discharged December 18, 1862.

Isaac Miller (wagoner), discharged February 18, 1863.

Joseph Roe, transferred to company I December, 1861.

Jackson Roe, transferred to company I December, 1861.

James Sowers, transferred to company I December, 1861.

John R. Benton (1862), died at Cleveland, Ohio, August, 1863.

Jeremiah Congdon (1862), sick in hospital.

Edward W. Farr (1862), discharged June 29, 1865.

James C. Hammond (1862), died at Dumfries, Virginia, March 14, 1863.

Eli C. Joles (1862), killed at Dug Gap, Georgia, May 8, 1864.

Henry J. Knapp (1862), discharged May 18, 1865.

William Lutz (1862), discharged June 29, 1865.

Hartwell A. Parker (1862), discharged January 10, 1863.

Elisha H. Pursell (1862), died in 1865.

John H. Wright (1862), discharged September 21, 1864.

Hiram Boyd, substitute, discharged with company.

John Buck, (1864), mustered out with company.

Allen Brown (1864), mustered out with company.

Newton Barkhammer (1864), mustered out with company.

John V. Cummings (1864), substitute, mustered out with company.

John Cowan (1864), drafted, discharged June 5, 1865.

William Durant (1864), died at Resaca, Georgia, discharged May 25, 1864.

Anton Ehrlar, substitute, discharged June 23, 1865.

John Funk (1864), mustered out with company.

William Ford (1864), drafted, sick in hospital.

Samuel Flesher (1864), drafted, discharged June 5, 1865.

James Heathman (1864), mustered out with company.

Henry N. Hullinger (1864), substitute, mustered out with company.

Henrick Hoyer (1864), substitute, discharged June 5, 1865.

Selburn H. Hall (1864), substitute, discharged June 5, 1865.

John J. Jones (1864), substitute, discharged June 5, 1865.

Daniel Kilso (1864), discharged June 1, 1865

John Kreps (1864), drafted, mustered out with company.

Emanuel Kaley (1864), died at Nashville, Tennessee, March 25, 1864.

Benjamin Lee (1864), killed at Peach Tree Creek, Georgia, July 20, 1864.

George B. Myers (1864), mustered out with company.

William Shameon (1864), drafted, discharged June 5, 1865.

Peter Leuzler (1864), mustered out with company.

William McVay (1864), drafted, discharged June 5, 1865.

Stephen Nettle (1864), mustered out with company.

Ira S. Nash (1864), mustered out company.

James R. Purine (1864), discharged April, 1865.

Charles Osburn (1864), killed at Dug Gap, Georgia, May 8, 1864.

Augustus Richards (1864), mustered out with company.

Martin Smith (1864), killed at Dug Gap, Georgia, May 8, 1864

Salathiel Shurtzer (1864), substitute, mustered out with company.

Harvey J. Smith (1864), mustered out with company.

David Smith (1864), mustered out with company.

Phillip Stadler (1864), mustered out with company.

Mortimer Van Hyning (1864), discharged May 27, 1865.

James Wild (1864), discharged June 23, 1865.

Edman Wiswell (1864), substitute, discharged July 18, 1865.

----

## COMPANY I.

Mustered into service September, October and November, and December, 1861.

Captain Russell B Smith, resigned June 12, 1863.

Captain Edwin B. Woobury, promoted second lieutenant March 13, 1862; first lieutenant, April 14, 1863; captain, June 29, 1864; major, July 12, 1865; mustered out with company.

First Lieutenant Augustus Philbrick, resigned March 3, 1862.

First Lieutenant Seth E. Wilson, resigned May 10, 1862.

First Lieutenant Stephen Kissinger, promoted from first sergeant to first lieutenant January 21, 1865; mustered out with company.

Second Lieutenant William J. Hall, resigned January 25, 1862.

First Sergeant John G. March (brevet first lieutenant—not commissioned), killed at Gettysburg, Pennsysvania, July 3, 1863.

Sergeant Ransom D. Billings, killed at Atlanta, Georgia, July 28, 1864.

Sergeant Zaccheus Farnsworth, died May 5, 1862.

Sergeant George Rorke, died May 14, 1862.

Sergeant Martin G. Owen, discharged September 11, 1862.

Sergeant Clark Beach, mustered out with company.

Sergeant Henry Rex, mustered out with company.

Sergeant James Hawk, mustered out with company.

Sergeant Almon Woodruff, mustered out with company.

Sergeant John Rupp, mustered out with company.

Sergeant Thomas Henderson, died September 10, 1864.

Sergeant Cassius C. Lord, transferred to non-commissioned staff.

Sergeant Norton B. Adams, transferred to Veteran Reserve corps January 23, 1865.

Corporal Warren F. Wilbur, died May 16, 1863.

Corporal John Sage, absent without leave.

Corporal Joel J. Bair, discharged November 18, 1862.

Corporal Horace H. Heath, discharged June 12, 1862.

Corporal J. R Polley, discharged June 1, 1862.

Corporal Charles F. Gove, mustered out with company.

Corporal William Abbott, mustered out with company.

Corporal James Walsh, mustered out with company.

Corporal James Sowers, mustered out with company.

Corporal DeWitt C. Stevens, mustered out with company.

Corporal Eli Rushon, mustered out with company.

Albert Bishop, killed at Kenesaw Mountain, Georgia, July 2, 1864.

Joseph Baker, killed at Atlanta, Georgia, July 18, 1864.

Jonathan Everhard, killed at Pine Knob, Georgia, June 16, 1864.

James Grine, killed at Gettysburg, Pennsylvania, July 3, 1863

Cass M. Nims, killed at Cedar Mountain, Virginia, August 9, 1862.

Tobias Phinney, killed at Dug Gap, Georgia, May 8, 1864.

Henry Rupp, killed at Dug Gap, Georgia, May 8, 1864.

John Craig, died April 15, 1862.

George M. Craighl, died October 7, 1862.

William Dickinson, died of wounds, June 13, 1863.

David N. Hubbard, died March 25, 1862.

William Wildy, died December 15, 1861.

O. O. Wakeman, died April 29, 1862.

William Campbell, substitute, died February 18, 1865.

Harrison Gordon, drafted, died December 11, 1864.

Alvah Holden (1861), died at Savannah, Georgia, March 27, 1865.

Charles Link, drafted, died December 3, 1864.

Hiram Newcomb (1861), died at Ringold, Georgia, of wounds received at Dug Gap, Georgia, May 15, 1864.

Andrew Ream (musician), transferred to non-commissioned staff, September 1, 1863.

Spencer Atkins, transferred to company B, January 5, 1863.

H. W. Horton, transferred to Veteran Reserve corps July 1, 1863.

Lewis Pegg, transferred to company F, Seventh Ohio veteran volunteer infantry, December 24, 1863

John Patchen, transferred to Veteran Reserve corps March 5, 1864.

Roswell Krahl, transferred to Veteran Reserve corps February 15, 1864.

A. W. Holdredge, transferred to Veteran Reserve corps April 1, 1865.

Charles Hawkins, absent without leave.

Charles Dudley, absent without leave.

William N. Dewitt, absent without leave.

Robert Hill, absent without leave.

Edwin Holcomb, absent without leave.

Roswell Trall, absent without leave.

William Trall, absent without leave.

Charles Welton, absent without leave.

George Jarvis, absent without leave.

Alderman Bidwell, teamster June 10, 1862.

William Babcock, discharged April 27, 1863.

William H. Cooper, discharged May 15, 1862.

John C. Cauley, discharged October 29, 1862.

William Dewitt, discharged November 1, 1862.

Martin Elliott, discharged July 14, 1862.

Michael Greenwall, discharged December 5, 1862.

Theodore N. Harrington, discharged May 20, 1862.

Sidney Kennedy, discharged April 4, 1863.

Henry Kennedy, discharged April 4, 1863
Nathan Miller, discharged July 2, 1862.
Mandleburt Manley, discharged September 11, 1862.
Milton H. Murdock, discharged February 23, 1863.
Bryon McArthur, discharged December 4, 1862.
Thomas J. Nichols, discharged April 27, 1863.
William Pond, discharged November 5, 1862.
Jackson Roe, discharged August 9, 1862.
Joseph Roe, discharged August 9, 1862.
Orville O. Rockwell, discharged April 12, 1863.
Euclid Suplee, discharged June 16, 1862.
Ira Scott, discharged November 1, 1862.
Thomas Sharkey, discharged August 29, 1863.
Stephen Sturdephant, discharged April 3, 1864
Alpha Thompson, discharged August 12, 1862.
E. C. Whitticher, discharged July 28, 1863.
Albert Alderman mustered out with company.
Uriah Cook, mustered out with company.
William E. Dickey, mustered out with company.
William Eldred, mustered out with company.
William Gilbert, mustered out with company.
Philip Hawk, mustered out with company.
Cosom M Kindig, mustered out with company.
James Miller, mustered out with company.
Michael McNerny, mustered out with company.
Albert Squires, mustered out with company.
George W. Reed, mustered out with company.
Sereno F. Sawyer, mustered out with company.
William Waterman, mustered out with company.
Ferdinand Cutler, mustered out with company.
Willard Trall, mustered out with company.

### RECRUITS.

Joel J. Bair (1861), mustered out with company.
Gordon Case, mustered out with company.

Henry H. Hibbard, mustered out with company.

William Kelley mustered out with company.

Francis Kelley, mustered out with company.

Edwin Mabry, mustered out with company.

William Mabry, mustered out with company.

Hudson Merritt, mustered out with company.

Frederick Newmyer, mustered out with company.

William P. Rushon, mustered out with company.

William Stille, in hospital.

Milo Sharp, mustered out July 3, 1865.

Owen Woohes, mustered out with company.

William Akres, substitute, mustered out with company.

Percival Bever, drafted, mustered out July 10, 1865.

Joseph Deal, drafted, mustered out with company.

George W. Mead, drafted, in hospital.

McClane J. Marfier, drafted, mustered out with company.

Isaac Welch (February, 1865), mustered out July 3, 1865.

Abel Archer, veteran, discharged June 6, 1865.

Robert A. Bloomer, drafted, discharged June 5, 1865.

James Ensler, drafted, discharged June 5, 1865.

Christian Fetterhoff, drafted, discharged June 5, 1865.

John Ford, drafted, discharged June 5, 1865.

Theodore Hawk, discharged June 5, 1865.

Thomas Hill, substitute, discharged June 2, 1865.

Christopher Letherer, drafted, discharged June 5, 1865.

Dennis McGunnigal, substitute, discharged June 5, 1865.

David Miller, substitute, discharged June 5, 1865.

Henry May, drafted, discharged June 5, 1865.

John Nesbit, drafted, discharged June 5, 1865.
James Perkins, veteran, discharged June 22, 1865.
James Reed (1862), discharged June 5, 1865.
Elisha Robinson, drafted, discharged May 27, 1865.
John Shannon (1862), discharged May 4, 1865.
Henry H. Turner, drafted, discharged June 5, 1865.
Daniel Truman, drafted, discharged June 5, 1865.
Reuben Wilson (1862), discharged June 5, 1865.
James Winters, veteran, discharged September, 1864.
Richard Adams, substitute, discharged July 3, 1865.
Horace Stevens, drafted, discharged June 5, 1865.

James H. Freeman, killed at Port Republic, Virginia, June 9, 1862.

## COMPANY K.

Mustered into service September, October, November and December, 1861.

Captain Alden P. Steele, resigned April 13, 1862.

Captain Charles W. Kellogg, promoted second lieutenant June 20, 1862; first lieutenant January 26, 1863; captain April 1, 1865; mustered out with company.

Captain David E. Hurlburt, promoted to captain April 13, 1863; discharged August 29, 1864.

Lieutenant William Neil, transferred to company E Januay 5, 1863.

First Lieutenant Marcus F. Roberts, sergeant of company A, promoted to first lieutenant of company K May 31, 1865; mustered out with company.

First Lieutenant Wilbur A. Chamberlain, promoted to captain of company E, October 12, 1864.

Second Lieutenant Benjamin N. Smith, promoted May 1, 1862; discharged March 16, 1864.

Sergeant William E. Gray, shot at Frederick, Maryland, December 10, 1862.

Sergeant Christopher C. Johnson, discharged April 3, 1863

Sergeant Ansel O Benjamin, discharged March 13, 1863

Sergeant George C. Judd, discharged March 2, 1863.

Sergeant Lewis Wrisley, discharged August 12, 1863.

Sergeant Luther L. Kinney, discharged

Sergeant Joseph C. Hammond, mustered out with company.

Sergeant Cornelius O. Hinkle, mustered out with company.

Sergeant Michael F. Haldman, drafted, mustered out with company.

Sergeant Ulysses S. Hoxter, promoted.

Sergeant Charles Potter, discharged June 19, 1865.

Sergeant Harlow H. Fenton, discharged June 7, 1865.

Corporal Fayette N. Johnson, discharged December 27, 1864

Corporal Thaddeus Marsh, died· at Cumberland, Maryland, March 3, 1862

Corporal Joel Ritter, absent without leave.

Corporal Alfred D Eddy, mustered out with company.

Corporal Daniel Turner, mustered out with company.

Corporal Frederick A. Rounds, mustered out with company.

Corporal James Spain, mustered out with company.

Corporal Esick Blanchard (1862), discharged June 19, 1865

Corporal James C. McCleary, discharged June 19, 1865.

Alber M. Alderman, discharged September 28, 1864.

David McIntyre, served three years, discharged October 20, 1864.

William Law, discharged, no date.

Hezekiah Davenport, served three years; discharged December 6, 1864.

Joseph M. Marsh (1862), killed at Dallas, Georgia, May 28, 1864.

Mathias Soden (1862), killed at Gettysburg, Pennsylvania, July 3, 1863.

Byron Bulfinch (1862), died at Frederick, Maryland, October 28, 1862.

Orlando Clark, died at Strasburg, Virginia, May 13, 1862.

Philander M Griggs, died at Alexandria, Virginia, October 3, 1862.

John L. Haywood, died at Back Creek, Virginia, March 13, 1862.

Oney McLee, died at Camp Wade, Virginia, July 17, 1862.

Sylvester Pierce, died at Frederick, Maryland, October 20, 1862

Martin Banney, died at Alexandria, Virginia, July 11, 1862.

Daniel Phillips, missing in action at Cedar Mountain, Virginia, August 9, 1862.

George P. Strong, missing in action at Cedar Mountain, Virginia, August 9, 1862.

William Fitzgerald, missing in action at Cedar Mountain, Virginia, August 9, 1862.

Osmond O. Oliver, missing in action at Chancellorsville, Virginia, May 3, 1863.

George Bullis, absent without leave.

John Blodgett, absent without leave.

Elias H Durfee, absent without leave.

Reuben Alderman, discharged April 4, 1863.

James Alexander, discharged June 19, 1863.

Lewis Brown (minor), discharged December 15, 1861

Charles W. Bancroft, discharged May 1, 1862.

Aaron C Baker, discharged July 10, 1862.

Wellington Burns (1862), discharged April 4, 1863.

Thomas Cook (minor), discharged December 23, 1861.

William Chalmers (1862), discharged February 6, 1863.

Francis M. Cutler, discharged July 9, 1862.

Rufus N Daniels (1862), discharged December 2, 1862.

Almond T. Mills, deserted August 18, 1862.

Foster W. Eggleston, discharged January 3, 1863.

Luther Fowler, discharged May 1, 1862.

William Fletcher, discharged September 29, 1862.

James Goldsmith, discharged July 9, 1862

Hiram Griggs, discharged May 31, 1862.

Renslo C. Griffin, discharged October 3, 1862.

Alonzo Hurlburt, claimed by Sixth Ohio volunteer cavalry, December 10, 1861.

William Houston, left at Camp Giddings December, 1861.

Judson Hunt, discharged June 10, 1862

Horace Holcomb, discharged May 31, 1862.

Martin H. Hammond, discharged December 2, 1862.

Edwin A Johnson, discharged June 13, 1862.

John Jenks, discharged February 17, 1862.

William Knox, discharged August 1, 1862.

Franklin Love, discharged July 28, 1862.

William Luce (1862), discharged October 1, 1862.

Delos Marsh, discharged June 9, 1862.

John McLoud, discharged June 7, 1862.

Joseph Matthews, discharged July 31, 1862.

Joseph B Partch, discharged June 30, 1862.

George Perry, discharged April 4, 1863.

John Randall, discharged August 27, 1862.

Solon Squires, discharged July 14, 1862.

John St. Clair, discharged, date unknown.

John Swinton, discharged November 3, 1862.

Albert J. Wightman, discharged June 9, 1862.

Harmon Wilder, discharged October 2, 1862.

George W. Weeks (1862), discharged November 3, 1862.

Charles W. Wilson, discharged October 10, 1862.

George W. Cargle, transferred to company I, December 27, 1861.

Thomas Shultz, transferred to company E, December 18, 1861.

James Williams, transferred to invalid corps, December 1, 1863.

William J. Pond, transferred to company I, December 29, 1861.

Christian Conrad, discharged July 22, 1865.

George W. Deem, mustered out with company.

Francis J. Hibbard, mustered out with company.

George W. Light, mustered out with company.

John Sarsfield, mustered out with company.

Jonathan Tyler, mustered out with company.

William H. Stratton, mustered out with company.

Clinton B. White, mustered out with company.

Sylvester W. Collins, drafted, mustered out with company.

Levi H. Greene, drafted, left in hospital.

Henry Garden, drafted, mustered out with company.

James B. Haskins, substitute, mustered out with company.

Jacob Lenox, substitute, mustered out with company.

John Loudon, drafted, mustered out with company.

Antoine Miller, substitute, mustered out with company.

James Ritchendoller, substitute, mustered out with company.

George H. Wilson, drafted, mustered out with company.

Joseph White, drafted, mustered out with company.

Thomas J. Failes, veteran, killed at Pine Knob, Georgia, June 15, 1864.

Amos Long, killed at Dug Gap, Georgia, May 8, 1864

Joseph Herman, drafted, died at Savannah, Georgia, February 13, 1865.

Morris Madison, drafted, died at Jeffersonville, Indiana, November 29, 1864

William Reed, veteran, died at Atlanta, Georgia, September 29, 1864.

Henry Swarts, drafted, died at Savannah, Georgia, June 9, 1865.

Daniel W. Abbott, drafted, discharged June 19, 1865.

James Amsdill, drafted, discharged June 19, 1865.

Ferdinand Burt, veteran, discharged February 6, 1866.

Daniel Barber, drafted, discharged June 19, 1865.

Michael Bulyer, drafted, discharged June 19, 1865.

Harmon Baker, drafted, discharged June 19, 1865.

Theodore M. Cochran, substitute, discharged June 19, 1865.

Charles Eberle, substitute, discharged June 19, 1865.

William Finiarty, substitute, discharged June 19, 1865.

John H. Finneman, drafted, discharged June 18, 1865.

Henry C. Farnsworth, drafted, discharged June 19, 1865.

John Grun, drafted, discharged June 19, 1865.

John W. Hutchinson, drafted, discharged June 19, 1865.

Henry C. Hardnock, drafted, discharged June 19, 1865.

Andrew Horn, drafted, discharged June 19, 1865.

Edson G. Holcomb (1862), discharged June 19, 1865.

John W. Joslin (1862), discharged June 19, 1865.

Daniel V. Lowary, substitute, discharged June 19, 1865.

William Norris (1862), discharged June 19, 1865.

William H. Parker (1862), discharged April 1, 1865.

Alonzo S. Pelton, drafted, discharged June 19, 1865.

Gabriel Quesino, drafted, discharged June 17, 1865.

Samuel Ripple, substitute, discharged June 19, 1865.

Frederick Schrapel, drafted, discharged July 19, 1865.

Samuel B. Emmons (1864), discharged July 18, 1865.

Asa A. Sanford, discharged July 28, 1865.

# CASUALTIES.

The following list of casualties is prepared from the records in the War Department, and contains the name of every member of the regiment, whose disability was reported to the department. It is believed to be perfect.

RECORD OF DEATHS IN TWENTY-NINTH REGIMENT OHIO VOLUNTEERS, EXCEPT KILLED IN ACTION.

### 1861.

Private Charles A. Clap, company D, December 8, 1861.

### 1862.

Private John A. Austin, company F, April 2, 1862.

Corporal Augustus Belden, company G, May 1, 1862.

Private Albert H. Beardsley, company C, February 17, 1862.

Private Hiram E. Balch, company F, February 18, 1862.

Private Marshal A. Brown, company A, March 10, 1862.

Private Conant Brunian, company B, April 30, 1862.

Private Oren Brewer, company E, May 23, 1862.

Private Charles F. Bauer, company B, April 19, 1862.

Private Andrew Beardsley, company E, July 29, 1862.

Private Byron Bulfinch, company K, October 28, 1862.

Private John Craig, company I, April 15, 1862.

Private Oliver P. Crosby, company C, April 23, 1862.

Private Orlando Clarke, company K, May 15, 1862.

Private Lewis D. Clements, company G, September 7, 1862.

Private George M. Cargill, company I, October 7, 1862.

Private Charles E. Dudley, company C, February 17, 1862.

Private Franklin Dimock, company F, February 28, 1862.

Private Ethan Davis, company E, March 6, 1862.

Private Alma Dalrymple, company A, May 2, 1862.

Private Michael Dowling, company F, May 18, 1862.

Private William Dickinson, company I, June 13, 1862.

Corporal John W. Ewell, company G, March 6, 1862.

Sergeant Zaccheus Farnsworth, company I, May 3, 1862.

Private Orvid Fairbrothers, company B, May 27, 1862.

First Sergeant Charles Fairchild, company H, September 11, 1862.

Sergeant William E. Grey, company H, December 19, 1862.

Private Wellington G. Gillett, company C, May 21, 1862.

Private Philander M. Griggs, company K, October 3, 1862.

Corporal Seth N. Hubbard, company A, April 12, 1862.

Private John L. Hayward, company K, March 13, 1862.

Private David N. Hubbard, company I, March 20, 1862.

Private Elisha Hamilton, company D, June 9, 1862.

Private Herman O. Holmes, company B, April 6, 1862.

Private Clark Hall, company B, July 14, 1862.

Private Newton P. Humiston, company G, July 28, 1862.

Private William C. Ives, company A, March 5, 1862.

Private William Johnson, company E, April 6, 1862.

Private William H. Jones, company D, July 21, 1862.

Sergeant John H. Knox, company D, May 22, 1862.

Private Joseph Loomis, company G, February 21, 1862.

Corporal William Liggitt, company H, May 25, 1862.

Musician Thaddeus Marsh, company D, March 5, 1862.

Private George W. Miles, company B, June 20, 1862.

Private Robert McFall, company B, June 27, 1862.

Private Oney McGee, company K, July 14, 1862.

Private Alvin W. Newman, company D, February 13, 1862.

Private Peter Nicholas, company D, April 19, 1862.

Private James Pike, company E, January 14, 1862.

Private Joseph Pierson, company H, May 3, 1862.

Private Sylvester Pierce, company K, October 20, 1862.

Sergeant George Rorke, company I, May 14, 1862.

Private Emerson Richerson, company A, March 10, 1862.

Private John Rowland, company G, May 1, 1862.

Private Harvey A. Reaves, company E, May 28, 1862.

Private Martin Ranney, company K, July 11, 1862.

Private Ellson Reed, Jr., company F, November 1, 1862.

Private Norman Salisbury, company H, April 3, 1862.

Private Hiram Sly, company E, July 6, 1862.

Private Leonard Squires, company D, September 4, 1862.

Private James Thomas, company C, March 9, 1862.

Private William H. Vanscoit, company B, April 5, 1862.

Sergeant Edwin Williams, company F, May 23, 1862.

Private O. O. Wakeman, company I, April 29, 1862.

Private Andrew A. Wolcott, company D, May 11, 1862.

Private James H. Whitney, company F, June 3, 1862.

Private Rufus Wilson, company B, June 21, 1862.

Private Eben H. Wright, company D, December 7, 1862.

### 1863.

Private John W. Baur, company B, captured at Port Republic, Virginia, June 9, 1862, supposed to be dead.

Private George W. Batchelor, company E, March 8, 1863.

Private John R. Benton, company H, June 28, 1863.

Private Edward I. Brown, company A, July 20, 1863.

Private Romeo Churchill, company C, January 13, 1863.

Corporal Roderick M. Gates, company A, August 27, 1863.

Private George Gale, company B, April 14, 1863.

Private Robert W. Hall, company G, January 15, 1863.

Private James C. Hammond, company H, March 14, 1863.

Private Charles D. Hine, company G, March 23, 1863.

First Sergeant John H. Knox, company D, May 22, 1863.

Private Julius Lavelee, company C, May 7, 1863.

Private Abram W. McNaughten, company A, January 28, 1863.

Private Tallis E. McCain, company G, August 12, 1863.

Private Dyer Newcomb, company B, January 29, 1863.

Private Moses Pennington, company E, May 15, 1863

Private George A. Root, company A, March 19, 1863

Private C. Robinson, company E, June 21, 1863.

Private H. M. Ryder, company C, September 25, 1863.

Sergeant George Shabondy, company G, April 24, 1863.

Private James L. Smith, company G, March 4, 1863.

Musician Oscar F. Stickney, company F, April 28, 1863.

Private Thomas Shultz, company E, May 12, 1863.

Private Robert Sills, company B, supposed to be dead.

Corporal Warren Wilbur, company I, May 10, 1863.

Private Elias Waltz, company D, April 10, 1863.

1864.

Private Albert W. Atwater, company E, July 4, 1864

Private George F. Braginton, company G, May 16, 1864.

Private Andrew J. Breght, company B, June 2, 1864.

Private John J. Belnap, company F, June 18, 1864.

Private Levi Baughman, company D, September 2, 1864.

Private Barney Brick, company E, September 8, 1864.

Private Christopher Beck, company D, September 17, 1864.

Private Charles S. Blake, company A, November 14, 1864.

Private Mitchell Babbington, company G, December 11, 1864.

Private Richard Conn, company F, December 8, 1864.

Private John T. Best, company F, December 25, 1864.

First Lieutenant George W. Dice, company D, June 17, 1864.

Private Charles A. Downey, company D, May 14, 1864.

Private Charles Demlin, company D, December 8, 1864.

Private William Durant, company H, May 25, 1864.

Private John Denneland, company D, December 8, 1864.

Private Thomas Dowling, company F, 1864.

Private Charles Ellis, company B, July 16, 1864.

Private Thomas J. Fales, company K, June 17, 1864.

Private Jacob Gardner, company D, May 24, 1864.

Private James Gaule, company G, supposed to be dead.

Private Nelson Gillett, company E, July 15, 1864.

Private Harrison Gordon, company I, December 17, 1864.

Private William H. Hartley, company G, July 15, 1864.

Sergeant Thomas F. Henderson, company I, September 10, 1864.

Private Henry A. Hane, company D, May 26, 1864.

Private W. B. Hoyt, company A, October 20, 1864.

Private Morgan Johnson, company G, February 29, 1864.

Private Emanuel Kaley, company H, March 28, 1864.

Private James H. Lane, company G, November 25, 1864.

Private Charles Link, company I, December 3, 1864.

Corporal Allen Mason, company C, May 29, 1864.

Private John H. Montgomery, company D, June 2, 1864 (June 8, 1864).

Private George Murray, company G, May 9, 1864.

Private Thomas S. McCartney, company E, July 16, 1864.

Private Morris Madison, company K, November 29, 1864.

Private Hiram Newcomb, company I, May 31, 1864.

Private William Potter, company B, July 6, 1864

Private Simeon J. Peters, company D, July 2, 1864.

Private William Reed, company K, September 2, 1864

Private Levi Yanke, company D, December 17, 1864.

Corporal Theodore Smith, company A, March 24, 1864.

Private John Smith, company H, May 25, 1864.

Private Elmore Stevens, company F, July 10, 1864

Private John A. Stewart, company G, November 19, 1864

Private Jacob Scott, company B, December 24, 1864.

Sergeant Samuel Woodbridge, company D, May 8, 1864.

Private Truman Williams, company E, February 29, 1864.

Private John Woodard, company G, May 11, 1864.

Private George W. Write, company B, May 31, 1864.

Private Aaron Warner, company C, June 3, 1864.

Private George Williams, company F, June 2, 1864.

Private William Wirt, company G, June 20, 1864.

Private George W. Warden, company B, October 29, 1864.

1865.

Private William F. Boal, company E, April 2, 1865.

Private Thomas Clifford, company F, March 2, 1865.

Private William Campbell, company I, February 18, 1865.

Private Joseph Datson, company F, March 2, 1865.

Private Jacob Dunkal, company C, April 17, 1865.

Private Jacob D. Foster, company G, March 29, 1865.

Private Levi H. Green, company A, March 7, 1865.

Private Alvah Holden, company I, January 25, 1865.

Private Joseph Herman, company K, February 13, 1865.

Private Adam Hulbert, company G, March 26, 1865.

Private George Huntwork, company F, May 26, 1865.

Private Lysander T. King, company T, May 6, 1865.

Private Henry Miller, company A, February 4, 1865.

Private Robert McKee, company A, April 6, 1865.

Private Charles Mullett, company D, June 22, 1865.

Private Ephraim Odell, company F, February 1, 1865.

Private Melancthon Poe, company B, February 13, 1865

Private Samuel Perry, company E, April 8, 1865.

Private Henry Swartz, company K, January 9, 1865.

Private James Simms, company A, March 4, 1865.

Major M. Wright, January 7, 1865.

Private Addison A. Way, company E, April 19, 1865.

Corporal George J. Young, company D, June 14, 1865.

RECORD OF KILLED, WOUNDED AND CAPTURED IN THE
TWENTY-NINTH OHIO VOLUNTEERS DURING THE YEAR
1862.

### COMPANY A

First Lieutenant Everson J. Hulbert, wounded, June
9, 1862, Port Republic, Virginia.

Second Lieutenant Martin D. Norris, wounded, June
9, 1862, Port Republic, Virginia.

Corporal Joseph B. Dalrymple, wounded, June 9,
1862, ·Port Republic, Virginia.

Private Franklin B. Mowry, wounded, June 9, 1862,
Port Republic, Virginia.

Private Henry P. Turner, wounded, June 9, 1862,
Port Republic, Virginia.

Private James E. March, wounded June 9, 1862, Port
Republic, Virginia.

Private Theodore Smith, wounded June 9, 1862, Port
Republic, Virginia

Private Montezuma St. John, wounded June 9, 1862,
Port Republic, Virginia.

Private Nelson W. Simmons, wounded June 9, 1862,
Port Republic, Virginia.

Private Perry A. Decker, wounded June 9, 1862, Port
Republic, Virginia.

Private Eli P. Young, wounded June 8, 1862, Port
Republic, Virginia.

First Lieutenant Everson J. Hulbert, wounded August
9, 1862, Cedar Mountain, Virginia.

First Sergeant Winthrop H. Grant, wounded August
9, 1862, Cedar Mountain, Virginia

Sergeant Silas G. Elliott, wounded August 9, 1862, Cedar Mountain, Virginia.

Corporal James M. Loomis, wounded August 9, 1862, Cedar Mountain, Virginia.

Private S. M. Coon, wounded August 9, 1862, Cedar Mountain, Virginia.

Private Mortimer Canfield, wounded August 9, 1862, Cedar Mountain, Virginia.

Private Daniel Thatcher, wounded August 9, 1862, Cedar Mountain, Virginia.

Private Rosalva W. Graham, wounded August 9, 1862, Cedar Mountain, Virginia.

Private Nathaniel Wilder, wounded August 9, 1862, Cedar Mountain, Virginia.

Private S. E. Colburn,* captured March 23, 1862, Winchester, Virginia.

Sergeant T. E. Hoyt,* captured June 9, 1862, Port Republic, Virginia.

Private H. P. Turner,* captured June 9, 1862, Port Republic, Virginia.

Private P. A. Decker,* captured June 9, 1862, Port Republic, Virginia.

Private E. J. Maltby,* captured June 9, 1862, Port Republic, Virginia.

Private A. L. Rickard,* captured June 9, 1862, Port Republic, Virginia.

Private J. A. Exceen,* captured June 9, 1862, Port Republic, Virginia.

Private John Ellis,* captured June 9, 1862, Port Republic, Virginia.

Private Albert Frazier,* captured June 9, 1862, Port Republic, Virginia.

Private F. B. Mowrey,* captured June 9, 1862, Port Republic, Virginia.

Private J. E March,* captured June 9, 1862, Port Republic, Virginia.

Corporal W. 'B. Hoyt,* captured August 9, 1862, Cedar Mountain, Virginia.

Private C. Covert,* captured June 9, 1862, Port Republic, Virginia.

Private C. Roth,* captured June 9, 1862, Port Republic, Virginia.

Private John Sylvester,* captured June 9, 1862, Port Republic, Virginia.

Private J. B. Broughton,* captured June 9, 1862, Port Republic, Virginia.

Private Eli P. Young,* captured June 9, 1862, Port Republic, Virginia.

Private Leonard Grover,* captured May 25, 1862, Strasburg, Virginia.

## COMPANY B.

Private Harvey Beckwith, killed March 20, 1862, Winchester, Virginia.

Corporal Levi K. Bean, killed March 23, 1862, Winchester, Virginia.

Private Monroe Burgett, wounded June 9, 1862, Port Republic, Virginia.

Private George McNutt, wounded June 9, 1862, Port Republic, Virginia.

Private N. A. Germond, wounded June 9, 1862, Port Republic, Virginia.

Private Alvinson Kinney, killed August 9, 1862, Cedar Mountain, Virginia.

Sergeant Rush Griswold, wounded August 9, 1862, Cedar Mountain, Virginia.

Corporal Elbridge Potter, wounded August 9, 1862, Cedar Mountain, Virginia.

Corporal Frank Chapman, wounded August 9, 1862, Cedar Mountain, Virginia.

Private George Wright, wounded August 9, 1862, Cedar Mountain, Virginia.

Private Henry Hicks, wounded August 9, 1862, Cedar Mountain, Virginia.

Private Henry Brainard, wounded August 9, 1862, Cedar Mountain, Virginia.

Private Oscar Burbanks, wounded August 9, 1862, Cedar Mountain, Virginia.

Private Lewis Montgomery, wounded August 9, 1862, Cedar Mountain, Virginia.

Private D. Newcomb, wounded August 9, 1862, Cedar Mountain, Virginia.

Private Robert Sills,* captured May 25, 1862, Strasburg, Virginia.

Private J. C. DeWolf,* captured May 25, 1862, Strasburg, Virginia.

Musician J. H. SeCheverell, captured May 14, 1862, Winchester, Virginia.

Lieutenant Andy Wilson,* captured June 9, 1862, Port Republic, Virginia.

Sergeant J. E. Tanner,* captured June 9, 1862, Port Republic, Virginia.

Corporal A. J. Longworthy,* captured June 9, 1862, Port Republic, Virginia.

Private Spencer Atkins,* captured June 9, 1862, Port Republic, Virginia.

Private Albert H. Benham,* captured June 9, 1862, Port Republic, Virginia.

Private John W. Baur,* captured June 9, 1862, Port Republic, Virginia; died in prison.

Private Job Brazee,* captured June 9, 1862, Port Republic, Virginia.

Private William D. Potter,* captured June 9, 1862, Port Republic, Virginia

Private L. J. Phinney,* captured June 9, 1862, Port Republic, Virginia.

Private S. A. Stanley,* captured June 9, 1862, Port Republic, Virginia.

Private S. B. Wilder,* captured June 9, 1862, Port Republic, Virginia.

Private G. W. Atkins,* captured June 9, 1862, Port Republic, Virginia.

### COMPANY C

Second Lieutenant Frank F. Stewart, wounded August 9, 1862, Cedar Mountain, Virginia

Sergeant George W. Britton, killed June 9, Port Republic, Virginia

Sergeant Henry W Ryder, wounded June 9, Port Republic, Virginia.

Corporal William A Burwell, killed June 9 Port Republic, Virginia.

Corporal John Chapell, wounded August 9, Cedar Mountain, Virginia

Corporal Algernon Kingsley, wounded August 9, Cedar Mountain, Virginia.

Corporal Allen Mason, wounded March 23, Winchester, Virginia

Private George Eastlick, wounded June 9th, Port Republic, Virginia.

Private Joseph Hall, wounded August 9th, Cedar Mountain, Virginia.

Private Beneville Miller, wounded March 23d, Winchester, Virginia.

Private David B Parker, mortally wounded August 9th, Cedar Mountain, Virginia.

Private William H. Runyan, wounded June 9th, Port Republic, Virginia.

Private Allen A. Monty, killed June 9th, Port Republic, Virginia.

Private Willis Sisley, killed June 9th, Port Republic, Virginia.

Private Thomas Davis, wounded June 9th, Port Republic, Virginia

Private Joseph Wimby, wounded June 9th, Port Republic, Virginia.

Private John Williams, wounded August 9th, Cedar Mountain, Virginia.

Private John Yokes, killed August 9th, Cedar Mountain, Virginia.

Private H. M. Rice,* captured May 25th, Strasburg, Virginia.

Private George D. Brockett,* captured May 25th, Strasburg, Virginia.

Sergeant R. L. Jones,* captured June 9th, Port Republic, Virginia.

Captain Edward Hayes,* captured June 9th, Port Republic, Virginia.

Corporal H. C. Lord,* captured June 9th, Port Republic Virginia.

Private Johnson Noble,* captured June 9th, Port Republic, Virginia.

Private Benjamin F. Sperry,* captured June 9th, Port Republic, Virginia.

Private James Turton,* captured June 9th, Port Republic, Virginia.

Private N. H. Bailey,* captured June 9th, Port Republic, Virginia.

Private S. O. Crosby,* captured June 9th, Port Republic, Virginia.

Private D. L. Lindley,* captured June 9th, Port Republic, Virginia.

Private R. W. Cross,* captured June 9th, Port Republic, Virginia.

Private J. Fleming,* captured June 9th, Port Republic, Virginia.

Private M. Maloney,* captured June 9th, Port Republic, Virginia.

Private John A. Frazier,* captured June 9th, Port Republic, Virginia.

### COMPANY D.

Captain Myron T. Wright, wounded March 23, 1862, Winchester, Virginia.

Private Valentine Viers, wounded March 23, 1862, Winchester, Virginia.

Private John Snyder*, wounded March 23, 1862, Winchester, Virginia

Lieutenant James H. Grinnell, wounded June 9, 1862, Port Republic, Virginia.

Corporal Frederick C. Remley, killed June 9, 1862, Port Republic, Virginia.

Corporal William A. Hart, wounded June 9, 1862, Port Republic, Virginia.

Private William Mendleson, wounded June 9, 1862, Port Republic, Virginia.

Private* F. R. Johnson, killed June 9, 1862, Port Republic, Virginia

Private Henry W. Morrel, wounded June 9, 1862, Port Republic, Virginia.

Private Theron W. Smith, wounded June 9, 1862, Port Republic, Virginia.

Lieutenant George W. Dice, wounded August 9, 1862, Cedar Mountain, Virginia.

Sergeant Lewis B. Stark, wounded August 9, 1862, Cedar Mountain, Virginia.

Corporal George Foust, wounded August 9, 1862, Cedar Mountain, Virginia.

Corporal James S. Alexander, wounded August 9, 1862, Cedar Mountain, Virginia.

Private Leonard E. Squares, wounded August 9, 1862, Cedar Mountain, Virginia.

Private William C. Finney, wounded August 9, 1862, Cedar Mountain, Virginia.

Private William D. Haynes, wounded August 9, 1862, Cedar Mountain, Virginia.

Private John G. Steinhour, wounded August 9, 1862, Cedar Mountain, Virginia.

Private Henry A. Thompson, wounded August 9, 1862, Cedar Mountain, Virginia.

Private Jacob Gardner, wounded June 9, 1862, Port Republic, Virginia.

Private Norman Cochran, wounded June 9, 1862, Port Republic, Virginia.

Private Marshall Hoagland, wounded June 9, 1862, Port Republic, Virginia.

Private Leonard Gaylord*, captured August 9, 1862,

Sergeant S. Woodbridge*, captured August 9, 1862, Cedar Mountain, Virginia

Private O. Brewster*, captured August 9, 1862, Cedar Mountain, Virginia.

Private W. H. Jones*, captured August 9, 1862, Cedar Mountain, Virginia.

Private J. Waite*, captured August 9, 1862, Cedar Mountain, Virginia.

Private E. Randall*, captured August 9, 1862, Cedar Mountain, Virginia.

Private J. Replogle*, captured August 9, 1862, Cedar Mountain, Virginia.

Private John Hughes*, captured August 9, 1862, Cedar Mountain, Virginia.

## COMPANY E.

Private Peter Vanskoik, wounded March 23, Winchester, Virginia.

Captain Horatio Luce, killed June 9, Port Republic, Virginia.

Corporal Isaac Dalrymple, killed June 9, Port Republic, Virginia.

Private Frederick Brown, wounded June 9, Port Republic, Virginia.

Private Lewis Weber, wounded June 9, Port Republic, Virginia.

Private William Robinson, wounded June 9, Port Republic, Virginia.

Private James P. Bagley, killed August 9, Cedar Mountain, Virginia.

Private Thomas McCarty, wounded June 9, 1862, Port Republic, Virginia.

Corporal Charles Howard, wounded June 9, 1862, Port Republic, Virginia.

Corporal N. L. Parmeter, wounded June 9, 1862, Port Republic, Virginia.

Private S. J. Rockwell, captured March 23, 1862, Winchester, Virginia.

Lieutenant William Neil, captured June 9, 1862, Port Republic, Virginia.

Private L. Hill, captured June 9, 1862, Port Republic, Virginia.

Private James C. Jones, captured June 9, 1862, Port Republic, Virginia.

Private Elijah Curtiss, wounded accidentally.

Private M. Mayhew, captured June 9, 1862, Port Republic, Virginia

Private Nelson Gillett, captured June 9, 1862, Port Republic, Virginia.

Musician John S. Bellows, captured May 25, 1862, Strasburg, Virginia.

Private Frances Colver, captured May 25, 1862, Strasburg, Virginia.

Private Herman Sly, captured May 25, 1862, Strasburg, Virginia

Private David W. Hall, captured May 25, 1862, Strasburg, Virginia

### COMPANY F.

Private Alexander Neil, killed March 23, 1862, Winchester, Virginia.

Private A. Case, wounded March 23, 1862, Winchester, Virginia.

Private Sidney M. Smith, killed June 9, 1862, Port Republic, Virginia.

Private Frederick R. Johnson, killed June 9, 1862, Port Republic, Virginia

Captain Eleazer Burridge, wounded June 9, 1862, Port Republic, Virginia.

First Lieutenant Hamblin Gregory, wounded June 9, 1862, Port Republic, Virginia

Sergeant Roland H. Baldwin, wounded June 9, 1862, Port Republic, Virginia.

Private Asa E. Sanford, wounded June 9, 1862, Port Republic, Virginia.

First Sergeant Joseph Jerome, wounded June 9, 1862, Port Republic, Virginia.

Private Almer B. Paine, wounded June 9, 1862, Port Republic, Virginia.

Private Sheridan B. Smith, wounded June 9, 1862, Port Republic, Virginia.

Corporal Burton Pickett, killed August 9, 1862, Cedar Mountain, Virginia.

Private George N. Meno, killed August 9, 1862, Cedar Mountain, Virginia.

Sergeant Almer B. Paine, wounded August 9, 1862, Cedar Mountain, Virginia.

Private Spencer E. Balch, wounded August 9, 1862, Cedar Mountain, Virginia.

Private Thomas Dowling, wounded August 9, 1862, Cedar Mountain, Virginia.

Private Peter Dowling, wounded August 9, 1862, Cedar Mountain, Virginia.

Private Simpson McLeon, wounded August 9, 1862, Cedar Mountain, Virginia.

Private George A. Patchen, wounded August 9, Cedar Mountain, Virginia.

Private Jabin S. Duston, wounded August 9, 1862, Cedar Mountain, Virginia.

Private Charles F. Waldron, wounded August 9, 1862, Cedar Mountain, Virginia.

Corporal George Gray, wounded August 9, 1862, Cedar Mountain, Virginia.

Private John C. McLeon, wounded August 9, 1862, Cedar Mountain, Virginia

Private L. Walker*, wounded August 9, 1862, Cedar Mountain, Virginia.

Private Pomeroy Smith*, captured August 9, 1862, Cedar Mountain, Virginia.

Private Ellison Reed, Jr., killed June 9, 1862, Port Republic, Virginia.

Lieutenant H. Gregory*, captured June 9, 1862, Port Republic, Virginia.

Sergeant Solon Hall,* captured June 9, 1862, Port Republic, Virginia.

Corporal George Woodford, captured June 9, 1862, Port Republic, Virginia.

Corporal N. B. Noyes,* captured June 9, 1862, Port Republic, Virginia.

Private J. J. Belknap,* captured June 9, 1862, Port Republic, Virginia.

Private C. VanValkenburg,* captured August 9, 1862, Port Republic, Virginia.

Private C. V. Clark,* captured June 9, 1862, Port Republic, Virginia

Private Charles Cain,* captured June 9, 1862, Port Republic, Virginia.

Private William Call,* captured June 9, 1862, Port Republic, Virginia.

Peter Dowling,* captured June 9, 1862, Port Republic, Virginia.

Private Martin P. Durkee, captured June 9, 1862, Port Republic, Virginia.

Private Jason Manley,* captured June 9, 1862, Port Republic, Virginia.

Private M. Malcom,* captured June 9, 1862, Port Republic, Virginia.

Private Eliphalet S. Ontis,* captured June 9, 1862, Port Republic, Virginia.

Private Peter Smith,* captured June 9, 1862, Port Republic, Virginia.

Private Edson Reed,* captured June 9, 1862, Port Republic, Virginia.

Private Ferris Townsend,* captured May 25, 1862, Strasburg, Virginia.

Private Newton Hummiston,* captured May 25, 1862, Strasburg, Virginia.

Private George F. Hewitt,* captured May 25, 1862, Strasburg, Virginia.

Private James Whitney,* captured May 25, 1862, Strasburg, Virginia.

## COMPANY G.

Second Lieutenant W. P. Williamson, killed March 23d, Winchester, Virginia.

Corporal Charles Robinson, killed June 9th, Port Republic, Virginia.

Private Jacob Rosenbaum, killed June 9th, Port Republic, Virginia.

Captain J. J. Wright, wounded August 9th, Cedar Mountain, Virginia.

Sergeant Alexander C. French, killed August 9th, Cedar Mountain, Virginia.

Private James W. Smith, wounded June 9th, Port Republic, Virginia.

Private M. Grenewald, wounded August 9th, Cedar Mountain, Virginia.

Lieutenant Cary H. Russell,* captured June 9th, Port Republic, Virginia.

Sergeant W. F. Chamberlain,* captured June 9th, Port Republic, Virginia.

Sergeant C. W. Martin,* captured June 9th, Port Republic, Virginia.

Sergeant George Strohl,* captured June 9th, Port Republic, Virginia.

Private C. F. Remley,* captured June 9th, Port Republic, Virginia.

Private William Fisher,* captured June 9th, Port Republic, Virginia.

Corporal C. Zeittle,* captured June 9th, Port Republic, Virginia.

Corporal John Kummer,* captured June 9th, Port Republic, Virginia.

Corporal E. T. Green,* captured June 9th, Port Republic, Virginia.

Private C. Bragington,* captured June 9th, Port Republic, Virginia.

Private C. Lantz,* captured June 9th, Port Republic, Virginia.

Private T. McCain,* captured June 9th, Port Republic, Virginia.

Private J. Burns,* captured June 9th, Port Republic, Virginia.

Private J. Campbell,* captured June 9th, Port Republic, Virginia.

Private H Geer,* captured June 9th, Port Republic, Virginia.

Private William Wirt,* captured June 9th, Port Republic, Virginia.

Private J. Gross,* captured June 9th, Port Republic, Virginia.

Private William Gorrington,* captured June 9th, Port Republic, Virginia.

Private D. Stevens,* captured June 9th, Port Republic, Virginia.

Private John Worth,* captured May 9th, near Edenburg, Virginia.

### COMPANY H.

Private Lewis Harris, mortally wounded March 23, 1862, Winchester, Virginia, died April 7, 1862.

Private Robert M. Wilkins, killed August 9, 1862, Cedar Mountain, Virginia.

Private Reuben Farnam, wounded June 9, 1862, Port Republic, Virginia.

Private Hiram Root, wounded June 9, 1862, Port Republic, Virginia.

Private Samuel W. Hart, wounded June 9, 1862, Port Republic, Virginia.

Captain Jonas Schoonover, wounded August 9, 1862, Cedar Mountain, Virginia

Private Alfred Hazzen, wounded August 9, 1862, Cedar Mountain, Virginia.

Private L. Rodgers, wounded August 9, 1862, Cedar Mountain, Virginia.

Lieutenant Thomas W. Nash, captured June 9, 1862 Port Republic, Virginia

Corporal E. Oberholtz, captured June 9, 1862, Port Republic, Virginia.

Private John Heffiefinger, captured June 9, 1862, Port Republic, Virginia.

Private S. W. Hart, captured June 9, 1862, Port Republic, Virginia.

Private J. C. Stall, captured June 9, 1862, Port Republic, Virginia.

Private W. H. Connell, captured May, 1862, near Edenburg, Virginia

### COMPANY I.

Corporal Alfred Bishop, wounded August 9, 1862, Cedar Mountain, Virginia.

Private James H. Freman, killed June 9, 1862, Port Republic, Virginia

Private John Everhard, killed June 9, 1862, Port Republic, Virginia.

Sergeant Ransom D. Billings, wounded June 9, 1862, Port Republic, Virginia.

Private William H Abbott, wounded June 9, 1862, Port Republic, Virginia.

Private Albert Alderman, wounded June 9, 1862, Port Republic, Virginia.

Private William Dickison, wounded June 9, 1862, Port Republic, Virginia.

Private William Pond, wounded August 9, 1862, Cedar Mountain, Virginia.

Private Ransom Craigl, wounded August 9, 1862, Cedar Mountain, Virginia.

Private Michael Greenwalsh, wounded August 9, 1862, Cedar Mountain, Virginia.

Private W. J. Waterman, killed June 9, 1862, Port Republic, Virginia.

Lieutenant B. N. Smith, wounded August 9, 1862, Cedar Mountain, Virginia.

Sergeant John G. Marsh, wounded August 9, 1862, Cedar Mountain, Virginia

Private R. S. Krahl, killed August 9, 1862, Cedar Mountain, Virginia.

Private B. McArthur, wounded August 9, 1862, Cedar Mountain, Virginia.

Private James Winters, wounded August 9, 1862, Cedar Mountain, Virginia.

Lieutenant R. B. Smith, captured June 9, 1862, Port Republic, Virginia.

Lieutenant E B. Woodbury, captured June 9, 1862, Port Republic, Virginia.

Private William Gilbert, captured May 25, 1862, Strasburg, Virginia.

Private M. McNerny, captured June 9, 1862, Port Republic, Virginia.

Private J. Roup, captured June 9, 1862, Port Republic, Virginia.

Private W. J. Eldred, captured June 9, 1862, Port Republic, Virginia.

Private W. Waterman, captured June 9, 1862, Port Republic, Virginia.

Private A. A Woodruff, captured June 9, 1862, Port Republic, Virginia.

Private C C Lord, captured June 9, 1862, Port Republic, Virginia.

Private James M. Perkins, captured August 9, 1862, Cedar Mountain, Virginia.

Private James Sowers, captured May, 1862, near Edinburg, Virginia.

Sergeant G. Cowgill, captured June 9, 1862, Port Republic, Virginia.

Sergeant J. Walsh, captured June 9, 1862, Port Republic, Virginia.

Corporal C Gove, captured June 9, 1862, Port Republic, Virginia..

Corporal C. Beech, captured June 9, 1862, Port Republic, Virginia

Corporal A. Woodruff, captured June 9, 1862, Port Republic, Virginia.

## COMPANY K,
### AND FIELD AND STAFF.

First Sergeant Christopher C. Johnson, wounded June 9, 1862, Port Republic, Virginia.

Color Sergeant Ulysses S. Hoxter, wounded June 9, 1862, Port Republic, Virginia.

Private Frederick A. Rounds, wounded June 9, 1862, Port Republic, Virginia

Private Ferdinand Burt, wounded June 9, 1862, Port Republic, Virginia.

First Sergeant Christopher C. Johnson, wounded August 9, 1862, Cedar Mountain, Virginia.

Sergeant William E. Gray, wounded August 9, 1862, Cedar Mountain, Virginia.

Corporal Cornelius O. Hinkle, wounded August 9, 1862, Cedar Mountain, Virginia.

Corporal Jonathan Taylor, wounded August 9, 1862, Cedar Mountain, Virginia.

Sergeant V. S. Horter, wounded June 9, 1862, Port Republic, Virginia.

Private Frank Hibbard, wounded June 9, 1862, Port Republic, Virginia.

Private David McIntyre, killed June 9, 1862, Port Republic, Virginia.

Private Ph. M. Griggs, wounded August 9, 1862, Cedar Mountain, Virginia.

Lieutenant-Colonel Thomas Clark, wounded and captured June 9, 1862, Port Republic, Virginia.

Major John S. Clemmer, wounded June 9, 1862, Port Republic, Virginia.

Captain David E. Hurlburt, captured June 9, 1862, Port Republic, Virginia.

Lieutenant William Neil, captured June 9, 1862, Port Republic, Virginia.

Sergeant G. C. Judd, captured June 9, 1862, Port Republic, Virginia.

Private F. Rounds, captured June 9, 1862, Port Republic, Virginia.

Private F. J. Hibbard, captured June 9, 1862, Port Republic, Virginia.

Private G. W. Dean, captured June 9, 1862, Port Republic, Virginia.

Private D. Phillips, captured August 9, 1862, Cedar Mountain, Virginia .

Private William Fitzgerald, captured August 9, 1862, Cedar Mountain, Virginia.

Private G. P. Strong, captured August 9, 1862, Cedar Mountain, Virginia.

Private H. H. Fenton, captured June 9, 1862, Port Republic, Virginia.

Private J. Williams, captured June 9, 1862, Port Republic, Virginia.

Private John Sarsfield, captured June 9, 1862, Port Republic, Virginia.

Sergeant A. D Benjamin, captured June 9, 1862, Port Republic, Virginia.

Corporal W. S. Hoxter, captured June 9, 1862, Port Republic, Virginia.

Corporal Luther Kinney, captured June 9, 1862, Port Republic, Virginia.

Private F. Johnson, captured June 9, 1862, Port Republic, Virginia.

Private D. McIntyre, captured June 9, 1862, Port Republic, Virginia.

Private J. Jenks, captured June 9, 1862, Port Republic, Virginia.

---

RECORD OF KILLED, WOUNDED AND MISSING OF THE TWENTY-NINTH OHIO VOLUNTEERS AT THE BATTLE OF CHANCELLORSVILLE, VIRGINIA, ON THE 1ST, 2D AND 3D OF MAY, 1863.

Private F. B. Mowrey, company A, wounded.

Private R. E Woodbury, company A, wounded.

Private M. M. Canfield, company A, wounded.

Private Isaac Monger, company A, wounded.

Private D. Thatcher, company A, wounded.

Private L. M. Johnson, company A, missing.

Corporal Daniel J. Baur, company B, wounded.

Corporal Nathan G. Germond, company B, wounded.

Sergeant Rush Griswold, company B, missing.

Private Vaness Jordan, company B, missing.

Second Lieutenant Henry M. Ryder, company C, wounded and died.

Sergeant Charles C. Fitts, company C, wounded.

Private Julius Lavelle, company C, wounded.

Private Andrew W. Mann, company C, wounded.

Private M. Maloney, company C, wounded.

Private George D. Brockett, company C, missing.

Private Samuel E. Fay, company C, missing.

Private Henry C. Lord, company C, missing.

Private William Yokes, company C, missing.

Private John Warren, company C, missing.

Private Samuel Shanefelt, company D, killed.

Private Norman Cochran, company D, wounded.

Private Andrew Hunsicker, company D, wounded.

Private Edward Spicer, company D, wounded.

Private Henry Thompson, company D, wounded.

Private George J. Young, company D, wounded.

Private John H. Hill, company D, killed.

Private Thomas Shultz, company E, wounded and died.

Private Lorenzo Norton, company E, wounded.

Private Rufus Hurlburt, company E, wounded.

Private Sherman Tuttle, company E, wounded.

Private D. B. Franklin, company E, missing.

Private Roby Dewey, company E, missing.

Private Daniel Platt, company E, missing.

Corporal Alonzo Cole, company F, wounded.

Private Orlando Wilson, company F, wounded.

Private Jehial Johnson, company F, wounded.

Private Charles Canfield, company F, wounded.

Sergeant Charles T. Waldron, company F, missing.

Corporal Isaac J. Houghkirk, company F, missing.

Private Peter Dowling, company F, missing.

Private William Sober, company F, missing.

Sergeant Edward F. Smith, company G, killed.

Private William Wirt, company G, wounded.

Private Thomas White, company G, wounded.

Private Justus Townsley, company G, wounded.

Private Julius McCain, company G, wounded.

Private Andrew Halman, company G, wounded.

Private Henry Ewell, company G, wounded.

Private John F. Weidle, company G, wounded.

Private George Guest, company G, wounded.

First Sergeant Wilbur F. Chamberlain, company G, missing.

Private Albert Hall, company G, missing.

Private William H. Hartley, company G, missing.

Private Eli Overholtz, company H, wounded.

Private Andrew Robinson, company H, wounded.

First Lieutenant Andrew J. Fulkerson, company H, missing.

Private Henry Wolf, company H, missing.

Private William Lutz, company H, missing.

Corporal Warren Wilbur, company I, wounded.

Private Thomas Sharkey, company I, wounded.

Private Ferdinand Cutler, company I, wounded.

Sergeant Newton B. Adams, company I, missing.

Corporal Almon Woodruff, company I, missing.

Private Joseph Baker, company I, missing.

Captain David E. Hurlburt, company K, wounded.

Private James Williams, company K, wounded.

Private Ferdinand Burt, company K, wounded.

Private Joseph Marsh, company K, wounded.

Private David Turner, company K, wounded.

Private Osmond O. Oliver, company K, missing, never heard from.

Private Edson G. Holcomb, company K, missing.

Private Fred Rounds, company E, wounded.

Lieutenant E. J. Hurlburt, company A, wounded.

### RECAPITULATION.

| | | | |
|---|---|---|---|
| Commissioned officers . . . . Killed o. | Wounded, 3 | Missing, 1 |
| Non-commissioned officers and | | |
| privates . . . . . . . . . . . . . . . . . Killed 2 | Wounded, 42. | Missing, 26 |
| Total . . . . . . . . . . . . . Killed 2. | Wounded, 45. | Missing, 27 |
| Casualties . . . . . . . . . . . . . . . . . . . . . . . . . . . . . . . . . . . . . . . . . . . . . . . . . 72 |

RECORD OF KILLED AND WOUNDED OF THE TWENTY-NINTH OHIO VOLUNTEERS AT THE BATTLE OF GETTYSBURG, PENNSYLVANIA, JULY 2D AND 3D, 1863.

First Lieutenant J. G. Marsh, company D, killed.

First Sergeant George Hayward, company E, killed.

Private Benjamin F. Pontius, company D, killed.

Private J. Johnson, company F, killed.

Private John Williams, company C, killed.

Private Mathias Soden, company K, killed.

Private Jacob Gardner, company D, wounded.

First Sergeant J. Kessinger, company I, wounded.

Corporal J. Reed, company I, wounded.

Private Sidney A. Kennedy, company I, wounded.

Corporal Eli Rushon, company I, wounded.

Corporal George Putney, company E, wounded.

Private James Rounds, company B, wounded.

Private M. A. Rowe, company B, wounded.

Private William Jennings, company H, wounded.

Private Hiram C. Hill, company G, killed.

Private M. B. Haskins, company B, wounded.

Private Ed. Farr, company H, wounded.

Private O. O. Wright, company H, wounded.

Sergeant C. Woodford, company F, wounded.

Corporal G. McLain, company F, wounded.

Private Thomas Dowling, company F, wounded

Corporal Loren Frisby, company F, wounded

Private E. L. Gray,* company F, wounded

Private Alpheus Hardy,* company F, wounded.

Private A. W. Hardy, company F, wounded

Private E. F. Mason, company C, wounded.

Private B. Miller, company C, wounded

Private E. O. Miller, company C, wounded.

Private T. J. Merrell, company C, wounded.

Private W. H. Runyon, company C, wounded.

Private Obed Knapp, company C, wounded.

Private Esick Blanchard, company K, wounded

Sergeant John A. Kummer, company G, wounded.

Private Tallis E. McKain, company G, wounded.

Private Harry Gould, company G, wounded.

Private Isaac Munger, company A, wounded.

Private F. B. Mowery, company A. wounded

Private Ed. J. Brown, company A, wounded

Private C. Hedrick, company A, wounded.

RECAPITULATION

| | |
|---|---|
| Killed . | 7 |
| Wounded | 33 |
| Total. | 40 |

RECORD OF CASUALTIES OF THE TWENTY-NINTH REGIMENT OHIO VOLUNTEERS, FROM MAY 3, 1864, TO JANUARY 27, 1865.

First Lieutenant Winthrop C. Grant, company A, killed, Dug Gap, Georgia, May 8, 1864

Private Adrian M. Knowlton, company A, killed, Dug Gap, Georgia, May 8, 1864.

Private Franklin Potter, company A, killed, Dug Gap, Georgia, May 8, 1864

Private John Keppler, company C, killed, Dug Gap, Georgia, May 8, 1864

Private John Gray, company C, killed, Dug Gap, Georgia, May 8, 1864

Sergeant Samuel Wooldridge, company D, killed, Dug Gap, Georgia, May 8, 1864.

Corporal George Foust, company D, killed, Dug Gap, Georgia, May 8, 1864.

Private Thomas J. Bare, company D, killed, Dug Gap, Georgia, May 8, 1864.

Private John W. Steese, company D, killed, Dug Gap, Georgia, May 8, 1864.

Sergeant Ellis T. Treen, company G, killed, Dug Gap, Georgia, May 8, 1864

Sergeant Christian F Remley, company G, killed, Dug Gap, Georgia, May 8, 1864.

Private Curtis M. Lanty, company G, killed, Dug Gap, Georgia, May 8, 1864.

Private W. H. Connell, company H, killed, Dug Gap, Georgia, May 8, 1864.

Private Eli C Joles, company H, killed, Dug Gap, Georgia, May 8, 1864.

Private Charles Osborne, company H, killed, Dug Gap, Georgia, May 8, 1864.

Private Martin Smith, company H, killed, Dug Gap, Georgia, May 8, 1864

Private Tobias R. Phinney, company I, killed, Dug Gap, Georgia, May 8, 1864.

Private Henry Rapp, company I, killed, Dug Gap, Georgia, May 8, 1864.

Private Cass M. Nimms, company I, killed, Dug Gap, Georgia, May 8, 1864

Private Amos Long, company K, killed, Dug Gap, Georgia, May 8, 1864.

Private Cyrus Roath, company A, killed, Pine Knob, Georgia, June 16, 1864.

Private Ebet F. Bennet, company D, killed, Pine Knob, Georgia, June 16, 1864.

Sergeant Andrew L. Rickard, company A, killed, Pine Knob, Georgia, June 15, 1864.

First Sergeant Joel E. Tanner, company B, killed, Pine Knob, Georgia, June 15, 1864.

Private Jabin S. Dusten, company F, killed, Pine Knob, Georgia, June 15, 1864.

Private Lewis J. Phinney, company B, killed, Dallas, Georgia, May 29, 1864.

Private A. W. Atkins, company B, killed, Dallas, Georgia, May 29, 1864.

Private C. A. Davis, company B, killed, Dallas, Georgia, May 29, 1864

Private W. Hasting, company D, killed, Dallas, Georgia, May 26, 1864

Sergeant J. H. Marsh, company K, killed, Dallas, Georgia, May 25, 1864

Private James Baker, company I, killed, near Kenesaw, Georgia, July 2, 1864.

Sergeant Thomas Davis, company H, killed, Pine Knob, Georgia, June 16, 1864.

Corporal James Gunn, company I, killed, Pine Knob, Georgia, June 16, 1864.

Private W. F. Harrington, company G, killed, Peach Tree Creek, Georgia, July 20, 1864.

Private Benjamin R. Lee, company H, killed, Peach Tree Creek, Georgia, July 20, 1864.

Sergeant D. Ransom (James ?) Billings, company I, killed, near Atlanta, Georgia, July 28, 1864.

Private C. W. Kellogg, company C, wounded, Pine Knob, Georgia, June 16, 1864.

COMMISSIONED OFFICERS WOUNDED.

Colonel William T. Fitch, Dug Gap, Georgia, May 8, 1864.

Lieutenant-colonel Edward Hayes, Dug Gap, Georgia, May 8, 1864.

Adjutant James B. Storer, Dug Gap, Georgia, May 8, 1864.

First Lieutenant George W. Dice, Dug Gap, Georgia, May 8, 1864.

First Lieutenant W. F. Chamberlain, Dug Gap, Georgia.

First Lieutenant George W. Dice, Pine Knob, June 16, 1864, since died.

Captain W. F. Stevens, Dallas, Georgia, May 25, 1864.

Captain Myron T. Wright, Peach Tree Creek, Georgia, July 20, 1864.

Major Myron T. Wright, December 19, 1864; died at Savannah, Georgia, January 7, 1865.

Sergeant Thaddeus E. Hoyt, company A, wounded, Dug Gap, Georgia, May 8, 1864.

Sergeant A. L. Rickard, company A, wounded, Dug Gap, Georgia, May 8, 1864.

Private John Ellis, company A, wounded, Dug Gap, Georgia, May 8, 1864,

Private N. A. Germond, company B, wounded, Dug Gap, Georgia, May 8, 1864.

Private George Wright, company B, wounded, Dug Gap, Georgia, May 8, 1864.

Private William Potter, company B, wounded, Dug Gap, Georgia, May 8, 1864.

Private John Edwards, company B, wounded, Dug Gap, Georgia, May 8, 1864.

Private Andrew Bright, company B, wounded, Dug Gap, Georgia, May 8, 1864.

Corporal Allen Mason, company C, died of wounds, Dug Gap, Georgia, May 8, 1864.

Private D. C. Lindsley, company C, wounded, Dug Gap, Georgia, May 8, 1864.

Private George D. Brackett, company C, wounded, Dug Gap, Georgia, May 8, 1864.

Private William Yokes, company C, wounded, Dug Gap, Georgia, May 8, 1864.

Private Samuel E. Fany, company C, wounded, Dug Gap, Georgia, May 8, 1864.

Private James Wenham, company C, wounded, Dug Gap, Georgia, May 8, 1864.

Private Henry C. Lord, company C, wounded, Dug Gap, Georgia, May 8, 1864.

Private Obed Knapp, company C, wounded, Dug Gap, Georgia, May 8, 1864.

Corporal M. Hougland, company D, wounded, Dug Gap, Georgia, May 8, 1864

Private Rufus T. Chapman, company D, wounded, Dug Gap, Georgia, May 8, 1864.

Private Jabin S. Duston, company F, wounded, Dallas, Georgia, May 25, 1864.

Private John Montgomery, company D, wounded, Dug Gap, Georgia, May 8, 1864.

Private Jacob Gardner, company D, wounded, Dug Gap, Georgia, May 8, 1864.

Private Charles A. Downey, company D, wounded, Dug Gap, Georgia, May 8, 1864.

Private Henry Hane, company D, wounded, Dug Gap, Georgia, May 8, 1864.

Private John H. Hughes, company D, wounded, Dug Gap, Georgia, May 8, 1864.

Private Levi Baughman, company D, wounded, Dug Gap, Georgia, May 8, 1864.

Private Charles Steese, company D, wounded, Dug Gap, Georgia, May 8, 1864.

Private John Burkert, company D, wounded, Dug Gap, Georgia, May 25, 1864.

Private D. C. Stevens,* company I, wounded, Dug Gap, Georgia, May 8, 1864.

Private Seth M Thomas, company D, wounded, Dug Gap, Georgia, May 8, 1864.

Private Theron W. Smith, company D, wounded, Dug Gap, Georgia, May 8, 1864.

Private David M. Brown, company D, wounded, Dug Gap, Georgia, May 8, 1864.

Private Thomas White, company G, wounded, Dallas, Georgia, May 27, 1864.

Private Isaac Medsker, company D, wounded, Dug Gap, Georgia, May 8, 1864.

Private John J. White, company D, wounded, Dug Gap, Georgia, May 8, 1864.

First Sergeant A. J Andrews, company E, wounded Dug Gap, Georgia, May 8, 1864.

Corporal Hiram Thornton, company E, wounded, Dug Gap, Georgia, May 8, 1864.

Corporal Hiram Dalrymple, company E, wounded, Dug Gap, Georgia, May 8, 1864.

Private Barney Buck, company E, wounded, Dug Gap, Georgia, May 8, 1864.

Private J Bennet Powers, company E, wounded, Dug Gap, Georgia, May 8, 1864

Private Thomas Franklin, company E, wounded, Dug Gap, Georgia, May 8, 1864.

Private Franklin Flood, company F, wounded, Dug Gap, Georgia, May 8, 1864.

Private Alonzo Cole, company F, wounded, Dug Gap, Georgia, May 8, 1864.

Color Corporal Hammond W. Geer, company G, wounded, Dug Gap, Georgia, May 8, 1864.

Private George F. Braggington, company G, wounded, Dug Gap, Georgia, May 8, 1864 (died).

Private George I. McCormick, company G, wounded, Dug Gap, Georgia, May 8, 1864.

Private John Woodard, company G, wounded, Dug Gap, Georgia, May 8, 1864.

Private William Woodard, company G, wounded, Dallas, Georgia, May 27, 1864

Private George Murray, company G, wounded, Dug Gap, Georgia, May 8, 1864.

Corporal Floyd Morris, company H, wounded, Dug Gap, Georgia, May 8, 1864.

Private Henry J. Knapp, company H, wounded, Dug Gap, Georgia, May 8, 1864.

Private James Perrine, company H, wounded, Dug Gap, Georgia, May 8, 1864.

Private John Smith, company H, wounded, Dug Gap, Georgia, May 8, 1864.

Private John H. Wright, company H, wounded, Dug Gap, Georgia, May 8, 1864.

Private James Wild, company G, wounded, Dug Gap, Georgia, May 8, 1864.

Sergeant Newton B. Adams, company I, wounded, Dug Gap, Georgia, May 8, 1864.

Private William Gilbert, company I, wounded, Dug Gap, Georgia, May 8, 1864.

Private Abel Archer, company I, wounded, Dug Gap, Georgia, May 8, 1864.

Private A. W. Woldridge, company I, wounded, Dug Gap, Georgia, May 8, 1864.

Private Theodore Hawk, company I, wounded, Dug Gap, Georgia, May 8, 1864.

Private Alvah Holden, company I, wounded, Dug Gap, Georgia, May 8, 1864

Private C. H. Kindig, company I, wounded, Dug Gap, Georgia, May 8, 1864.

Private Hiram Newcomb, company I, wounded, Dug Gap, Georgia, May 8, 1864.

Private James Perkins, company I, wounded, Dug Gap, Georgia, May 8, 1864

Private John Shannon, company I, wounded, Dug Gap, Georgia, May 8, 1864.

Private William Stetle, company I, wounded, Dug Gap, Georgia, May 8, 1864.

Private James Reed, company I, wounded, Dug Gap, Georgia, May 8, 1864.

William Roshon, company I, wounded, Dug Gap, Georgia, May 8, 1864.

Private James Winters, company I, wounded, Dug Gap, Georgia, May 8, 1864.

Private William Waterman, company I, wounded, Dug Gap, Georgia, May 8, 1864.

First Sergeant N. S. Hoxter, company K, wounded, Dug Gap, Georgia, May 8, 1864

Private David Hartigan, company D, wounded, Dallas, Georgia, May 15, 1864.

Sergeant L. L. Kinney, company K, wounded, Dug Gap, Georgia, May 8, 1864.

Sergeant J. C. Hammond, company K, wounded, Dug Gap, Georgia, May 8, 1864.

Private F. A. Rounds, company K, wounded, Dug Gap, Georgia, May 8, 1864.

Private W. H. Stratton, company K, wounded, Dug Gap, Georgia, May 8, 1864.

Corporal G. B. Mowrey, company A, wounded, Pine Knob, Georgia, June 15, 1864.

Private J. O. Latimer, company A, wounded, Pine Knob, Georgia, June 15, 1864.

Sergeant George McNutt, company B, wounded, Pine Knob, Georgia, June 15, 1864.

Private Dudley Brown, company B, wounded, Pine Knob, Georgia, June 15, 1864.

Private John Davis, company B, wounded, Dallas, Georgia, May 27, 1864.

Private John Davis, company B, wounded, Pine Knob, Georgia, June 15, 1864.

Private G. W. Stocking, company B, wounded, Dallas, Georgia, May 27, 1864.

Private George W. Stocking, company B, wounded, Pine Knob, June 15, 1864.

First Sergeant R. L. Jones, company C, wounded Pine Knob, Georgia, June 15, 1864.

Private David Clark, company C, wounded, Pine Knob, Georgia, June 15, 1864.

Private James Fleming, company C, wounded, Pine Knob, Georgia, June 15, 1864.

Corporal George J. Young, company D, wounded, Pine Knob, Georgia, June 15, 1864.

Private D. W. Powell, company D, wounded, Pine Knob, Georgia, June 15, 1864.

Private Daniel Schaaf, company D, wounded, Pine Knob, Georgia, June 15, 1864.

Private John Snyder, company D, wounded, Pine Knob, Georgia, June 15, 1864.

Private H. A. Thompson, company D, wounded, Pine Knob, Georgia, June 15, 1864.

Private J. B. Yohey, company D, wounded, Pine Knob, Georgia, June 15, 1864.

Sergeant C. Howard, company E, wounded, Pine Knob, Georgia, June 15, 1864

Corporal R. H. Hurlburt, company E, wounded, Pine Knob, Georgia, June 15, 1864.

Private D. W. Hall, company E, wounded, Pine Knob, Georgia, June 15, 1864

Private M. Mahan, company E, wounded, Pine Knob, Georgia, June 15, 1864.

Private T. S. McCartney, company E, wounded, Pine Knob, Georgia, June 15, 1864

Private J. W. Kinnear, company E, wounded, Pine Knob, Georgia, June 15, 1864

First Sergeant, A B Paine, company F, wounded, Pine Knob, Georgia, June 15, 1864.

Corporal J. J. Houghkirk, company F, wounded, Pine Knob, Georgia, June 15, 1864

Corporal J W. Foot, company F, wounded, Dallas, Georgia, May 31, 1864.

Private J. B. Belknap, company F, wounded, Pine Knob, Georgia, June 15, 1864.

Private Charles Cook, company F, wounded, Pine Knob, Georgia, June 15, 1864.

Private J Johnson, company F, wounded, Pine Knob, Georgia, June 15, 1864.

Private George Williams, company F, wounded, Pine Knob, Georgia, June 15, 1864

Private H Edson, company G, wounded, Pine Knob, Georgia, June 15, 1864.

Private W. Hartley, company G, wounded, Pine Knob, Georgia, June 15, 1864

Private George Guest, company G, wounded, Pine Knob, Georgia, June 15, 1864

Private Evander Turner, company H, wounded, Pine Knob, Georgia, June 15, 1864

Private Henry Wolf, company H, wounded, Pine Knob, Georgia, June 15, 1864.

Private William Sperr, company II, wounded, Pine Knob, Georgia, June 15, 1864.

First Sergeant S. Kissinger, company I, wounded, Pine Knob, Georgia, June 15, 1864.

Private William Trall, company I, wounded, Pine Knob, Georgia, June 15, 1864.

Private E. Newberry, company I, wounded, Pine Knob, Georgia, June 15, 1864.

Private T. J. Fales, company K, wounded, Pine Knob, Georgia, June 15, 1864.

Private Daniel I. Turner, company K, wounded, Pine Knob, Georgia, June 15, 1864.

Private Jeremiah Congdon, company H, wounded, near Kennesaw, Georgia, June 24, 1864.

Private Robert D Lutz, company D, wounded near Atlanta, Georgia, July 28, 1864.

Private Charles H Beckwith, company E, wounded, Pine Knob, Georgia, June 25, 1864.

Private I. E. Haggett, company A, wounded near Marietta, Georgia, July 1, 1864.

Sergeant N. H. Bailey, company C, wounded near Marietta, Georgia, July 1, 1864.

Private Louis Crocker, company G, wounded near Marietta, Georgia, July 1, 1864.

Private Tobias Nettles, company H, wounded near Marietta, Georgia, July 1, 1864.

Private H. Farnsworth, company K, wounded near Marietta, Georgia, July 1, 1864.

Private H. C. Rood, company A, wounded, Dallas, Georgia, May 25, 1864.

Private E. W. Herrick, company A, wounded, Dallas, Georgia, May 26, 1864.

Private O. J. Parkill, company A, wounded, Dallas, Georgia, May 26, 1864.

Private John Burns, company B, wounded, Dallas, Georgia, May 26, 1864.

Private Charles E. Parkill, company C, wounded, Dallas, Georgia, May 26, 1864.

Private Israel Beck, company C, wounded, Dallas, Georgia, May 26, 1864.

Sergeant J. T. Parks, company D, wounded, Dallas, Georgia, May 26, 1864.

Private B. Holton, company D, wounded, Dallas, Georgia, May 25, 1864.

Private J. C. Greenlee, company E, wounded, Dallas, Georgia, May 25, 1864.

Sergeant George McNutt, company B, wounded, Dallas, Georgia, May 28, 1864.

Corporal S. E. Balch, company F, wounded, Dallas, Georgia, May 25, 1864.

Private John Goss, company G, wounded, Dallas, Georgia, May 25, 1864.

Private J. Townsley, company G, wounded, Dallas, Georgia, May 25, 1864.

Private William Demmings, company H, wounded, Dallas, Georgia, May 25, 1864.

Private William Lutz, company H, wounded, Dallas, Georgia, May 25, 1864.

Private A. Richards, company H, wounded, Dallas, Georgia, May 25, 1864.

Corporal C. F. Gove, company I, wounded, Dallas, Georgia, May 25, 1864.

Private James Hawks, company I, wounded, Dallas, Georgia, May 25, 1864.

Private James Walsh, company I, wounded, Dallas, Georgia, May 25, 1864.

Private G. W. Deem, company K, wounded, Dallas, Georgia, May 25, 1864.

Private T. J. Failes, company K, wounded, Dallas, Georgia, May 25, 1864.

Corporal N. J. Smith, company D, wounded, Pine Knob, Georgia, June 18, 1864; Kenesaw Mountain, Georgia, June 22, 1864.

Private Elias Shutt, company D, wounded, Kenesaw Mountain, Georgia, June 22, 1864.

Private Stephen Griffith, company G, wounded, Kenesaw Mountain, Georgia, June 22, 1864

Private W. Harrington, company G, wounded, Kenesaw Mountain, Georgia, June 22, 1864

Sergeant C. Woodford, company F, wounded, Pine Knob, Georgia, June 18, 1864

Corporal S. McLain, company F, wounded, Pine Knob, Georgia, June 18, 1864

Private O. E. Wilson, company F, wounded, Pine Knob, Georgia, June 18, 1864

Private George Williams, company F, killed, Kenesaw Mountain, Georgia, June 23, 1864.

Sergeant C. F. Sawyer, company I, wounded, Kenesaw Mountain, Georgia, June 20, 1864.

Private N. Wilder, company A, wounded, Pine Knob, Georgia, June 16, 1864.

Private John Hague, company A, wounded, Pine Knob, Georgia, June 16, 1864

Private L. M. Coon, company A, wounded, Pine Knob, Georgia, June 16, 1864

Sergeant B. A. Isham, company B, wounded, Pine Knob, Georgia, June 16, 1864.

Private S. S. Andrews, company B, wounded, Pine Knob, Georgia, June 16, 1864.

Private F. A. Rounds, company K, wounded, Pine Knob, Georgia, June 16, 1864.

Private Ezra Spidel, company D, wounded, Pine Knob, Georgia, June 16, 1864.

Private Jacob Winters, company D, wounded, Pine Knob, Georgia, June 16, 1864.

Private G. W. Holloway, company D, wounded, Pine Knob, Georgia, June 16, 1864.

Private C. Vanvalkenburg, company F, wounded, Pine Knob, Georgia, June 16, 1864.

Private P. E. Wilson, company F, wounded, Pine Knob, Georgia, June 16, 1864.

Private S. McLean, company F, wounded, Pine Knob, Georgia, June 16, 1864

Private William Cline, company G, wounded, Pine Knob, Georgia, June 16, 1864

Private William Harrington, company G, wounded, Pine Knob, Georgia, June 16, 1864.

Sergeant Alphonzo Hazzen, company H, wounded, Pine Knob, Georgia, June 16, 1864.

Private Lester Bruno, company H, wounded, Pine Knob, Georgia, June 16, 1864.

Private Samuel Heathman, company H, wounded, Pine Knob, Georgia, June 16, 1864

Private George Manning, company H, wounded, Pine Knob, Georgia, June 16, 1864.

Private John Sarsfield, company K, wounded, Pine Knob, Georgia, June 16, 1864

Private F. N. Johnson, company K, wounded, Pine Knob, Georgia, June 16, 1864.

Private C. O. Hinkle, company K, wounded, Pine Knob, Georgia, June 16, 1864.

Private George G. Guest, company I, wounded, Resaca, Georgia, May 15, 1864

Private Daniel Kelsea, company A, wounded, Resaca, Georgia, June 16, 1864

Private W. A. Frisbie, company A, wounded, Dallas, Georgia, June 28, 1864.

Private John N Wise, company G, wounded, Kenesaw Mountain, Georgia, June 28, 1864.

Private A. B. Durfee, company A, wounded, Dallas, Georgia, May 26, 1864.

Private B. F. Holten, company E, wounded, Dallas, Georgia, May 26, 1864.

Private George W. Reed, company I, wounded, Dallas, Georgia, May 30, 1864.

Private Frank Culver, company E, wounded, Pine Knob, Georgia, June 16, 1864.

Private Thomas Dowling, company F, wounded, Pine Knob, Georgia, June 16, 1864

Private W. F. Harrington, company G, wounded, Dallas, Georgia, May 25, 1864.

Color Bearer M. McNerney, company I, wounded, Dallas, Georgia, May 25, 1864.

Private W. H. Stratton, company K, wounded, Dallas, Georgia, May 25, 1864

Private A. B Durfee, company A, wounded, Peach Tree Creek, Georgia, July 20, 1864.

Private B F. Holton, company E, wounded, Peach Tree Creek, Georgia, July 20, 1864.

Private Frank Culver, company E, wounded, Peach Tree Creek, Georgia, July 20, 1864.

Private Thomas Dowling, company F, wounded, Peach Tree Creek, Georgia, July 20, 1864 (died).

Color-bearer M. McNerney, company I, wounded, Peach Tree Creek, Georgia, July 20, 1864.

Private W. H. Stratton, company K, wounded, Peach Tree Creek, Georgia, July 20, 1864.

Private Christopher Beck, company D, wounded, near Atlanta, Georgia, August 1, 1864.

Private Robert Williams, company A, wounded, near Marietta, Georgia, June 27, 1864.

Private Peter Dennis, company B, wounded, near Marietta, Georgia, June 27, 1864.

Sergeant B. F. Manderbach, company G, wounded, near Marietta, Georgia, June 28, 1864.

Private R. E. Woodbury, company A, wounded, near Marietta, Georgia, July 20, 1864.

Private John H. White, company B, wounded, Mill Creek Gap, Georgia, May 8, 1864.

Private William Porter, company D, wounded, Mill Creek Gap, Georgia, May 8, 1864.

Private Dennis Stevens, company I, wounded, Mill Creek Gap, Georgia, May 8, 1864.

Private J. S. Deshore, company F, wounded, Resaca, Georgia, May 25, 1864.

Corporal G. B. Mowry, company A, wounded, Pine Knob, Georgia, May 15, 1864.

Corporal A. J. Langworthy, company B, wounded, Pine Knob, Georgia, May 15, 1864.

Corporal H. Harlow Fenton, company K, wounded, no record.

Private Levi Baughman, company D, wounded, Mill Creek, Georgia, May 8, 1864.

Private George Bason, company B, wounded, Dallas, Georgia, May 25th to June 4, 1864.

Private James Brands, company D, wounded, Kenesaw Mountain, Georgia, June 26 and 27, 1864.

Private G. W. Drew, company K, wounded, Dallas, Georgia, May 25, 1864

Private Ferdinand Burt, company K, wounded, Mill Creek, Georgia, May 8, 1864.

Private G. W. Heern, company K, wounded, Pine Knob, Georgia, June 15, 1864.

Private George Hammerstein, company G, wounded, Atlanta, Georgia, July 20, 1864.

Private James Nardham, company C, wounded, Mill Creek, Georgia, May 8, 1864.

Private John Cooper, company E, wounded December 11, 1864.

Private James Rounds, company B, wounded June 16, 1864.

Private Jacob Foster, company G, wounded May 25, 1864

Private Charles Cain, company F, missing, Mill Creek Gap, Georgia, May 8, 1864.

Private James Gaule, company G, missing, Peach Tree Creek, Georgia, July 20, 1864.

Corporal H. C. Rood, company A, missing, Peach Tree Creek, Georgia, July 20, 1864.

First Sergeant Rush Griswold, company B, missing, Peach Tree Creek, Georgia, July 20, 1864.

Corporal H. E. Clark, company B, missing, Peach Tree Creek, Georgia, July 20, 1864.

Private J. C. Shaw, company C, missing, Peach Tree Creek, Georgia, July 20, 1864

Private Alonzo Cole, company F, missing, Peach Pree Creek, Georgia, July 20, 1864

Private H. Merrill, company I, missing, Peach Tree Creek, Georgia, July 20, 1864.

Corporal Hiram Thornton, company E, missing November 20, 1864.

Private M. Babington, company G, missing November 20, 1864.

Those killed near Dallas were buried on a ridge just to the right of the Burnt Hickory and Dallas road, i rear of our works. Those killed June 15th and 16th, were buried on a ridge near Kenesaw Mountain, 100 yards in rear of the front line of our works; the graves all marked and easily distinguished.

GEORGE W. HOLLOWAY,
Late Co. D, 29th Regiment.

REPORT OF CASUALTIES IN THE TWENTY-NINTH OHIO VOLUNTEER VETERAN INFANTRY, FROM JANUARY 27 TO MARCH 26, 1865.

Private John Rape, company G, killed February 12, 1865.

Private James Baller, company D, wounded February 12, 1865.

Private James Miller, company I, wounded February 12, 1865.

Sergeant Charles Potter, company K, wounded February 12, 1865.

Private William H. Abbott, company I, wounded February 12, 1865.

First Sergeant Ulysses S. Hoxter, company K, missing March 11, 1865.

Private David W. Hall, company E, missing March 15, 1865.

Corporal Rufus Hulbert, company E, missing March 15, 1865.

Private Charles Upham, company G, missing March 14, 1865.

Private Milo Sharp, company I, missing March 19, 1865.

Corporal John A. Exceen, company A, wounded March 24, 1865.

Private Adam Hulbert, company G, wounded March 24, 1865.

Private Thomas Bonner, company A, missing March 11, 1865.

AGGREGATE LOSSES OF KILLED, WOUNDED, AND MISSING OF THE TWENTY-NINTH REGIMENT OHIO VETERAN VOLUNTEER INFANTRY IN EACH BATTLE, FROM THE ORGANIZATION OF THE REGIMENT, SEPTEMBER, 1861, TO JUNE 1, 1865.

| Names of Battle. | Place. | Date. | Killed. | Wounded | Missing. | Aggregate. |
|---|---|---|---|---|---|---|
| | | **1862** | | | | |
| Winchester . .......... | Virginia ... .... | March 23.. | 5 | 7 | 2 | 14 |
| Port Republic . , ...... .. | Virginia ...... | June 9.. . .. | 12 | 33 | 105 | 150 |
| Cedar Mountain .. ... .. | Virginia .... | August 9.... | 11 | 26 | 12 | 49 |
| Chancellorsville , . ...... . | Virginia .. .... . | May 1, 2, 3.. | 4 | 42 | 25 | 71 |
| | | **1863** | | | | |
| Gettysburg ........... | Pennsylvania | July 3 .... | 9 | 35 | 1 | 45 |
| | | **1864** | | | | |
| Mill Creek Gap.... ... | Georgia ... .... | May 8.... | 26 | 67 | 1 | 94 |
| Resaca............... | Georgia ........ | May 15 .... | .. | 2 | .. | 2 |
| New Hope Church...... | Georgia ........ | May 25. .... | 6 | 24 | 1 | 31 |
| Pine Knob. .......... | Georgia ...... . | June 15 ... | 9 | 30 | .. | 39 |
| Kenesaw Mouutain.... . | Georgia ...... | June 26..... | 1 | 9 | 2 | 12 |
| Peach Tree Creek...... | Georgia . ...... | July 20 .... | 2 | 7 | 5 | 14 |
| Atlanta.............. | Georgia . .. ... | September 2. | .. | .. | .. | .. |
| Savannah .. . ........ | Georgia ........ | December 21 | 2 | 2 | .. | 4 |
| | | **1865** | | | | |
| North Edisto River. .. | South Carolina., | February 12 | 1 | 3 | .. | 4 |
| Goldsboro . ... . ... | North Carolina.. | March 23... | 1 | 2 | 9 | 12 |
| Grand Total......... | . . .. | . . | 89 | 289 | 163 | 541 |

N. B —A remarkable fact, the Twenty-ninth fought its first battle on the 23d of March, and its last on the same date.

# ERRATA.

Page 192—eighth line, "Steur" should be "Steen."

Page 193—Captain Luce was killed June 9, 1862.

Page 194—ninth line, for "October 17" read "October 27,", twenty-fourth line, for "Francis" read "Frances"

Page 196—twelfth line, "Haddock" should be "Hadlock."

Page 197—seventeenth line, "Bivius" should be "Bivins."

Page 198—twenty-first line, "Vanskoyt" should be "Vanskoik."

Page 203—fourth and fifth lines, instead of "Buele" read "Beede"; eleventh line from bottom, "Outis" should be "Ontis"

Page 204—tenth line, John J Belknap was wounded June 15, 1864.

Page 206—fifth line, "Vins" should be "Viers", nineteenth line, George Williams was killed at Kenesaw Mountain, Georgia; twenty-second line, the last date should be June 17, 1865

Page 207—third line, last date should read May 22, 1865; twelfth line from bottom, insert the word "major" between the word "promoted" and date.

Page 209—fourth line from bottom, instead of "Martin M Mills" read "Mills M Martin."

Page 210—fourth line, William Fisher was captured June 9, 1862; fourth line from bottom "Tallio" should be "Tallis"

Page 213—twelfth line from bottom, "Sures" should be "Sines."

Page 214—first line, for "Bubbington" read "Babbington."

Page 216—last line, for "Murgan" read "Morgan."

Page 220—third line, for "discharged" read "mustered out"; eleventh and twelfth lines, take out word "discharged."

Page 221—fourth line from bottom, for "Woobury" read "Woodbury."

Page 222—sixth line from bottom, for "Norton" read "Newton."

Page 223—tenth line, Albert Bishop was a corporal, twenty-fourth line, for "M" read "W."

Page 224—ninth line from bottom, after "teamster" insert "discharged"

Page 225—twenty-first line, for "with company" read "in hospital", ditto with fifth line from bottom, twenty-third line, for " with company " read "July 5, 1865 "

Page 226—eighth line from bottom, "June 5" should read "June 2."

Page 227—twelfth line from bottom, for " 1863" read " 1862", sixth line from bottom, for "A" read "F"; next line, for "E" read "G"

Page 229—eleventh line, Philander M Griggs was wounded at Cedar Mountain, August 9, 1862

Page 231—ninth line, "Cargle" should be "Craighl "

Page 232—last line, for "Grun" read "Green."

Page 234—first name, for "Clap" read "Clapp", same line, for 'December 8 " read " 5"; ninth line from bottom, for "Bruman" read " Brainard "; sixth line from bottom, take " e " out of "Bauer "

Page 235—third line from bottom, for "June 9" read "June 24."

Page 236—sixteenth line, for " Newman" read "Niman", sixth line from bottom, for "Ellson" read "Ellison."

Page 237—sixth line, for "May 11" read "September 4."

Page 238—tenth line, for "Shabondy" read "Sherbondy"; twenty-first line, for "Braginton" read "Braggington", twenty-third line, for "Breght" read "Bright", twenty-fourth line, for "Belnap" read "Belknap "

CPSIA information can be obtained
at www.ICGtesting.com
Printed in the USA
BVHW041443310322
632868BV00001B/46